Streetwise: Mafia Memoirs

by award winning author Russell A. Vassallo

Not just another Mafia book

Published by
Krazy Duck Productions
Box 105
Danville, KY 40423

www.krazyduck.com

ISBN-978-0-9776739-3-3

LOC: 2008901008

Book layout design by: Jane Eichwald
Edited by Virginia G. Vassallo

This book is a non-fiction book and the names have been changed
not only to protect the innocent and their families, but to save my
own worthless hide. All photos except those of Alia, Sicily are from
the collection of Russell A Vassallo. Robert Battaglia gave permission
to use the Alia photos.

Dedication

In loving memory of the family that has gone before me, and to all those loving kin who made me who and what I am. I bear their name with honor. I bear their name with pride. I carry their memories, always in my heart, and their smiles, always in my soul.

Acknowledgments

I MUST IN PASSING mention the people besides those in this book, who made this book possible. First and foremost, my wife, Virginia G. Vassallo, who spent countless hours working to make both my books and Krazy Duck a success. All of the historical family information upon which I relied to refresh my recollection came from her tireless efforts at reconstructing the genealogy of my family lineage. My original thought was that she would not get further back than the late 1800s when my family emigrated from Sicily. She astounded me, not only in tracing the lineage to the 1700s, but in confirming many stories my father told me that I believed to be "fluff."

I did rely on other resources to jog my recollection of some events. I did not use information from these books so much as I used them as an outline to refresh my recollection of events and to connect events. Still, it would be unfair not to mention them here. Memory being the fleeting thing it is, they were of invaluable assistance in ensuring accuracy.

For nudging my ancient recollection, thanks is due to *The Godfathers: Lives and Crimes of the Mafia Mobsters*, by Roberto Olla, Alma Books, 2003-2007; *Man of Honor*, Joseph Bonnanno, Buccaneer Press, 1983; *Newark's Little Italy*, Rutgers University Press, 1997; *Murder Inc.*, Burton B. Turkus and Sid Feder, De Capo Press, 1951; *Bread and Respect*, A.V. Marganso and Jerome J. Salamone, Pelican Press, 2002; *Gangbusters*, Ernest Volkner, Faber and Faber, 1998; *Inside Out: Fifty Years Behind the Walls of New Jersey's Trenton State Prison*, by Henry Camisa and Jim Franklin, Windsor Press and Publishing, 2003.

Thanks are also due to Marilyn Henley who provided invaluable information and furnished the name of a gentleman who provided us with photographs of Alia. So I also thank Robert Battaglia for his email permission to reprint the photos. Thanks is also due to Count Charles de Branchforte Said who emailed us more information on the origin of the Vassallo family. If I have forgotten anyone I deeply apologize. A book of this undertaking is a monumental task and there is almost always some kind person who is forgotten or overlooked. Their contribution, however, was very much appreciated.

Honorable mention goes to Penny Woods, reviewer for *Kentucky Monthly Magazine* for reviewing *Streetwise* and refusing to take payment for her efforts. Penny felt that a review that was paid for could be attacked as biased and she therefore asked no recompense for her work. I am embarrassed, but honored.

Table of Contents

Foreword

I grew up in suburban north Jersey about 3 miles from Newark. It was a town of single family homes set amid green lawns with swing sets and sandboxes in the backyards. The kids could run from one yard to another while the stay-at-home moms kept an eye on them. Our mothers all wore dresses or skirts and blouses and flat shoes, but if they were going out, they dressed in heels and better dresses even if they were just going to the market. *Leave It to Beaver, Ozzie and Harriet* and *A Father Knows Best*—all those television shows of the 50s could have been filmed in my neighborhood.

All the fathers had white-collar jobs: doctors, lawyers, upper management. They either drove to work or drove to the nearest train station where they commuted to New York City. My father was upper management for Owens Illinois, a glass bottling company with the regional office in Manhattan. Sometime in the mid-1960s he was given the job of starting the first recycling operation in the Northeast. OI gave him a year to accomplish the task. I remember viewing a movie about the making of glass bottles and listening to his speech about how recycling would be good for the environment and good for business. Dad went to company after company and town manager after town manager explaining the benefits of recycling. None were interested, and Dad's year to get a contract for a recycling center was running.

Finally he contacted some people in the sanitation business. He had a number of meetings with them and, being good businessmen and innovative thinkers, they decided to take a chance on this new recycling concept. Dad was able to report to OI that he had a contract for the first recycling center in New Jersey.

I remember the night he came home and told Mom and me. She was cooking dinner, and I was sitting on the kitchen floor playing with my dog. Dad came in from work, and, after he changed out of his suit and tie, he came down and sat at the kitchen table and told us the good news. Mom was very happy because it meant my father's job wasn't in jeopardy. That is, she was happy until she found out who the businessmen were that Dad contacted.

The sanitation company was owned by the Mafia. These were the men with the foresight to recognize a new opportunity to make money and to help the environment—long before any of the environmental movements began.

This was the only conversation that occurred in our house about the Mafia because Mom didn't want to hear anything else. To her, they were men who shot people in the streets. She didn't want that topic raised in her house. Dad did try to explain that the men he dealt with were not like that but she was adamant.

For years afterwards I often wondered how the same men who we read about in the newspapers could have been so helpful to my father.

Skip forward twenty or so years. I met Russell Vassallo. The scuttlebutt around town was that he was a member of the Mafia. At least that's what his ex-wife told all their neighbors who told the rest of the town. In truth, he was never a member, but he did know many men who were.

During the years that Russ and I lived in New Jersey, I met a few of his friends. All of them were cordial to me and seemed just like the fathers of my childhood friends. At one point Russ was in Aruba on business and I had to drive the three miles to Newark for a class a couple of nights a week. There was a small parking lot next to the building. The first night or two I was able to get a parking spot in the lot but then there were a few nights when the lot was full, and I had to park in a lot a couple of blocks away. But I always tried the closer lot first because the area was very unsafe, especially for a single female.

Well, I was a dumb suburban girl. One night the lot was full but a black parking attendant said he'd take my keys and park my car for me when a space opened up. I was reluctant to hand over my keys, thinking that he wanted to steal my Datsun. But I'd talked to him before; he seemed nice enough so I trusted him. And I came out of my class to find my car parked, and the attendant waiting with my keys. He told me to come into the lot every night I was in the city, and he would make sure I had a parking spot. I thought that was so nice of him.

A few weeks later as I was driving home, I realized that I was being followed. Every lane change I made, a car behind me made the same change. I debated driving straight to the police station but decided, if they were out to get me, I'd never make it into the building. So I drove toward home and, when I made the last turn, realized that the car didn't follow me.

A few weeks later I happened to mention that night to Russ. He laughed and said, "Didn't you realize who they were?"

I was dumbfounded. At that time he had been out of state on Family business. He was concerned about me going to Newark at night, and he had arranged for me to have a parking space and protection on the drive. I was later to discover it was his friend Benny who was watching and protecting me.

A few years later we were living in Montclair, the town where I had grown up. Russ's teenage daughter was enamored with a twenty-something, young man from Newark who worked on the docks. She finally convinced him to take her out on a date. When he came to pick her up, Russ and the young man had a very pleasant conversation while his daughter and I listened. She heard one conversation and related to me: "They are getting along so well. Daddy really likes him." Russ and the young man discussed life in Newark, how it hadn't changed, friends they had in common and men Russ knew but the young man had never met.

As I listened to the conversation, I actually heard two conversations. One was based on the spoken words. The second conversation taking place in that room was unspoken—or spoken in the code of the streets of Newark. "This is my young daughter. I would not want to be the man who harms her." "Sir, I understand and will treat her like my sister." And he did.

The distance between suburban Montclair and Newark is only three miles—yet they are a world apart.

Virginia G. Vassallo

Chapter One

————— ◆ —————

Newark, New Jersey, Circa 1940

I t was a city of cobblestone streets, brass bands on Monday nights, and electric buses that ran on long, overhead double cables. It was a city united by its diversity. A city of immigrants, of varied languages and exotic customs. A city divided into sections: First Ward, Ironbound (or Down Neck), Weequahic, Vailsburg, Forest Hill and Wilson Avenue Section. And into those sections migrated the Italian, the Jew, the Negro, the Portuguese, the Hispanic, the German, the Polish, even the Russians. They ranged in profession from stevedores to lawyers, doctors and judges, and they were all part of the Newark I knew as a child.

It was safe back then. The parks did not harbor drug dealers, and the streets did not harbor thugs. On Monday summer nights, we strolled around Independence Park, its winding, blacktop paths crossing and criss-crossing between grassy lawns and dignified elms and sycamores. Teens and adults listened to the blaring bands that came there while the young boys of puberty were ferreting out willing young ladies.

We stole a kiss, but not their lives or dreams. There were police there, but they were a relaxed police because they were not impeded by liberal courts, nor did they have much to do because the people policed their own sections. There were no Civilian Review Boards so if you gave the cop any lip, he cracked you with his nightstick or whapped you across the gut with the flat of his hand. But, if you respected him and conceded his authority, he left you alone. In times of need, he could be your friend, your strength, your protection. But it wasn't often we called upon him.

It was a communal city, composed of legends and common people. It was safe because some people carried concealed weapons while others used their fists. Everyone carried a knife of some kind. Switch blades were in vogue but those who were sensible carried a small sheath knife and concealed it inside their pants. Because it was a communal city, we knew how to take care of our own. The Pacific Loafers—dock workers, stevedores, union men, laborers, crane operators, fork lift drivers, truckers—tucked the young neighborhood guys under their wings and kept them out of dutch. They strutted down the streets with their dark blue jackets, a white stripe down the arms, gold lettering spelling out the name of the organization. On the front, scrolled in inch-high letters, the name of the Loafer . . . Tony . . . Bull . . . Ponzi . . . Duffy . . . Punchy . . . Squash, names that delineated the man, the culture, the pride in himself and his occupation. In many ways, the Loafers were a brotherhood, a chain of humanity, bonded by the common thread of their geographic location. It did not matter what your race or creed. It only mattered who and what you were. If you were Italian or Irish so much the better, but it did not need to be so. What mattered was the code that one followed and his conduct, his honor.

It was the area from which I hailed, and it was called Down Neck or the Ironbound because it was bounded on each side by railroad tracks. At the Southeast tip laid the Port of New York and the docks where international and national ships slipped into port to be loaded or unloaded. Great tractor trailers rumbled into the yawing chasms of the wharves. Day or night, hundreds of trailers lay ready to be loaded and shipped to foreign places. The dock workers reported at the Union Hall every morning. When the ships came in, those who paid their union dues and voted the Union way were assigned to a ship. They worked long hours for triple the pay of ordinary men. Some days they did not work because ships were being fumigated or Customs had to search the ship before it docked. And other days, the workers were idle and when they did shape up, a hundred men might report for duty while ninety-five returned home or to the club house without work. It would not matter, though, for when they did work they earned excellent pay.

Sometimes those who worked did not return home. The dock was a dangerous place. One slip with the heavy equipment, and someone paid the price for carelessness. Men were swept off the boats by the huge cranes and carried under water by the weight of the cargo they hauled. By the time they were recovered, the men were dead and the cargo lost. Or a man might tumble into the deep holds of the ship and the cargo after him so, when he was recovered, he was hardly recognizable.

But the stevedores were kings. They ruled the docks and they ruled the streets; there was not a kid among us who did not aspire to be one of them. When they worked, they lost men. They also lost crates of watches, televisions, radios, power tools, stereos, copy machines, cameras and anything capable of being crated and shipped. The packing crates were not really lost. They were just reported as such. The insurance company paid the claims. The goods were diverted to a waiting union boss. The products contained within the packing showed up in parking lots, sports parks, on busy street corners and the rear of cars. If you didn't want what they had, they'd find what you did want—all at a bargain price, too.

Yes, the stevedores were kings and the union bosses were the emperors. Those who rebelled never worked. Those who did not belong did not gain entrance to the union halls. The emperors decided who would live and who would die or who would eat and who would starve. The workers obeyed and, for their obedience, they were rewarded with high wages and contraband.

On one occasion I received a telephone call from an acquaintance who asked if I needed any meat. Apparently someone had pilfered a shipment of beef and wanted to unload it quickly. I placed an order and was told to look for a white Chevrolet van near the West Side Highway in New York, and there, for a pittance, I purchased a side of beef which I promptly delivered to my father's luncheonette. It was probably the only profitable deal my father ever got into, but, at least, the beef turned him a nice profit for several days afterward. Now that I think of it, the deal was very profitable for my father because he didn't pay for the meat. I got stuck for what I paid. Dad liked to borrow from his enterprising son, but he always developed a palsy of the hand when it came time to pay. That was part of the city too . . . beating the other guy before he beat you. If one wasn't streetwise, he was a mark and a mark always got beaten. Even the stevedores dealt this way. They earned their pay and some gambled it away. Others salted it away for that special girl they'd make their wife. They drove fancy, sleek cars and dated fancy, sleek women. They sported themselves with open-collared dress shirts and flashy jackets, and the women dressed in short, revealing dresses tight around their bosoms. And all this was the soul of Newark.

The Port was one of the hearts of Newark, but not its only heart. The railroad was another heart. And its people, yet another. It was a smoke-filled, industrial complex, home to hundreds of businesses, home to frame houses stacked neatly in long rows, or more spacious dwellings in the exclusive end of town. It was a city of breweries, paint and chemical factories, oil refineries, truck companies, salvage yards and machine shops. They were businesses that hummed and thumped by day and hissed at night; factories that pounded and groaned and squealed; great hearts that thudded to a stop at five o' clock and commenced again at six a.m.; sirens that beeped the warning of a moving vehicle and horns that blared the beginning of the work day, lunch hour and quitting time.

It was a city of excitement, of stories, of lives. It was the ships coming to port from faraway lands. Foreign-speaking captains who spilled into the local bars and rested their sea legs and guzzled rye whiskey. It was the commuter trains that brought people to and from New York City; it was the metropolis of Penn Station where trains chugged on steel rails to distant cities. It was the airport where one could climb the watchtower and see the planes land and take off. There was no security back then. It was a safer nation. It was dusty and dirty and noisy and ribboned with highways. It was cobblestone and cement and dirt and narrow alleys. It was tired, wood-frame houses. It was stifling summers and rain squalls when the streets flooded. Mosquitoes that rose up from the night swamps and the smell of mosquito coils holding them off. It was seven foot snows when winter swept in from the bay. It was people helping people who were bogged down in the snow. And plows with sweeping blades, scraping the cobblestone like fingernails scraping across a blackboard. Clanking chains on huge tires that shattered the crisp air. Plunk, plunk, ching ching, rattling along the cleared ground. It was the Meadowlands where the mob buried their honored dead, and the Newark Bay where those dishonorably executed were weighted down and sunk to the bottom.

It was a society of protection and a society of conflagration. It was both moral and immoral, those who climbed the ladder of success with dignity and honesty and those who rose by violence. It was their Newark. It was our Newark. It was my Newark. A nice place to grow, a nice place to live. It was a city with a pulse, a heartbeat and a city with a cry. Like a distant sea, the ebb and flow swept through time so that each sound had its place. Daytime initiated with the growl of the morning bus wallowing around a corner, its gears laboring to gain speed, and its poles attached to overhead lines that furnished electricity. By mid-morning the sound of the buses blended with a thousand other sounds, among them the first grating cries of the vendors, hawking their wares. The initial clamor might be the old rag man, plodding along on his open wagon, a bay gelding melodically pulling the wagon, halting on command, then shaking his harness to rid himself of flies.

"Rags, old rags. Buying. Selling. New ones; old ones. Rags." This was the song, the pulse of the morning. And before the song faded, another began.

"Peaches. Apples. Tomatoes. Nice tomatoes. Corn. Cherries. Bananas. Ripe bananas." Old man Memoli's horse-drawn wagon ambling to a stop while he rang out his ditty, again and again.

The women poked their heads out like moles testing the weather, then clambered out of basement doors, signifying interest. The vegetable man waited as they waddled across the street to the wagon to bargain and criticize the garden goods. They halted to shout to one another and stood gossiping long after they had made their purchases. I can still see them haggling with the wagoneer about the price or quality of his fruit. But mostly they spoke to each other, trading the day's gossip or complaining about the price of food and clothing.

"And what kind of fruit is this? It's bruised and old. Old fruit. My dog would not eat it."

"Today, myself, I carried this fruit from the tree to the wagon. What's a little bruise? The fruit is sweet like sugar. Taste." And he sliced a piece of peach and handed it the woman. She'd buy it anyway because that was her thing. It was a game they played, the merchant and his patron. For some reason, she had to complain and he had to listen, but, in the end, she always bought his fruit and vegetables because she knew they were fresh, and she could not beat the price at the market.

The women were dowdy but not old. They wore musty, print dresses that made them seem older. Their hair was tied up in buns. And they slid wrinkled, hard hands into their pockets to pull out worn, cloth purses from which they extracted wrinkled dollar bills. Even the bills seemed as if they had been stored away forever. Then they dropped the fruit into cloth bags, made parting comments to the vendor, finished with their gossip and waddled back into the holes from which they escaped.

The scrap collectors came in the afternoons. And a new contingent of ragged, old women crystallized from their dwellings. The organ grinder with his roasted peanuts and chestnuts came with the hurdy-gurdy in the evening when pungent smells saturated the air. Some days, the photographer trudged along with his weary-looking pinto pony, hoisted excited children on its back and snapped their photographs for grinning parents. Two or three times a year, the knife grinder appeared, wielding his spinning stone wheel with a cry as sharp as the blades he produced as he manipulated the knives and scissors over the spiraling wheel. The afternoon was filled with different sounds. Moving traffic. Sirens. Fire alarms. Thriving factories alive with people, those ending their shifts, those beginning. The buses came more regularly at opening and closing time. But at dark the pulse subsided. The sounds faded away. The buses diminished. Traffic slowed and the night air stilled. From distant taverns drifted juke box music and clamorous voices rising in laughter or anger. Some time after midnight, the city slept. A restless sleep. A troubled sleep. The silence shattered, occasionally, by some vehicle burning rubber as it squealed away or bombarding the night with its broken exhaust belching smoke and fire. And this was Newark. Newark in the era of 1940. Newark before the Second World War thinned the ranks of the young men and made patriots of kids who never returned. And youngsters who gathered up scrap iron for the war effort and played at war with their friends, though all of them secretly wished the war would wait until they turned seventeen; and in time, when some of them returned from war, they were boys no longer for their youth had been betrayed.

It was a town with a code and a culture. Neither the Code of the West nor the code of any one culture. There were parades to elect the mayor and campaign parties with hot dogs and pizza. It was the once a year visit by the parish priest who blessed the houses and cast out the demons. It was school kids and parents, workers and bums, heroes and fags, flop houses and low cost movies. It was a place where one could buy a hamburger that made it though the night in some sleazy, discount restaurant. It was the morning cry of a vendor summoning housewives to buy sundries, shoe laces, razor blades, sewing scissors and thread. It was the Farmer's Market where damaged vegetables and fruit were parceled out to the needy, and it was crowded buses, tenements, dice games and pin ball machines. Newark was the corner where kids hung out because they had few places to go. It was a city of silence, a city of noise, a city of people. It was a city that lived in the shadow of New York but was never a shadow itself. It was the place to which prize fighters came: Charlie Fusari, Rocky Grazziano, Tony Galento and the like. It was the place where Minnesota Fats came to win at pool and a hundred pool hustlers lingered behind to con the marks.

In many ways it was a city of nobility, a city of illusion. It pretended to be one thing and it was quite another. One moment it was silent and cheery and sleepily lazing the day along, and the next moment the world was shaken when catastrophe collided with chemicals and oil refineries. I was nineteen when the refinery blew up. A sticky valve did not shut tightly enough and oil spilled over the ground. An open flame ignited it. The rising black smoke could be seen and smelled for tens of miles around, and the explosion of each and every oil tank shattered the windows of my father's store and jarred the streets. From the east came a flaming ball of molten fire as if a volcano erupted under the refinery. Every few minutes another tank would explode, and more sirens raced off into the distance. Windows shook and cracked. People raced away in fear, tracing and retracing the steps they had taken before. Others knelt in prayer. Still others lay flat on the ground expecting to be swallowed up. The land was ablaze with flame. Cannonades of smoke fumed into the sky and it was night then. And when night did come, it was not night at all but sunrise because there were balls of light and fire when other tanks exploded. Each blast gave the Ironbound another shake, then quieted and let the city settle again.

Newark was burning, exploding, erupting. A sea of flames engulfed a sea of water and the two met, sizzled, flamed and burned. It would continue for days just as the bombing of the ship, *Normandy*, and, when it finally burned itself out, the dead were numberless and the damage beyond estimate. When others were fleeing from the horrendous blasts, the shaking ground, the flumes of fire spurting into the air, I was driving toward Newark Bay hoping to catch a better glimpse. This was the story of the city . . . my city.

It was a city of radiance and a city with dark, mysterious places. It was an ocean swell of cultures and a sea of currents and undercurrents. The pulse of that city flows in the words that follow and ends when my own days are done. So I hailed from a city where bankers walked along side hit men. Mafia bosses strolled inconspicuously behind baby carriages. Some of the undercurrents involved codes. A Code of the East or the Code of Down Neck. Codes of conduct. Trust, loyalty to one another, respect, silence, manliness. We were men. We were Down-Neckers. We were Italians first, Americans second. We married Italians. If we were Catholic, we married a Catholic girl. We ate Italian food and drank home-made wine. No meal was complete without pasta and crusty Sicilian bread. We voted for the Italian. We protected Italian enterprises and did business with them. As part of the city, we wore guinea tees and went shirtless in hot weather. In summertime we strolled to the lemon ice stands and enjoyed gelatto. We nodded respectfully to the wives and sisters of other Italians and venerated their mothers. And we respected the mob bosses because they held the power of life and death or economic success or failure. We did not regard the mob as evil nor did we regard Dons as men to be feared. We respected them as heroes.

Pretty Boy Floyd, Baby Face Nelson, the Barkers, Bonnie and Clyde, they were evil. They killed for money and for sport. The Mafia killed only for business and with reason. And the men who presided were immigrants fighting their way out of the slums and into society. They were among us. Not conspicuously. They were low key. Established members of the community, generous to the Church, helpful to those in need, they fought their way from immigrant status to wealth and power. They were integrated into the system to such a degree that in many cases they controlled the system.

They kept odd hours so that they were rarely seen in public. They left home before dawn, varied their schedules and their routes of travel, and returned after many hours of work. In their line of work it was not healthy to present too easy a target. We, in the streets, did not regard the numbers racket, or gambling, or illegal whiskey, or even prostitution as evil. On the contrary, these were enterprises fashioned from the minds of uneducated men who pandered to the needs of men and profited by it. They did not lavish money nor draw attention to what they owned. In many cases, they lived in unembellished homes, drove modest cars and wore casual clothing, far from the image painted by the movies.

Yes, there were Capones, but they were rare and not the rule. And, yes, men had to be killed when they transgressed the Code by which the mob existed. This was a code we adopted as well. The law of *Omerta*, the Code of Silence, was our code as well. We would not rat on a friend. We would furnish no information to the police. The very word *omu* means the art of never placing a friend in trouble, and it is a noble concept rather than a dread law of murder. Those who took the vow were like saints to us, not murderers. Though we took no vow, we kept the Code of Silence as well as the next man.

This law of silence was not an oath we took. It was something we understood. It was one of the first principles of being streetwise. Those who kept the silence were rewarded by their own conscience, if nothing else. Those who broke the Code paid a price. If we saw something, we kept our mouths shut. If we heard, we heard with deaf ears. We saw only with blinded vision. We said nothing to authority. When in difficulty we learned to speak, to reason, to convince. If we failed, it sometimes meant death. At the very least, a beating. If we succeeded, we lived to make amends but never to be trusted.

Though I grew up with these men as my gods, I knew nothing of their employment. Hit men did not carry a sign that said: "For hire. Hit man." They were professionals. Men who studied their craft, had a mind for detail and an artistic quality of their work. They did not butcher with shot gun blasts. No, the true hit man placed two bullets almost side by side in the head of his victim and left with no trace. The weapon he used would never be found. It would be melted down with scrap iron and a replacement given.

When we read of a hit, we did not recoil in horror. We were filled with respect and admiration for how well the task was accomplished. There was no compassion for the deceased because, to merit retribution, he violated some rule and was punished for it. We had our Captain Midnights and our Lone Rangers but we also had the Don and his soldiers. We discussed proudly how effectively the hit was done and wondered if the hit men had families or feelings and how it felt to snuff out a life. Later, when some of our friends were gunned down, some of them mere innocent bystanders, we lost some of our enamor for the hit men but never for their professionalism and their cool execution. But we feared them then.

Hit men were professionals. They did not survive by trusting others. On the contrary, they survived by stealth and detail. Did they have feelings? At least one I knew did. For years Benny had been an amateur heavyweight boxer. And he looked like a prizefighter because he stood square, tall and muscular. He had a puffy, roundish face, with cheeks that looked as if his wisdom teeth had just been pulled. When he was serious, his eyes narrowed into razor sharp slits, though I could never tell when he was serious and when he was kidding. Benny was good with his fists. Good, but not good enough to make the pros. I wish I could say he had a poor childhood and that's the reason he turned to crime. But that would not be true. He was an average kid, with an average family and average intelligence. So he did not become a hit man because of poor family life. Nor was he mean. Nor did he set out to be a killer. He had to earn a living like everyone else. That living was collecting funds from reluctant gamblers or late payers on their loan shark debts. At first, it was small stuff. Threatening a bum who didn't pay or punching in his ribs because his "boss" meant business. Eventually, though, the pay from that work was insufficient to support a family. So Benny graduated. He developed a cool detachment that one could detect from the distant glare in his eyes. Although we were friends, I never knew his real occupation until later in life. Benny was married and had a son. A son who was special and dear to him. For whatever reason, his son turned twenty-one and never grew any older. He placed his father's thirty-eight against his temple and squeezed off a round. The shot charged through his brain and splattered blood over the floor and walls.

Benny was never the same after that. Always towering, straight and even tempered, Benny turned sour, blaming his son's fate on his own occupation. He no longer stood tall but stooped like an old man when he walked. He became distant to his wife and most friends, drank heavily, locked himself in his room for days. He ate little. Spoke little. It was as if he buried himself with his son. And, he refused assignments. He avoided the mob. He even became argumentative when asked to work.

I met Benny in the Pennington Bar where he always spent his idle time. Such men have plenty of time between jobs. He always had affection for me, a trust I never understood. He often told me that if I ever needed anyone busted up, he'd do the job. When I began dating my second wife, he suggested I remove her "problem" his way. It would save the cost of a divorce. He meant it. It was not an idle promise. He had a way of gazing into your soul with light blue, intensive eyes. When Benny gazed into someone's eyes, it was as if he were searching for something. And he was a philosopher, deliberating the meaning of life and death, and an avid soothsayer who mastered the interpretation of dreams as somber communications from the beyond. He once told me that just before his son committed suicide, he dreamed of having a tooth pulled. "Such a dream always imparted the loss of a loved one," he said. By then, I knew what he was and what he did for a living. It struck me as odd that someone so nearly associated with death should find it such a fascinating subject. In his heart, he was a prizefighter. In his mind, he was a person who eliminated wrongdoers. Somehow, it never fazed me. He was just Benny to me. When I had to travel to Aruba and Venezuela on mob business, Benny made sure my fiancée was guarded and protected. He followed her husband to make certain she wasn't molested in any way. When she parked her vehicle—in a parking lot that was normally full—she always had a spot reserved for her right near the school entrance. She had never experienced this before. Her husband was fortunate he refrained from trouble while I was away. I am certain Benny would have acted without the slightest hesitation. I can recall how often he tactfully suggested that I free his hands. My greatest fear was that her then-husband would do something that might trigger a real problem. Benny had a cruel side to his nature. He had a loyal side as well.

I met with him often after his son's death. There had been so many years of friendship, it seemed cruel not to offer him some consolation or comfort. We always met at the Pennington Bar where Bob served drinks in the front room during legal hours, and in the back room until everyone tired and went home. Entering the bar, day or night, one entered a dismal world of dim lights and fleeting shadows. The only window was the front window and that was obscured by signs and curtains. On the left was the linear bar that coursed along seventy feet of dingy wooden floor. Faded red bar stools lined along the bar as if someone yelled "Attenhut!" Behind the bar, on wooden shelves, whiskey, a few cordials, some inferior wines, a blackboard that listed what food was available. Straight back lay the rest rooms and beyond that, a curtained room reserved for private poker games and meetings. Bob was as old and jaded as the room itself, as if he had become a fixture that moved only when requested and then remained innocuous and inconspicuous. Occasionally, the back telephone rang and Bob shuffled over to it, noting a wager and writing it in code. "Five bottles of bar gin to be delivered to Mr. Mo, apartment three, first floor, five dollars per bottle." This simply meant that a bet was being placed on the fifth race at Monmouth Race Track, post position three, in the sum of five dollars to win. Each kind of whiskey coded a different race track. If the bettor wanted to bet the horse for second place, then he designated it as second floor and so on.

This was the decrepit place into which Benny had sunk. No more the alert philosopher, the cherubic-faced boxer, with no marks or broken face bones. Just an indiscriminate solitary figure hunched over the bar staring at the polished wood before him. On each occasion that I met him there, he was high on rye whiskey. He stared at me with no recognition as the whiskey had dulled his brain. His sad, distant eyes were listless and blurry, but he still searched my face for answers I could not give. Then recognition spread over his face, and then the light went out of it again.

"Why'd he do it, Russ? Why? I give him everything a father could give."

Then he would hesitate, his mind still working.

"You think he knew (he drew out the word *knew*) what I did for a living? Could he have found out, maybe?"

"No way." I shot back rapidly. "No way. Even I didn't know and how long were we friends?"

He smiled, looking down at his glass, each time. "Long time, Russ. Long time." His eyes widened as he drifted. "Long time," he whispered pensively. "I always liked you, Russ. Trust you," he'd conclude.

"Benny, you've got to put it behind you. It probably was something wrong with his chemistry. Hormones can do that. Something went haywire inside. It had nothing to do with you or your wife, and it's not something you could help. It just happened. He wouldn't want you doing this to yourself. Sal always worried about you, you know that. He wouldn't want you boozing it up and spilling your mouth." I reverted to Down Neck dialect so he associated me more on his level than that of a lawyer.

He snickered. "Yeah, I could put a lot of guys in jail, couldn't I? I only talk to you, though . . . I think." He chuckled, a little spittle slobbering down his chin. "When I get boozed up, I forget who I talk to." Then, he swigged down a drink and tapped his glass on the bar, motioned Bob to pour another. And Bob shook his head but complied. It was as if the whole scenario was written out because it played the same way each and every time I saw him.

"I never meant it personally," he started up. "I bumped people because it was business. Some of them deserved it. I didn't judge. The Bible says don't judge or you'll be judged." He whined to a stop and began crying.

"You think he knew how I made my living, Russ?"

"No, Benny. He couldn't know."

I needed to steer him away from his depression. "Was it bad . . . when you did a job? I mean, did you have any feeling about it?"

"First time I felt bad. Almost backed out. That's not a good thing to do, huh? I felt bad but it was business. After that, I didn't think about it except how I was going to do the job. And I was good. Yeah, good. I'd watch a guy for months. Get his routine down. Did he have a girlfriend? That was a biggie. A guy almost always had a girlfriend. Sometimes you found a guy who was clean. Family man. Didn't drink. No women. Even went to church on Sunday." He pounded his fist into his hand, and I watched the palm turn white with the weight of each blow. "Never hit a guy going or coming from church. Bad luck. Some guys did. They had no respect. Just meat hunters and no respect. I never did."

"And if he was clean, what then?"

"Had to find some clue. Did he do his own banking? Where'd he go at night? What sports did he like? Where'd he place his bets? Have his hair cut? Favorite restaurant? Yeah, I was thorough." He laughed. "I took pride in my work. It was hard work, not easy. People think you just walk up and shoot a guy? Stupid cruds. It takes time and talent. Detail, you got to pay attention to detail. And I was small time. I know that. Just a corner hood."

In one of his drunken stupors, he spilled that God had punished him for his line of work. All those lives he snuffed out. All the people he contracted to kill. He could see their faces. He could hear their pleas. And he knew that God had punished him by taking his son. After a year, he was no better. His wife deserted him. He lived and drank alone. There were nights the police called me to come and pick him up. He had been found sitting by his son's grave, crying and babbling incoherently. I never shirked my obligation. After all, Benny was willing to put me on the cuff and tap some enemy of mine into oblivion. Why should I desert him when he needed someone desperately?

I kept warning him to be silent. He had to stop shooting his mouth off. The last time I saw him, he remarked about one of my questions. He was sitting at Bob's bar. The worse for wear. When I saw him, he was slumped over, half drunk, half asleep. He stirred when I neared him, the instinct of his profession rousing him. He fixed me with a hazy, unfriendly eye, and then, as recognition flowered, he smiled and tapped me on the shoulder with his fist.

"Remember Joey Boops?"

I nodded.

"He was a good guy. We palled around together. Did you know that? He was a crazy coot. His head was two sizes too big for his body, and he had those big rubber lips, deep black, curly hair. Remember when he chased that guy off his girlfriend's stoop? Drove the ratty car right up the stoop, broke the steps, busted his front end, blew the blinking tires out. I can still see that car moving up on the steps while the guy was backing up to the wall."

"I remember that. The old man came out with a shotgun and put a hole in Joey's radiator. Crap, there was water all over the street and Joey went nuts. Tried to run the guy down and blew his engine all to hell. I had tears running down my face, I was laughing so hard. What a bimbo. "

"We spent a lot of time together, Joey and me. He came to all my fights. Wanted to be my manager. I told him he couldn't manage his way out of the lady's room." He hesitated, swigged down another drink. "Did you know Joey introduced me to my wife? Yeah, he did. I think he was interested in her. But he saw I was thunderstruck with her. He told her I was a good guy, honorable, he said. Me? Honorable?"

"You are, Benny. You are an honorable guy. A noble savage."

"Poetry. You should be a writer. Always with the words, the poetry."

"Maybe someday I'll write about you, Benny."

"Just make sure I'm dead or the Mob will hire me to hit myself," he laughed.

"I remember Joey," I said. "He came with me to my grandfather's house. Had a glass of wine or two. You know my grandfather's wine. Hell, we just got out the door and he keeled right over."

Benny was laughing. His eyes were sparkling with laughter, too. "He never could hold a drink. Or take a punch. He wanted to be my sparring partner. Little, 5'4" Joey. I hit him one left, and he spun down for the count. Two hours later he was still out. Glass jaw. Lord, was he game!"

Then, the laughter merged into tears.

"We ate pasta together. Went swimming at Palisades Park. Snuck into the Rialto Theater to watch Westerns. Hoot Gibson, Lash La Rue. Wild Bill Elliot. Every time he saw a new movie, he wanted to be like the guy on the screen. Then, we'd go to Nathan's and get a hot dog and a Jewish knish. Joey ate more mustard than hot dog."

"I lost track of him when I went to school," I said.

"You did good. Got out of Newark. Now you're a fancy lawyer."

"Not too fancy for my friends, Benny."

He motioned Bob for another drink. The somber barkeep slid it before him and remained laconic. "Yeah, you never got uppity. Never forgot your roots."

"So what happened to Joey?"

"He went into the paper business. Became a runner for the family. Our family." He chortled. "Collected money from the local books and ran it to the controllers. Except sometimes all the money didn't make it home. He used to say a few of the birds got lost in migration. Huk, huk huk, can you believe that? Lost in migration?"

"Shame. . . what happened, I mean. Or, maybe, I shouldn't ask."

Benny gripped me by the lapel and tugged me face to face. "This don't go no further. Right?" He exhaled his liquor breath on me. "Right?"

"When did I ever betray your confidence?"

"Joe P doesn't call me in. Too smart for that. He sends Bones to talk to me. 'Benny,' he says, 'where do you want to go in the organization?' He's acting like a big shot, like I don't know who really sent him."

"'I'm happy Bones,' I says. 'I guess I'd like more dough. But I'm not complaining.'"

"'I got a job. A special job. I could hire someone outside the state or ask for an accommodation from our friends in New York or Philly. But it's a tacky job. It needs someone with just the right touch.'"

"'I'm interested,' I say. I'm still wondering what he's talking about but it's an opportunity. I can't pass it up."

"'Once I tell you about it, you're in. No backing out.'"

"Bones gives me that stern look that is supposed to scare me."

"I shrugged. 'If I'm in, I'm in.'"

"'We got this guy. Nice kid. Known him a long time. But he's got a dame, and she's bleeding him for the big stuff. Diamonds, fancy car, gowns, furs. You know the scene. He's taking bread from the mouths of our children. When it was small amounts, the guys overlooked it. Everybody steals a little. But now, he's hitting us big time, and the vote was against him.'"

"'A hit?'"

"'You taking the job?'"

"'I'm in.'"

"'It pays $20,000.00. And it's gotta be done soon. Our losses are mounting every day.'"

"'I'm in. Who is it?'"

"He pushed back into his swivel chair, paused a moment. 'Joey Boops!'"

"He searched my face like you search for gold in the ground. I never flinched but, inside, I was hooked. My friend. Joey Boops. I was going to make my bones on the back of my friend."

I knew he shouldn't be spilling his guts. I protested, but I knew he wouldn't stop. "Benny, you should stop. Leave it alone."

"I got to tell somebody. Who else can I trust? So, you're my Father Confessor."

I tried pulling away, but he held me fast. I was still inhaling his sour breath.

"Joey and I go out drinking. I need to have him off guard. I'm sitting in his car, laughing with the guy, and all the time knowing I have to blow his friggen' brains out. If I don't, they do it anyway and I go with him."

"You got yourself into a box."

"A box," he muttered.

"Joey looks at me. 'I'm in deep,' he says. 'Deep trouble.'"

"'I know.' Joey's shoulders sag like boiled pasta. That's because he knows why I'm there."

He squints at me a little. His eyes show some recognition. Benny isn't seeing much.

"'You know?' Joey asks."

"'I know.' I answer."

"Joey settles back against the window and heaves a sigh. 'I'm glad it's you. I'm glad it's over. That lousy broad drove me like a car. Now, she'll be layin' everything in sight, and Joey Boops is dead. Bum break.'"

"'I know. I wish there was something . . . but it's business. I didn't know until I took the job. They're testing me. If I make my bones, I'm part of the Family. If not, they dump me in Newark Bay.'"

"'Yeah, that's the rackets for ya.' He smiled, his eyes lighting for the first time since I pulled the gun. 'What do ya think they'll do with me?'"

"'The body? You mean the body?'"

"'Yeah! They going to dump me in the Bay or in the back of my car?'"

"'I'll take care of it, Joey. You get a first class burial.'"

"'Thanks, Pug. Hey, I always enjoyed watching you fight. I should a been your manager.'"

"'Bump you, buddy. I never had a chance, manager or not. You have to play the game or you don't get the fame.'"

"His voice turned serious. 'Will it hurt, Benny?'"

"'Naw. It's a .22. The shock will stun you so bad you won't feel nothing.'"

"'A .22?'"

"'Yeah. It don't penetrate the other side. Makes a nice small hole and breaks up. The fragments rattle around in your head, and there ain't much blood. Okay, so maybe I put two or three, but see, when it hits the brain, everything goes dead, and you don't feel nothin'.'"

"'Like all the circuits is blown?' Joey asks."

"'Right.'"

"Joey nodded again. 'What happens when we die? I mean, is there a Heaven and Hell? I always knew they'd catch me one day. Nicking those bucks. Bad move.'"

"'I can't answer that one. Give you time to make your peace. I'm sorry, Joey. It's just business, ya' know. Nothing personal.'"

"'I'm glad it was you. I figured it would be some stranger. Somebody who didn't give a plugged nickel. It makes a difference. This way I got to see you one last time. It got so bad I couldn't sleep, couldn't eat. Couldn't even sleep with my girl. Woke up one night and had peed my underwear. Every shadow was going to kill me. And still, I didn't stop. Dames will do that to you. Wouldn't do any good to run. So, I been waitin'. I'm glad it's you.' He sighed heavily. 'Don't tell me when.'"

"'I won't.'"

"'I'll make peace with the Man.'"

"He dropped his chin a little, turned his head and recited an Act of Contrition and an Our Father. Then, he looked at me, and I see there is peace in his heart. He's resigned. I never lift the gun. I shoot right from the lap. The bullet strikes him dead on the bridge of the nose and punches him up against the window. I see blood and brains splattered against the car window, and I know a .45 is too sloppy for a job like this. The silencer did a lousy job. Ya know, Russ, it's not like in the movies where ya hear nothing. In a closed car the sound is loud, but I got a job to do, and I punch another one into his head. I don't worry about people. People don't matter. They're scared witless at the first sound, confused, gutless; they rubberneck and then they scram because they figure the next crash is going to be them. I don't know now many times I walked into a bar, pointed a gun and blew five shots into a guy while people were frozen with their mouths open. They're not even looking at me, and if they do, ten minutes later they won't remember what I am wearing if I was dressed like a clown.

"Anyway, I check the dude. He has no pulse and I fade out of the car. An hour later, I call the cops and tip them on where the body is. I figure that way, Joey gets his funeral."

There were tears slipping down his cheek. "That first one bothered me. After that, only one other job got to me. Only once." His cheeks puffed, and his eyes squeezed down into tiny channels of wisdom.

"A kid in Montclair. He was just there bowling. I goofed that one. I had a Contract on the owner of the place. He was into Joe P for a lot of bucks. Didn't pay after two warnings. Threatened to turn Joe P into the Feds for loan sharking. Not smart. I figured it was closing time and the joint was empty. So, I walk up to the bum, stick the gun out and blow two holes in his head. And then, the kid pops up from one of the alleys. His mouth sags like a wet noodle, and he's eyeing me square up and down. There is no question he can finger me if I let him go."

He upended his glass and tapped the bar.

"It's not something I want to do. The kid is scared. Maybe eighteen, not much younger than my kid."

"'Mister, I won't say nothin'. Honest. I didn't see nothin'. I don't even work here. Look! I got a girl. We're gettin' married in a month.'"

"'Kid, you promise?'"

"'I promise, Mister. I won't tell anyone I was here.'"

"The kid wet his pants. I could see the dark stain near his crotch."

"'O.K. Turn around and walk real slow to the back door. Go on through and don't turn around. You say a word to anyone, and I'll find you. Got that?'"

"The kid turns slowly around and creeps along. Believe me, Russ, there are tears in my eyes when I squeeze off the rounds. He staggers forward like somebody slipping on the ice. Then, he's down. I check him over and he's dead. Just a kid and he's dead. And that one hurt. I guess because he reminded me of my Sal. I kept thinking: How'd you like it, Benny, if it was your kid? I couldn't come up with an answer. That one bothered me. None of the others. Just that one. I could hear the family crying as they buried him. A young life. Shit! Why'd the dumb kid have to be in the wrong place at the wrong time?"

"Benny, shut up! You're talking too much and in the wrong places. It can't keep up this way. Sooner or later, they'll shut you up."

"What's it matter? I'm all dead inside. That's why I got punished. That kid in Montclair. Maybe it wasn't his time, and I pushed him over the edge."

"Okay, but don't talk to anyone else."

"Got cha."

"Benny, did you ever muff a job?" There was no point in trying to stop him. He was going to talk anyway. I gambled that getting it all out of him might shut him up because it was off his chest.

He bolted upright and straightened his shoulders. "Never. Never bungled a job. I always hit clean. And I didn't torture nobody. A guy had to be snuffed, I did it with style. He was entitled to that kind of respect. Sure, some guys groveled. Most did. Maybe I got a soft heart or somethin'. I let 'em talk. Why not? Was the sky gonna fall because I let a guy talk?"

"No, I guess it wouldn't."

"Sometimes I let the guy think he was talking me out of it. You'd be surprised how some wise guys would think they had me snowed. I enjoyed snuffing those guys. But some guys were sincere, and, if they were, I'd let 'em talk."

"You always had a soft heart."

"Hey, mostly they talked about their wife and kids. One guy even included his girlfriend. Her birthday was in two days, and he bought her this special necklace. Would I give him two days so he could spend one last birthday with her?"

"You didn't, did you?"

"I told him to get out of the car. I told him I couldn't hit no guy two days before his girlfriend's birthday." His lips drew wide into a snide smile. "He starts to get out of the car, and I wham him in the back of the head. He never knew what hit him. Hey, the way I figure, his last moments were thinking he was off the hook. That had to make him happy, didn't it?"

I shifted and motioned Bob for another drink and pointed to Benny's glass as well. I figured that if I got him good and drunk, I'd take him home. "He died a happy man . . . if he believed you," I said, pushing away from the bar.

"Bob wants to close, Benny. Drink up and let's go."

"A bullet in the head that way has got to take you out fast. A lot of amateurs in the business today. They hit the body and get you down, then stand over you like Clint Eastwood and pump two more into your head. Amateurs. You hit 'em in the head, and they go out fast, stunned, no time to hurt, no time to even think. The bullet cuts right through the brain tissue, and it kills the switch on everything."

He stared out across the bar and into the mirror. "Like my kid. He knew what he was doing. Put the gun right where it would cut the switch. Split-second."

"Not your fault, Benny. For all you know some chemical in his brain went crazy and the kid wasn't thinking right. Nobody's fault."

"Yeah, that's what the priest said. We were good parents, and only God understands why these things happen."

"Let's talk about something else. How about that fight you had with Tony Marco?"

"Yeah, fight. Did I ever tell you how I got into this business?" Another drink downed.

"I never asked. That's not the kind of thing you ask somebody."

"Did you know, Russ? Did you know I was a hit man?"

"I had an idea."

"And it didn't bother you?"

"Not my place to judge. If a guy is right with me, I have no beef with him. Benny, you've got to clam up now. I don't need to know all this stuff. "

I stared into his face. His eyes were dull and sad. He was still handsome, though the tears had reddened his cheeks, and he brushed them away with crusty, thick fingers. Two men pushed through the barroom door and shoved the chairs around, making a racket. Then, noting Benny, they quieted down and asked the bartender for drinks. After a time, they both squirmed a little and hoisted their drinks quickly. One of them spoke to the other, nervously glancing at the malevolent gaze emanating from Benny. They handed Bob some cash, moved silently away from the bar and left. Benny's glare remained for a few seconds, then he turned again, faced the endless bottles lined up against the back of the bar and continued speaking.

"Two of Joe's torpedoes had a hit to make. One of them is called Dizzy, and he ain't too bright. He has this mother-in-law, see. She's a whiner. Complains about everything. Dizzy is up to here with her." He places his open hand across his throat. "Nothing is good enough for the old bag, and she's hanging by a thread. Heart problems, brittle bones. All the time I see Dizzy he moans about his mother-in-law so I tell him 'why don't you get rid of the old bat?'"

"'How?' he says."

"'You throw her out a friggen' window.' I says."

"'We live in a ranch. Nellie won't climb no stairs anyway.'"

"'So, you figure it out.'"

"Well, does he?" I asked.

"Dizzy buys a two story house, split-level or something. He walks the old douche up to the second floor to show her the upstairs, and she's cranky every step of the way. 'Hold on to me,' he says, and she grabs hold of his belt and he's pulling her up. Tells her they got a nice, comfortable bed for her. Just a few steps more and they'll be there. So she huffing and puffing when she gets to the last step. Dizzy turns, and with a sneer on his face, says 'Goodbye Grandma', and he heaves her down the stairs. Fourteen stairs and she lands like rocks . . . but she ain't dead. The old gal ain't dead. What's more, she clocks him in the nose with her right and it stings. She's swearing like an old sailor, but he's mad because of the punch and the fact that she ain't dead."

"So what does he do then?" Benny asks.

I shrugged, waiting for the punch line.

"He carries her up the stairs and tosses her down again. This frail, little old lady, with brittle bones and a bum ticker, and he has to throw her down the stairs three times and all the time she is wailing , 'sumnabitch, I killa you.' Finally Dizzy don't hear no more hollerin', but he tosses her down one more time for good measure."

"Don't they have an investigation?"

"Sure, but the County Coroner is connected to the mob, and he's not going to commit suicide. Dizzy's wife don't buy the Coroner's report, and Cindy takes her belongings and heads out to Vegas to her old job as a cocktail waitress. So Dizzy got rid of the old fart, but I think he missed the old bat more than he did Cindy. Like I said, he was never any too bright. I think the Dons felt sorry for him, and they gave him easy work. That's why they gave him this easy hit too." He turned to stare toward the front of the bar as if to see if anyone is coming in. Satisfied we are alone, he turns again to me.

"The mark Dizzy is to hit is a pimp. He works his girls, and he don't pay the bosses. And he takes more out in trade than he pays over. Then he propositions the sister of one of the Dons. They don't need no more excuse than that. They don't even vote on the hit. The offended patron doesn't ask because he doesn't have to. He orders the rub, and Dizzy gets the job because a school kid on lunch could do the hit.

"The hit is coming out of the bar, and Dizzy's waiting to plug him. All of a sudden there's a big crash inside the bar, and the mark ducks back into the door. Dizzy fires a shot, but the guy is already back inside the door. Now, he realizes he's been shot at, and the pimp makes a leap into the street, turns the corner and he's runnin' like hell. Dizzy don't know which way to turn, but I follow the guy, and I take off runnin' up the parallel street. I figure the guy has to take a breath. He'll look back and see if he's being chased. Old Benny has got him figured to a tee. He's standin' on the corner and, boom-boom, I make the hit."

"You knocked him off without having the job?"

"Yeah. I wasn't in the mob. I broke a few fingers here and there but nothin' like a hit. I did it on my own. I figure who's going to get mad if I do the job instead of a jerk?"

"So, what then?"

"Then, nothin' because there is nothin' to do. I just sit back and wait. Pretty soon Tony Bones calls me on the carpet. He wants to know what happened. But I'm smart. I don't slam the other guy for missing his hit. I figure maybe I've proved something so I don't have to run Dizzy down. Well, nothin' happens for a month, and then Bones comes to see me. He's askin' me how work is and what I earn and am I interested in big dough and I tell him, yeah, I am. Interested in big dough."

"A week later, he comes to see me again. That's when he asks me if I would make a hit for him. He tosses a grand on the table. One thousand bucks and says it's live-on money. So, we live on it. A little time goes by and Tony comes to see me again. Hey, that Joe P is smart. He never gives a direct order. Always, it's from Tony. That's when they order the hit on Joey Boops. I had to make my bones by hitting a friend. It's the way they operate."

He wipes his face with his arm and holds up his glass to Bob. The bartender frowns and his eyes are steely like the eyes of a snake before it strikes, but he pours the drink and saunters down to the end of the bar. He pretends he's not listening, but Bob isn't missing a word, and all of it will go back to Joe P. But I can't shut Benny up. It's a dead night, and we've got the place to ourselves and he has a lot of baggage to unload. Besides, Tuesday nights are like that. People are still recovering from the long weekend. They're back to work and low on pay so they stay home.

Bob wipes a few glasses and pours himself some seltzer water. He notices me watching him and raises the glass. His face tells one story, and his eyes another. And I know Bob because he's a bookie for the syndicate and takes in big action on the weekend. Once a month there's an all-night poker game in the back room. The cops come in for a few free drinks, get their payoff and throw their weight around because it would hurt their pride if anyone thought they were crooked. So Bob is a company man, and it's not good for Benny to shoot off his mouth, but he continues talking and all I can do is listen and try to quiet him down.

"Now they've got this guy who is pretty cagey. He don't follow a schedule. He's got no girlfriend. Doesn't drink. Operates mostly from the house. Has just about everything sent in. His kids walk out the door and get the school bus. When they get home, they never leave the back yard. The shades are always pulled. I mean, the guy is impossible to spot." He slid off his chair. "I got to pee."

I watched him stagger back to the rest room, half expecting to hear gunshots, but there was an eerie pall as if the outside world cloaked and soundproofed the bar.

Benny returned, still zipping his fly.

"I got him. Know how?"

"I don't know how. And maybe we should leave it at that."

He smirked. "I found out the guy was a diabetic. Checked with his pharmacy and found out he was on insulin. A guy on insulin has to have his shot. He can miss a pill, but he can't miss his shot. So after I get the information from the pharmacists, I made an appointment with his doctor and got friendly with the secretary. Hey, she was a looker, you know?" He jabbed me with his elbow as if we shared a common joke. "So she told me the doctor has to see an insulin patient every six months. The guy has to come in or no more insulin. From there on in it was duck soup. I date the secretary a few times, nothing funny. Just good fun. I tell her my friend should be comin' in pretty soon. If she tells me when, I'll drive the guy to the doctor. After all, I say, he shouldn't be driving around anyway."

"Yeah, it's bad for his health." I laugh, as if sharing the joke, but I am starting to shake. Can this really be happening? Am I really listening to all this? Or am I going to wake up and the reality is that I imagined all of it?

"Now this bird is lookin' around every corner. He sits in the rear of the car, crouched down. His wife drives. She parks at the curb, and the rear door swings open. He crouches down as he exits, but he can't walk that way to the front door. This is the one time when he's vulnerable, and that's when he has to walk into the doctor's office. So, I come in the back door to the doctor's office, wait in the hall. I'm wearing my real dark sunglasses so when I take them off, my eyes adjust to the darkness, and here comes bimbo, just taking a deep breath because he thinks he's in the clear. Bingo!"

"Bingo? In the hallway?"

"Two shots dead center forehead and I'm out." He shakes his head. "The look on that guy's face was priceless. Surprise, shock, panic all rolled into one. Nobody even came out to look. Can you beat that, Russ? I walked out the front door like I just finished an appointment."

"What'd you do with the gun?"

"Returned it. I don't use my own gun. I rent one from a local gunsmith who works for the boys. He builds his own custom weapons. Hit a dime at twenty yards. He gets five hundred for a hit and a thousand for a heist. For that, you get the custom gun, a range to try it out, special ammo and thirty days to do the job. When the hit is made, I return the gun and he gets rid of it. Cycles the parts or dumps, I don't know. I only know there is nothing left to trace when he finishes."

"That is cool. Damn! That's cool."

"Want to hear the crazy part? The guy does repair work for the police department."

"What I don't understand is all these people. The pharmacists, the secretary, the doctor, they're all potential witnesses. How come you're not afraid they can make you?"

"You think Benny's stupid?" He punches my arm harder than I liked.

"I grow a beard and a mustache. I tint my hair with that Grecian formula. Wear dark glasses. Stuff my jeans with rags to make me look fatter. But it don't make any difference anyway. People get so scared they can't agree on anything. You collect ten witnesses, you have ten different stories. None of them the same."

"Benny," I said. "It's late. Let's call it a night." I motion toward the door with my chin.

"Come on, we gotta have another drink or two. Find a broad maybe and do some bedtime." He cast his eyes downward toward his crotch.

"Hey, did I ever tell you about that little Jewish girl I dated? Come on! I'll tell you while I'm driving you home."

He grabbed me by the arm and hummed the words: "Tell me now or I don't go."

"I got work tomorrow. I'm calling it a night. Let me drive you home."

"No, tell me now or I don't go."

I moved back onto my seat and pushed my glass to the far end of the counter.

"It was when I was in high school. You know I got bounced out of two schools before I graduated, right?"

"Right." He pushed me with a lusty shove. "Dumbo. Flunking out of two schools."

"Yeah, but I meet this little Jewish girl. Her name is Myra and she's a hot one. Really pretty. A little taller than me."

"Everybody's taller than you," he scoffed, "but I love you anyway, buddy."

"Well, Myra seems to like me, and I have this thing for her. I ask her on a date, and she says she'll go. She lives up on Chancellor Avenue when that was what they called Mocky Town. So I go up to meet the family, and they're real nice people for Jews. The father sits me down, and we have some Jewish wine and we talk. He's in the diamond business, and his wife is an interior decorator. His son is away at college, engineer or something, and his little girl couldn't cut it in regular high school so he sends her to the school where I'm going." I took a deep breath and eyed the door. No one was coming in so I kept talking.

"Anyway, the father is real nice to me, but just before we leave, he turns and tells me he needs to talk to me. I figure it's the 'keep-your-hands-off-my-daughter-speech.'

"So we go in this room.

"'Sit down,' he says. 'You're a nice boy and I like you. I understand about young people. They get hot hormones and things happen.' He raised his eyebrows and smiled. 'Things.'"

"'You don't' have . . .' I start to say but he cuts me off."

"'Listen! Don't talk. My daughter is a beautiful girl. Anyone in his right mind would want to bed down with her. I'm her father. I understand. I got two rules, and you don't break either one of them, understand?'"

"'Sure,' I say, wondering what the hell he is talking about."

"'Good. Now, you can enjoy my daughter, but you don't get her pregnant. Rule one. Understand?'"

"I stammered for two minutes and said: 'I understand.'"

"'Rule number two. You do not fall in love with my daughter because you are a Gentile, and she is a Jew and no child of mine will marry any Gentile. Understand?'"

"My mouth hung ajar and I couldn't blurt out the words. I was just in shock."

"'Understand?' he repeated."

"'Yes, sir.'"

"'Good. Then take her out. Have fun. But remember the two rules.'"

"I mean, I could not believe this. Hell, you know, Benny, in our culture, we'd cut the testicles off any guy that goofed around with our sister or daughter, and this guy is telling me it's all right, but not to fall in love with her. Hey, I was already falling in love with her."

"So. What did you do?"

"We dated for about three months. I never laid a hand on her. Maybe that was her father's notion all along. She goes with me one night and tells me she can't see me any more."

"'Why not?' I ask."

"'Because I'm falling in love with you, and you're a Gentile. I just can't hurt my father that way.' And she goes on to cry and tell me how much she loves me because I'm a fine individual and I am thinking I should maybe become a Jew, but I don't like the idea of being circumcised."

"Did you see her after that?"

"She dropped out of school. And when I telephoned, they told me she had gone to school in Florida near her grandparents. I guess she had it bad. I know I did."

"Yeah, it goes that way sometimes."

"So, I told you. Now let me take you home."

"Hey, Russ. Do you know why the pirates wore a patch over one eye?"

"Sure. The other eye was a glass eye."

"Un uh," he shook his head, smiling triumphantly. "It was an old pirate trick. See, they were coming out of the sunlight into the dark hallways below decks. When they did that, they switched the patch to the other eye so one eye was already adjusted to the darkness. If anybody was down there waiting to ambush them, they could see them. Smart, huh?"

"I didn't know that, Benny. How come you know that kind of thing?"

"That's my trade. People think a hit man is dumb, and he kills because he isn't savvy enough to find any other kind of work. I've read all the classics, Roman history, the Barbary Coast, every wartime novel I could get my hands on. You think I need a gun to kill somebody?"

"No, Benny, I don't. Not really."

"I studied karate, Japanese stick play. I could kill a man with a switch no rounder than a pencil. I could kill him in a strangle-hold around his neck without cutting off his wind." He slid off the stool and caught me by the throat. His hands were laced in my shirt collar, criss-crossed across the gullet, but I was still breathing. Yet, I could feel blood pulsing into my brain, could sense darkness overtaking me. I wanted to scream at Benny, to punch him in the gut, to wrest away, but I knew his strength well enough to comprehend that I was powerless. My head was churning, whirling around in concentric circles, and I knew that soon I was going to pass out. He must have sensed this because he released me and held me up.

"See? I cut the blood off to your brain. Faster than cutting off the air. A man can hold his breath and fight you for maybe forty or fifty seconds. But if you cut off the blood flow to his brain, he's out in a few seconds, and the more he struggles, the faster he goes down."

I shook my head, slid back up on my seat. My eyes were blurry and unfocused, and my head felt as if someone had pumped it up with air and then left it full. Benny reached over and pushed on one of my vertebras just down below the neck. My head cleared a little. My eyes sharpened a touch and then focused more keenly.

"Feel better?" he asked. "I didn't mean to hold you so long. You okay?" There was worry in his voice. He kept rubbing my neck, staring at me with a distant, concerned gaze.

"Gees, Benny, I never felt anything like that."

"I could kill a guy in under a minute. I don't need a rod to shoot a guy." He was boasting and he knew it. But then, his eyes went dull and distant, and he bent toward the bar again.

"Do you think he knew? My kid? Do you think he knew?"

"No, Benny. He didn't know. It was a chemical thing. Like a crossed wire in the head."

It was apparent that Benny was deeply troubled. The underworld could not permit him to keep sparking off about Mob business. A rumor began to circulate that they wanted to talk to Benny, to offer him some kind of consolation. When I heard the rumor, I knew what it meant. In the past, I had done some work for Joe P. In a sense, he owed me a favor, and the underworld repays its obligations no matter what they may do in business. The Mafia started as men of honor protecting their own. When one considers how many nations invaded and conquered Sicily, the need for protection is pretty evident.

After some nosing around, I made it known to Joe P that I wanted to parlay. He granted me an audience. This is not something to be taken for granted. An audience with a Don is a high honor. And the smiling man who gazed back at me harbored a rounded, tan face, gray, steely hair, and somber, brown eyes that said he already knew why I was there. He was sixty or so, yet his cheeks were unwrinkled as if someone had tightened the skin until it stretched like a drum. The rest of the man was slightly rotund and just average height, muscular and tautly preserved. But he had presence. The kind one sees on the movie screen. The kind that tells someone a man has a power.

We met at a very unassuming office building near Port Newark. Steel framed windows gazed out over the sprawling industrial complex while pictures of Italian boxers adorned one of the walls. There was no secretary in the outer office. The desk was a plain, gray metal structure almost totally devoid of paperwork or pencils. The telephone was as unassuming as was the man.

He smiled at me because he knew why I had come. There is a respect that flows from courage, a respect that men of power admire. It will not stop them at their work, but it placates them to know that one has guts. Still, he permitted me the option of stating my case.

"Don P, it was good of you to see me."

Translation: *You know damn well why I am here but we have to observe protocol. Besides, you have the power of life and death, and I'm not too proud to be scared.*

"It's always nice to see a loyal friend." He uttered the words cautiously and with drooping eyelids as if straining to see me clearly.

Translation: *I know you've done some favors here, and that is why I have seen you. But one cannot change fate. What you are going to ask is impossible.*

"I see your nephew is doing big things in the school system."

Translation: *You got your sister's kid a nice cushy job down town. Big pay. Few hours. Nice to be related to the Boss. Maybe I should be asking for a political favor instead of sticking my neck out for a friend.*

"Joey's a good boy. He's well suited to the job."

Translation: *He's my sister's kid, what else am I supposed to do with him? He's not fit for family business. And I wouldn't trust him to launder my shirt so I got him a job where he can do no harm.*

There was an uncomfortable silence as the conversation dead ended.

He moved impatiently. My silence irritated him. "So, what brings this visit?" he asked, staring down at his finger tips.

Translation: *My time is valuable so we need to end this little dance.*

"Don P, this friend of mine has bought himself some trouble." My voice was low and sweet, almost imploring to this man of power. "He is a good man. A loyal man. And for many years he did what was asked of him and never complained. Now, he's suffering the loss of his child, and he has not been wise in some things he's said. He means nothing by it. He is family true and true. No harm should come to him."

Translation: *Rumor has it that there is a contract out on Benny. He worked for the Family for many years and was always loyal and thorough. Never once did he foul anything up. And I am sticking my tail way out on a limb here and could be sitting right next to Benny when the hit comes.*

I went on. "He suffered a loss. Respect, Don P. His son committed suicide. With Benny's own gun. The guilt hangs heavily on my friend. Now, his wife has left him. He's alone, so he drinks out of guilt and shame."

Translation: *Don't all his years of loyal service mean anything to the Family? The guy is hurting. There must be something that can be done.*

I searched his face for a glimmer of emotion. He shrugged, disinterestedly.

I continued.

"Benny just needs time to mend. Time to think, and perhaps, to reconsider his actions." I halted again. Still, he was impassive. Not a flicker of any kind.

Translation: *I know Benny is shooting off his mouth. He's hurting and he's drinking but he's loyal and always has been. Surely, the Family can give him a break.*

Joe's eyes never wavered, but he set them on me and chills coursed up and down my spine. His words were measured and menacing, something in the tone that was frigid. "This friend of yours is angering a lot of people. Even if I could help him, there are others to be considered. His misery becomes the misery of someone else. There are some destinies that cannot be changed. Life? Death? Can we change these things?"

Translation: *He's putting people in jeopardy. Nothing can jeopardize business. It is our way of life. And even if I were*

inclined to overlook this indiscretion, there are others to whom
he is accountable. Sooner of later, the Feds will get hold of him
and ply him with liquor. Then, his misery becomes our misery.
There are some things I can do and some I cannot. I, alone, do
not make these decisions.

I nodded slowly, hoping something might occur to me.
"This friend knows the law of *Omerta*. He would never talk to
the authorities. Drunk or sober, he just would not."

Translation: *Benny is smarter than that. The Feds would*
never get anything out of him. He talks to me because he trusts
me. And I trust him.

Joe showed no emotion. "I agreed to see you because your
grandfather was *paisan*. We came over on the *Sicilia*. We slept

SICILIA — **The steamship on which my grandfather first traveled to the**
United States. From the Steamship Historical Society of America
Collection, University of Baltimore

on deck under tarps. Only when the weather was bad did we come inside. The women were sick. During rough seas, I tied my children to me with ropes, so they would not be washed overboard. Your grandfather held my children in his arms. When we—the Sicilians—came to America, we had no place. We faced the same prejudices, the same hatred, and the same humiliation as those who came before us. We waited in lines for humble work. The police shoved us around and ran us off when we congregated. We could not afford hospitals, and so, we either died, or we worked in spite of our illnesses. Most of us did not speak the language, and we dressed in dowdy, antiquidated clothing and high button shoes. We dressed and looked like greenhorns, and we were treated as such. Our children died for want of care. We did not wish it to be so, but that was our destiny, and thus, we had to survive."

He puffed on his cigar, blew the smoke away from me, then began again.

"We started working for others. Because we were poor, we ate at the homes of those who had food, homes where there was little more than bread and a little pasta. As the years passed, we were accepted no better than in the beginning so we started our own businesses. Your grandfather operated a leather shop in New Orleans because that was what he knew how to do. I settled here, in the Northeast, and took work as a construction laborer. When the unions took hold, I organized the workers and controlled the docks, the stevedores and the heavy equipment operators. Without them, there was no commerce. The ships lay idle in the harbor if my men did not work. There are those who despise us, call us butchers, murderers, and thieves. Even our own in government persecutes us because they paint us as mobsters and killers. Those who do not persecute us take our money and revile us in the private quarters of their high society clubs." He paused, catching me straight in the eyes.

"Did you know that around the turn of the century a tide of ill-feeling turned against the Italians? Innocent immigrants were hung from lamp posts and trees. They hung almost as many of us as they did Blacks ... and for nothing because many of them had nothing to do with La Cosa Nostra. And do you know who was hollering the loudest for our blood? It was the Blacks. The Blacks who they hung and burned and shot. They wanted our blood. So this should tell you how revered the Italians were in this country. Yes, they felt sorry afterwards, and the government paid money to the families, but the Italians were dead."

I shifted nervously in my seat, and his eyes lightened as if to calm me.

"We made money in illegal whiskey because we understood that you cannot eradicate vice. People want vice. They want whiskey. They want cigarettes. They want marijuana. The men want women. The day will come when illegal drugs, such as opium and morphine, will be the soul of business. It is not our fault that people want these things. We only cater to what they desire. End the demand for whiskey, cigarettes, prostitution, and drugs, and you call an end to our business and even our existence."

He cleared his throat then sipped at the coffee sitting in front of him. "But that will never happen because there are corrupt people and corrupt people corrupt. Can there be an honest government? Yes. Honest. Not as Plato or Socrates envisioned because an honest government is one without people controlling it. So, can there be such a thing? Not as long as there are people who are corrupt. Do you think I could operate in my business without corruption in government? In the police force? On the bench? And if we did not supply these things, do you think no one else would offer them?" He leaned back in his chair and swiveled to his left. "I listen to you out of respect for your grandfather. He was a good man. A loyal friend. Just as you are loyal to your friend."

I was astonished at his diatribe. One would not think this simple peasant so educated. And yet, he knew the history of his country, and he possessed an acute understanding of human weakness. His was a code based on loyalty and discipline. He was no ignorant savage as the Mafia has been painted to be. This was a self-educated man who read the great philosophers and understood the corruption of man. I could only shake my head in wonder. How unassuming this man. How complex this man. He conducted a business founded upon human corruption and immorality, and yet, he, himself, was refined and articulate, just a hint of his former accent, and no hint of the seriousness of his occupation. He held a power, and he knew how to apply it. In his hands lay the power of life and death, and yet, it surfaced only when business required it.

I licked my lips because they had no moisture. My mouth was dry, and my throat a little hoarse. My mind raced to compete with this man, this giant. I wanted to save my friend, and yet, I was engaged in a silent game of chess, and my opponent was winning. Still, I held a power of oratory. I had often been so told. I could not relinquish the game without one final move.

"In my grandfather's name, then, let me put to you a proposition. Suppose someone put this friend of mine in a private sanitarium? He could get treatment from a friendly doctor. Keep him silent until he is well. He is separated from his wife. He holds no job. No one would miss him. I would pay his bills until it is safe to release him. I know then that he'd be useful. Is this not within the realm of possibility?"

Translation: *This is a long shot, but worth asking. Maybe you can present it to the Board.*

It was a scant suggestion but one worth considering. It would not be the first time the Family kept someone under lock and key until danger was gone. The Don stared off into space, working his lips as if considering my proposition. Time halted. And began again each time it seemed he would speak. But he did not and time stopped again.

"But that is a risk in itself. This friend, he has been treated well during his employment." He shrugged, meaningfully, slid the cigar into his mouth and began puffing. "To ask the innocent to take such a risk is unfair, eh counselor?"

Translation: *It's not really up to me. He's shooting his mouth off, and he's disrupting Family business. If I protest too much because he's one of mine, others may get the notion I am weak and a pushover. I can't afford that.*

"As far as I know I am the only one he talks to. I take nothing seriously."

Translation: *He may not be talking to other people. Perhaps, I am the only one. Ah, but if I am, what's my position if Benny gets hit. Then I'm the liability and vulnerable.*

"I've heard different." He moved the cigar to the side of his mouth. Smoke emerged from the center of his lips, and his cold, dark eyes flashed with malevolence.

Translation: *You know nothing of what is going on. He is talking all over the place and to everyone who comes in contact with him. It's already too late.*

"Russell, take some advice from an old man." He croaked in a sweet, sincere voice. "Put it aside and forget it. Some friends do not want help. Some will not accept it. Some, honorable men like you, try too hard. The wise man knows when he cannot help someone, and he lets fate take its course."

Translation: *Benny is too great a risk. The wheels are already in motion, and there are others to be considered as well. And perhaps, if you persist, this risk might spill over to you. Already, you know too much.*

It was then I understood the hopelessness of Benny's problem. And I wondered if Benny had deliberately set about to terminate his own life. I stared at the photos of the Italian boxers posed in a boxing stance and moved my eyes to the other wall which held scenes of the Roman Villa at Casale, Mt. Etna with puffs of mist rising up from the barren terrain, the Cathedral at Palermo. As I studied them, I understood the futility of my visit. The Mafia traced back hundreds of years into the history of Sicily. The exact origin, even the exact meaning of the word, is not yet clearly understood, but the concept of the Mafia dates back into the thirteenth century. It is the essence of manliness, of protecting one's ego, his reputation, his family honor. It was spawned in rural Sicily, not among the intellectuals, but among country people who had to resolve their own problems. The towns and villages of Sicily were so remote and distant from the cities that police protection or law enforcement simply was not possible. And it arose from the need to exact justice because there was no other justice. Peasants paid fealty to the Don who, in turn, righted the wrongs committed in his territory. As the organization evolved, it corrupted into what the newspapers trumpeted in their headlines. Joe P was part of this system. He understood the rules as well as anyone. He had been *paisans* with my grandfather. They had grown up together near Alia, a small hill town of three thousand workers. When Mussolini conducted his scourge of the Mafia, others like Joe immigrated to the United States because they were hunted men. But men such as

ALIA OVERVIEW – **Alia is a hill town, step mountains and scattered caves, approximately sixty kilometers from Palermo. It is still very isolated.**

Joe saw the handwriting on the walls, and they abandoned their native lands near the century's turn.

Joe P landed in Ellis Island and settled in the North. My grandfather, Rosolino, landed there as well but, two years later, returned to Alia to marry my grandmother. When he and Concetta returned to America, they shipped to New Orleans and lived there for several years before coming North. By a remarkable coincidence the woman who married Lucky Luciano was also named Concetta Vassallo, and I am still investigating whether or not there was a relationship between my family and her. But my conversation was not about genealogy, but about a man's life.

It was then I understood where my conversation with Joe P was aimed. I wasn't pleading to save someone's life. I was arguing against a system that existed long before I was born. As I returned my eyes to Joe P, I understood that this was a favor he simply could not do. Others would be involved in the decision making. It was not his call alone.

"Is there nothing that can be done to help this friend of mine? We go back many years. He has been a protective friend." My thoughts must have registered because Joe leaned forward, and in a lowered voice, whispered: "All you can do is to find trouble for yourself. I admire you for trying to help your friend, but I would dishonor your grandfather if I did not advise you to let it alone."

Translation: *You've traded on my friendship with your grandfather for too long now, and my patience is wearing thin. By rights you know too much, and we are taking a risk you will remain silent, but if you push any further, I will not be responsible for the results. Your grandfather was a good man, but he is dead. Those alive now conduct the Family business.*

I nodded. My neck tightened as I did. I had just been warned.

He continued then. "Because you are my friend's grandson, this discussion stays between us. It goes no further. That is all I can do."

Translation: *If I reveal this conversation, you may also be in jeopardy. I will respect my friend and say nothing, but after this, I cannot help you. Mind your own business. Now!*

"*Mi Scusi, mi Don*. I ask the impossible. I understand that now. It was unfair of me to show such disrespect."

Translation: *I didn't assess the risk to myself. Benny has been talking to me. Now, I am a risk too. Not as great as Benny, but a risk. I'll let it drop.*

He held up his hand, commanding silence. Then, standing extended his hand. I bent forward and kissed his ring, the sign of fealty, of loyalty.

"I admire you for coming on behalf of your friend. I owe you many favors but you do not ask for yourself. I respect that.

You are your grandfather's blood. He would be proud of you. When you need something for yourself, come and see me."

Translation: *I don't hold anything against you for asking for your friend's life. I respect you for that, but I think you were a fool to even ask. Still, because I owe you a favor and your grandfather was my patron, you and I will forget this conversation.*

I nodded respectfully.

"You're a good friend, Russell. I can buy your friend a little time, perhaps. That is all I can do." He stood up and, as if on cue, someone came in from behind me. A shiver coursed up my neck, and I felt the fear convulse my muscles. The door behind me swooshed and I knew the audience was over. I wondered if my own existence was over. That was the way things were done. Very often, a victim was lulled into a sense of false security, perhaps out of humanity, perhaps to catch him off-guard. I held my breath and gave a slight bow.

As I gazed at this unassuming, quiet man, I wondered how such power came into the hands of one so ordinary. Yet, he did not seem ordinary at all. A man with a power seldom is. I exited the room, not once turning my back on him, feeling as if I were exiting royalty. At that point, my friend was worse off than before. Before, I could have told him to run. But I could tell him nothing now lest I implicate myself. I did not return to the Pennington Bar again. I did not try to see Benny again. I understood that the windmills which Don Quixote jousted with were not imaginary at all. I had just jousted with one—and lost.

In the end, Benny became a risk the mob could not afford, and my words to him became prophetic. I think he knew that. I think he was slowly committing suicide. He was Catholic, but he murdered for profit. He was Catholic so he could not pull the trigger on himself. The hit man did it kindly. I don't think

Benny suffered. The bullets were swift, side-by-side holes in the base of the skull angling upwards. Whoever took the assignment must have liked Benny because he plied my friend with whiskey, aimed the gun at his head and fired. They found him slumped over the bar as if asleep, but he was not asleep. The bartender, of course, was never found. Perhaps that is why they hit him at an off-street bar. Hit men do not survive by taking risks, nor do the lords who command them.

If nothing else, my friend Benny, the guy who always feinted a punch to my stomach but never harmed me, was finally at rest. He hurt no more. He was hurt no more. When I think of him now, I think of him as a hit man with a heart. If there can be such a thing, and it is not a contradiction, then hit men have feelings like the rest of us. They just know how to subvert them when it comes to business or protecting themselves. Some enjoy it because they are mad. Others perform the task like an everyday job. Each man is an individual. And feelings have nothing to do with business. Yet, this is how I knew I was not destined for mob affiliation. I missed Benny. I risked my life to save him. I did not have the killer instinct necessary for survival. Yet, I was a part of them as surely as if I had taken the blood oath. Loyalty was part of the code, even if one was not part of the Mafia.

There were other rules in this code we followed. It did not matter if we were Mafia or not. If silence was the first principle, respect for women was another. One did not disrespect another's mother, sister, wife or girlfriend. It simply was not tolerated. If a stranger in the group commented on the physical attributes of such a one, he was warned that the woman was a protected species. If he transgressed or was defiant, he usually paid the price in broken bones. Within the Family itself, members did not mess with the wives of others. Respect flowed from the Don to his family. It flowed from the common men of Newark no differently. One provided safe escort for such women, offered them a ride home, helped with carrying their packages, fixed flat tires for those who drove.

A cop who openly flirted with the sister of a mobster suddenly found himself pounding the beat along the cold and lifeless swamps near the Port Newark docks. Disrespect was not tolerated. For twenty-eight years, Newark was the hub from which my life radiated. For seventy years, its roots burrowed deeply into my fabric, and I mourned the passing of that power to punish when my life there ended. If I had that power now, those who shun and abuse me would not be unpunished. I would take from them the same dignity they have stolen from me. Even those who gained no admission to the Mafia could ask favors. And those who held favor with the mob had the same power because their power was my power.

As I am too old to care any more, I reveal the power because it is part of the story. We respected the women of our friends. It was an honor to escort them safely through the streets of Newark, to help with their groceries, or open a door for them. It was not just a matter of courtesy; it was a matter of honor.

To a Sicilian, honor and loyalty are great attributes. Disgrace is equally devastating to the Sicilian. When I was in grammar school, we enjoyed the company of Philip M. I remember Philip because he was thin, with black, wavy hair and serious, hazel eyes, but mostly, I recall him because he was the only boy in our class who wore a bow tie. Philip had to be home exactly fifteen minutes after school. He did not play boxball or kick the can with us during recess because he couldn't muss his clothing. When his father attended school functions, a smile never creased his lips. He was a dumpy, short man whose equally dumpy wife stood two inches taller. Both dressed as if they had just stepped off the boat from Palermo, the father wearing black, starched trousers, a stiff white shirt, a tie too long for his short frame and black, high laced shoes while Mrs. M dressed in a dowdy, gray dress with blue speckles and masculine looking black shoes. Neither smiled. Neither spoke more than necessary, but it was apparent Mr. M was the disciplinarian in the family and watched Philip and his sister, Angelina, with hard, diligent eyes.

That Mr. M's honor was steeped in Sicilian lore was evident from the manner in which he guarded his daughter. To breach that honor was to invite catastrophe. Philip graduated, and I never saw him again. His sister graduated two years later and went to West Side High School where she and her father were destined to make the newspapers.

One afternoon, Mr. M decided to investigate why it should take Gina twenty minutes to make a walk ordinarily completed in three. As he turned out the entrance to his butcher shop, he spied Angelina strolling along West End Avenue, hand in hand with a boy. It all transpired in seconds. Mr. M, infuriated by this dishonor and disgrace, stormed into his butcher shop. He raged into the streets, blasting away with a pump shotgun. The first blast tore his daughter in half. The next decapitated the shocked boy. He snatched his daughter from where she had fallen, wailing in both Italian and English.

"*Mio figlia, mio figlia, tale dishone.* Why, my daughter? Why do you disgrace me?" The dignity of that Sicilian honor was so deeply imbedded in Mr. M that he could not bear to live with the disgrace. His rage knew no limits. He was not a man anymore, but a raging animal. He did not see red. He did not see anything. He felt and experienced only the disgrace that his relatives and friends would malign his good reputation because his daughter was a whore. It mattered little that she was only holding hands. For a female to touch a man not her husband was the ultimate humiliation for a father. In Sicily the bonds of love are spoken only with the eyes. A boy sends a quick glance. A young lady smiles with her eyes and shyly turns away. When the boy signifies his interest to his father, there is a meeting of the families, discussions, a dowry to be arranged. From that day forward the two lovers are never left alone, always meeting with chaperones or in the presence of the families, never speaking, never giving more than a quick glance. And how long the courtship lasts depends upon the girl's father and when he feels it is appropriate to give his daughter in marriage.

Mr. M's daughter had violated the cardinal rule of courtship. Although she was an American citizen, born in Newark and reared in a new land, her father's customs did not alter. In his fury, Mr. M did not see his daughter or the boy or even himself. He saw only dishonor. So he struck at that dishonor in the only way he knew, choosing death to a life of disgrace.

With the blood of his daughter seeping through his fingers, Mr. M sprang to attention, thrust the barrel just back of his jaw and fired. The shot charged up through his chin and throat, killing him instantly. He simply could not live with the disgrace. In his mind, he would rather destroy his daughter than have her disgraced by being compromised. He could not face a tomorrow with people ridiculing him, as a father, or his daughter, as the child he had once been so proud of.

There are other instances of the intensity of the Sicilian. The movies portray the savagery of such instances by suggesting that the man's testicles were severed, leaving him to a life of celibacy. It was more likely that the man was first executed, and the severed organs stuffed into his mouth as a warning to others. The mob would never be so careless as not to leave a message. They were much more likely to eliminate anyone who could point a finger. And, rather than blatantly displaying their crime, they were much more likely to hide the crime unless some object lesson—such as a warning—was in fact its purpose.

I spoke moments ago about surrendering the clout I acquired by knowing those in power. A personal audience was not always required. Sometimes such a thing could be accomplished by a simple letter or even a handwritten note. Before I delve into that facet of knowing mobsters, I'll recount exactly how a favor could be done without much fanfare.

I was in my forties, divorced and dating a young woman. Ambitious as she was, she climbed the ladder of employment but could aspire no higher because she was blocked by the "in" crowd. In every pursuit, there is always an "in" crowd. Sometimes they were minority groups. Other times simply ambitious people. No matter how hard this young woman tried, no matter how qualified she was for the next higher position, her efforts were stonewalled by several people directly connected with the appointing authority. I wish I could say that they all belonged to minority groups but they did not. In fact, the most vehement opposition came from an Italian who shall remain nameless.

The young lady submitted an application. This adversary scrimmaged the application like a defensive lineman. It promptly found its path to the circular file. I advised her to check with the Federal Agency in Washington. She was to determine if the application had been received. None had. She submitted another. More time elapsed. No application was received in Washington. Not only did he intentionally block her access to the government position—which would have raised her salary substantially and launched her into a lucrative career—but he was openly abusive. He derided her at meetings. Ridiculed her in front of her peers. He even enlisted the aid of the remaining "in" crowd to assail her with insult. No amount of reason, no amount of negotiation moved this man to decent and respectable treatment. He defied the laws of respect and honor and boasted about it. A law suit against him would have been defended by the Board of Education and was of no value.

Finally, this gentlemen and I met at a political rally for a Negro politician. He denied subverting the applications and smirked when I suggested we hand him one there and then. In the presence of witnesses, I handed him a completed form. He seized it as if to tear it into pieces, then folded it and tucked it into his jacket pocket. He sneered as he boasted that he hoped it got where it was supposed to go. With that, he put his thumb on his upper teeth and launched it forward as if pulling an upper tooth and hurling it toward me. It was clearly a defiant gesture designed to insult and humiliate. Needless to say, not only did the application never reach Washington, but the insult was broadcast to every person at the affair.

Fate strikes in mysterious ways. This native born Italian-American was driving to work one morning. He must have wondered why his car was not responding when he applied the brakes but they seemed to hold so he mentally noted to have them checked by his mechanic. On the way to his school, the adversary coaxed his vehicle up a long hill. The path down was steep and somewhat curved. There was a traffic light at the bottom of the hill. Traffic there was usually heavy in the early morning hours. As he swept over the hilltop and began his descent, the roadway before him was unusually clear of traffic for that time of day. He pressed the accelerator, trying to make the green light at the bottom. But, as he approached, a vehicle ran the red light and crossed the intersection, causing him to jam the brakes. The peddle held for a second, then sagged to the floor. The car continued at its rate of speed, crossing the intersection. Another vehicle had entered on its green light. The disabled vehicle swerved to the right and jumped the curbing, knocking down a mail box and careening into a store front window. The momentum launched the vehicle through the window and into the store. The window penetrated the broken windshield and sprayed splinters of glass over the embattled driver. Although not seriously injured, the man was badly shaken, reclining in a totally demolished car.

Such things are not the stuff one brags about. The young lady saw her adversary in school, wished him good fortune in his recovery. Not a word was uttered to the man, but a single glint in her eyes told him everything he needed to know about who intervened on her behalf. The next application was submitted to Washington and was approved without opposition.

After five years of trying every legal means possible to obtain a vice-principalship for the young lady of my heart, it became apparent that the minority forces at work simply would never permit her to advance. We tried working with local politicians, and, although they made promise after promise, once the election was over, so was the promise. We tried petitioning the Board of Education with thousands of signatures requiring her appointment as vice-principal, all without result. We sued in the courts to have an appointment made on the basis of discrimination. The suit went nowhere. We met with high-end administrative officials and gained nothing for the effort. One, by the way, went so far as to suggest that the lady consider sexual favors to gain her administrative position. That was as detestable to the young lady as it was to

STREETWISE: MAFIA MEMOIRS ◆ 57

me. We asked the principal of her school to recommend her for appointment to the position. Nothing we tried was successful.

One afternoon, the door to my law office swung open and in walked an old acquaintance, the man whom I have referred to as Joe P. I had not seen him in some years, though we had talked on several occasions by telephone. Rather than walk in with a slough of bodyguards, he strolled in the door as casually as the postman delivering mail.

He had grown slightly paunchy, wearing an open-collared white shirt, black shoes and charcoal grey pants, and he had the appearance of a Boticelli angel with such innocence about his face that one would hardly have classified him as head of the local mob.

"Russell, I should have called for an appointment, right?" he shrugged sympathetically, with a slight smile. "I was in the neighborhood and thought you would not mind if I came in."

I was shocked by his appearance and was half standing behind my desk as he approached. He offered his hand which I quickly took and motioned him to sit down. "Don P needs no appointment in my office." I said, "Has he forgotten that he and my grandfather were *paisans*?"

He sat and pulled his chair up closer. "Close friends. And his grandson does his name honor. But you change your name from Rosolene to Russell, ah."

"Only to avoid the police mocking me. When they pull me over for speeding, they sound the name with derision. Their prejudice is apparent."

He shrugged again, looked uncomfortably around him. "Nice office, you have. I like the comfortable atmosphere."

"I try to make people comfortable." I searched his eyes, trying to determine the reason for his visit.

He caught me staring. "You wonder why I am here."

"You have something on your mind? Tell me."

With that he leaned back in his chair. "We can talk here? It's private?"

"We can talk."

"You know my sister, Rose?"

"I know of her. I don't know if I met her."

"She was often at my home in Long Branch. Poor woman. She never married. So I kept her with me when I was at the shore, but she wanted to live alone after Tutti died."

"She is well?" I asked, avoiding his gaze for there was always something sinister in his stare.

"She is not well. Her memory is going. She wanders the streets, and I have to send friends to find her. I need to put her away, but I cannot bring myself to do that."

"I'm sorry to hear that. What is it I can do?"

He lifted himself from the chair and wandered around my office, gazing at pictures on the wall, my law degree, some of the books sitting on my file cabinet. Then, he returned to his seat. "My sister is senile. She shops along the main street here, and, sometimes, she doesn't remember to pay. One time they found her with her brassiere outside her blouse. But three weeks ago, she went into a local dime store. She threw some items in a bag and didn't pay for them. The manager had her on the tape, and he made a charge at the police station. I had to go and bail her out."

"Couldn't the police see she was old and ill?"

"They care only for their pay checks. An old woman, senile, in poor health, what does she matter to them? They are busy molesting the female drug-addicts in the county parks."

"I know about that. I represent some of them."

"Rosolene, my son, this matter cannot come up in court. Too embarrassing for my family. My sister is not well, and she is confined. I need to have an end to this matter."

"I see," I said. I knew the store he was talking about. They had a strict policy of prosecuting shoplifters, and they usually presented a strong case. The local judge favored the town businesses so there was little chance of a not guilty plea once the case came before him. I recounted this to Don P and continued. "We need to talk the manager into dropping the charges. I don't know him, but let me contact him and see whether he is a reasonable man."

"Your efforts will not be forgotten," he replied, a glimmer twinkling in his somber eyes. I wondered what thoughts might lurk behind those eyes. I wondered what would happen if I failed. Failure was not an option within the mob. In all my law career I had never tried to persuade someone to abandon charges. It was not in me to be pushy or aggressive. I preferred to win by preparation and wearing my opponent down with a tremendous outlay of energy and work. I hated those smooth-talking lawyers who negotiated every point, chipping away at your arguments, knocking out the foundation of your position. They reasoned away your opposition until there was no opposition, and then, because I lacked any argument at all, I was compelled to just refuse their offers without a firm reason. He rose and disappeared out the door as quickly as he had appeared.

But now, that I had taken the assignment, there was no option. I'd have to contact the manager and reason with him, persuade him to abandon the charges. I wasn't even sure what kind of man I'd be dealing with. I knew the store because Bloomfield was a small town, an old town. The stores were reminiscent of better times when the residents sought higher-priced items in clothing, sundries, appliances and luxury items, but it also had its bargain stores such as Woolworth's Five and Dime, Grant's Bargain Store or Dollar Stores. In fact, all the merchants seemed to compliment one another rather than compete.

I admit I was jittery over the prospect of meeting with an unknown manager. Should I telephone him first? Make an appointment? Or should I casually stop by unannounced? Should I press the issue at first meeting? Or simply get to know him and then broach the topic later on?

I didn't have a court date as yet, and I knew that I could postpone the matter. I decided on a compromise course and pulled myself out of my chair. The exercise of walking to see the manager would not only give me much needed exercise, but it would defuse some of the tension I felt. I could just visualize myself explaining to the Don why I had failed, and his sister was humiliated with a jail sentence or a heavy fine. And in that visualization, I lived every movie scene I had ever viewed with a mob execution in transit. One fantasy was especially repugnant, and that was where they tied me with ropes and weighted me down with ponderous chains just before they hurled me overboard into the frigid waters of Newark Bay.

Dumb, I thought. What difference would the water temperature make? That man's thoughts would not be on the cold water but on the desperation of his situation. How long could he postpone the inevitable by holding his breath? How long before the shock of that icy water choked off his air and caused him to writhe and twist as he drowned? I realized then that I had walked the entire distance in this sordid frame of mind.

I was standing in front of the store, staring into its window. Large plate windows that angled in toward a narrower door and framed the marble walkway into the building. It wasn't turn-of-the-century construction. More like the 20s when wood-frame stores were cast up and later cloaked in stone or brick. The main floor held the store. The upper floors held other businesses which had rented space. Most of them held a rickety, ponderously slow elevator that bumped and shuddered its way to the upper floors, made by Otis elevator. The bigger stores actually had an elevator operator who read off the items stored on that floor. I could still hear the voice as it droned, "lingerie, underwear, men's shirts, boy's trousers and summer/winter sportswear."

But that was then and now, I was at the door and hoping for a miracle. The floor saleslady saw me standing inside the doorway and asked if I needed assistance. I asked for the manager if he had a moment to spare. She walked me to the rear of the store and knocked on a wood-frame door with opaque glass. There was no name on the door. When a voice answered, she walked in, holding the door only partially open. I couldn't see the manager but a moment later a weary-looking young man came out to greet me. I eased a little when he thrust out his hand to shake my own. I think he expected a complaint of some kind and motioned me into the office and toward a chair in front of his metal desk.

It was a simple room. Company not spending much on frills, I thought, and thudded down into the wooden chair. He stood for a moment, eyeing me curiously, and I can still see him standing there, light, brown hair, grey, questioning eyes, well-cut chin, ears close to his head. He cleared his throat and asked if he could do anything for me.

Indeed he could, as I explained who I was and what the business at hand was. I had decided only to meet him and not discuss the case at all, but he seemed so bored and weary that I thought perhaps he needed some excitement. So I abandoned my earlier plan and told him I was a local lawyer representing Mrs. Rose—against whom his company preferred charges for shoplifting. I told him I was waiting for a medical report from her doctor attesting to her deteriorating mental condition and that I would probably present that testimony in court. This woman was in such a state of health that she could not afford jail time or even a heavy fine. The humiliation suffered by the family would be enough for them to put her away. I was sure he had elderly people in his own family and might understand how dementia or Alzheimer's disease could bring them to such a sorry state.

He listened attentively but only committed that the store's policy was to prosecute vigorously all such shoplifting cases. I got off the topic and talked about him. He seemed like such a talented young man. Why was he working in such a menial job with no real authority? I asked about his family. His past experience. Did he live in Bloomfield? And in the course of that time, I discovered a good deal about him, but mostly, that he was a kind-hearted man who didn't especially like the concept of prosecuting older people. I pointed out to him that the local judge favored senior citizens and often let them off the hook which, if it happened in this case, could expose his company to a law suit for false imprisonment.

As we talked it became apparent he didn't have much to do, and it almost seemed as if he welcomed the opportunity to have a sane conversation with someone. We parted on pleasant terms. I told him I'd like to get to know him better, and I'd call him to see if there was a change in company policy about the shoplifting charges. He nodded agreeably, and I felt confident I'd eventually wear him down and get him to drop the charges.

In the ensuing months, I postponed the case several times. This was little problem since I knew the court clerk, and there is very little a court clerk cannot do administratively. Their power is more encompassing than that of the judge. If the clerk wants to lose a case indefinitely, it simply gets misplaced on his desk. And I am not suggesting that this is something that routinely happens, but it *can* happen. The manager and I lunched on several occasions. Sometimes we just talked about general matters. Other times, we discussed the case. I knew his heart wasn't in it to prosecute this demented old woman, but he also had a job to protect. I sensed he needed something to hang his hat on, something to persuade the home office that his actions were entirely appropriate in this single case where he deviated from company policy. I took pains to point out that it would do his company's image no commercial good to prosecute a sick and mentally deranged old lady. The word would spread to other seniors, and they, in turn, would stop trading in his store, for fear they might one day lose their senses. He seemed to blanch at that thought and conceded the point. At each juncture I felt I was coming closer and closer to simply asking him to drop the charges.

When I felt the time was right, I enlisted a large number of friends to telephone and write the store manager, telling him they had heard about the case and felt the store was unfairly persecuting a sick, old lady. Moreover, they would never again do business in that store if the harassment was continued.

The manager telephoned my office and told me he was being bombarded with protests. He had no idea I had enlisted the aid of friends and clients to make those telephone calls. I lied and told him I had also been receiving telephone calls asking what the status of the case was. In my sincerest voice I sympathized with his plight and asked if there were anything I could do.

A week later he telephoned my office and told me we had to appear in court two days later. I didn't know what to think at that point. Did he suspect my ruse? Did he simply throw up his hands?

We appeared in the judge's chambers two afternoons later. The kindly judge shook his head. "I don't know how you did it, Mr. Vassallo, but they are apparently willing to withdraw the charges. Now these seniors shoplifting will just not be tolerated," he continued, wagging his finger at me while smiling as if enjoying a private joke. "Case dismissed. The defendant need not appear."

I bid them goodbye and turned to leave.

"You did a very nice job, counselor," the judge concluded.

Naturally I was elated. I hurried back to my office, only to find Joe P sitting in my waiting room.

"I thought I'd stop by. See what is happening with Rose's case." There was no indication that he knew anything, but it was too coincidental that he just showed up.

I shook his hand and invited him into my office. The secretary was out to lunch so I didn't close the door.

"The case was dismissed. Your sister doesn't have to appear."

"You did a good job." He stood up and shoved a wad of bills into my hand. "This is for your trouble."

"No, no. I cannot accept money. This was an accommodation. Perhaps one day I will need a favor and can ask."

He clenched my hand and forced the money into it. They were all hundred dollar bills. "You can ask the favor anyway."

Two or three days later, I wrote a letter to the Don, simply recounting that my young lady friend was having trouble advancing in her career. I outlined all the steps we had taken, the politicians we had entreated, the school officials who were blocking the appointment. Nowhere did I directly ask anything.

Dear Don Provento:

I am embarrassed to have taken money for so trivial a thing. It was my honor to represent your sister and you. I received the Judge's Order dismissing the case, and I enclose a copy for your records. I will retain a copy for my own file.

I did not have time to discuss a very critical situation that requires a justice which I cannot provide. For some years now, I have been trying to aid a very close female friend in obtaining a position as a Vice Principal similar to that of your nephew's position. She is more than qualified. Her best efforts have failed due to political favoritism of the minorities.

We have tried using parents to pressure the Board of Education as well as direct contact with the Superintendent of Schools. We have mounted signed petitions from the local churches. We have instituted a law suit to compel an appointment, but that was unsuccessful. We have both joined various political campaigns, making it clear what we wanted in return for our financial and work contributions. Even when our candidates won, they did nothing to reward us for our work.

I feel that perhaps some greater motivation may be necessary to have this very qualified young lady appointed to the position. She has been in the school system for more than twenty years. She has been awarded any number of citations for outstanding work. She is Italian. She works in various programs including obtaining grants for the various governmental funds available. I can think of no one more qualified to the position of Vice Principal.

I admire your great business acumen and skill, and I would welcome any suggestions you might make as to how we should next approach this difficult problem.

I would be happy to introduce you to the young lady if you feel that is necessary, and I throw myself on your generosity to help us in this situation.

Sincerely,

Russell A. Vassallo

Two weeks later, my lady friend received a letter from the Superintendent of Schools advising her that she was appointed temporary Vice Principal to the school where she taught. Her appointment would be made permanent after a one year probationary period.

All favors did not require a personal appearance. And what was said in the letter could hardly be construed as asking anything more than advice. But a five-year struggle, hours and hours of work, disappointment after disappointment, stone wall after stone wall, came to an end with the writing of a single letter. It was the way powerful men tell you that you are in their favor. Say what you like about the mob but they repay their debts.

If there was another such code in lower Newark, it was that one did not desert another compatriot in need. If there was a gang fight, members gathered from the four corners where they hung out and stood united. There were race fights periodically. Not often because whites and blacks generally got along. But a younger generation did not observe the same rule, and sometimes the cry of "gang war" rang out. Everyone raced to the projects that were almost all minority, only to find two school girls locked in combat. When the real fights broke out, they seldom lasted for very long. Yes, there was a clear delineation between colored and whites, but it was not in the way blacks were treated. They simply lived differently. They were all poor. Most were hard-working. But they lived in substandard dwellings, and they wore shabby, hand-me-downs. But we were unified in Down Neck Newark.

In 1968, part of the new movement for blacks was rioting, burning, pillaging. Troublemakers poured into Newark from all over the country. Like the solider ants of South America, they looted, burned, destroyed anything in their paths. We'd heard about it happening in distant states, but it was coming to Newark. Already the central ward was devastated. Tenement apartments that housed the blacks had been razed by fire. Stores burglarized. Cars were overturned and smashed. White people were not safe in those areas, and landlords stayed away. The message was clear. America was no longer free, and it was no longer safe.

Yet, there were areas of Newark remaining unscathed. When looters attempted to invade the Ironbound, they found the elevated railroad tracks lined with angry men, armed and waiting for them to attempt a crossing. The rioters came with lighted torches, guns, tire-irons and weapons of any kind, but they did not cross the line. An entourage of whites, blacks, and Hispanics stood shoulder to shoulder, most armed with shotguns. Sporadic shouting echoed back and forth. The troublemakers encouraged the local blacks to desert their posts, to join them to free themselves from the oppression of whitey. None did. They held their posts like true soldiers. We were not blacks or whites or Hispanics. We were down-neckers, men from the Ironbound, and no outsider was coming into our turf to do any damage.

One man tossed a lighted torch. A shot rang out at his feet, and birdshot scattered the crowd behind him. No, they clearly were not prepared to fight resistance. These weren't freedom fighters. They were a mob. Bought and paid for by troublemakers to annihilate America. No one was safe from the violence born of hatred. It was a couple of hundred years of oppression boiling and fermenting like seething stew.

On Sundays, the Pacific Loafers often sponsored a dice game on one of the corners. When I watched them, I often thought of the Roman soldiers who crucified Christ. They cast lots for his garments as if he were a common thief. Gambling was part of the Down Neck area. Even the Italians invented ways of gambling. I had often seen my father play a two man game where each man held out a certain number of fingers while one of them called odd or even. On the count of three, out came the fingers. The winner was the man who correctly called the play. I never had much luck at the game. For some reason I could never extend the ring finger of my right hand without the pinkie coming out with it. That limited me to combinations that were easily discernable by my competitor. Not that I was much of a gambler anyway. My best luck was with horse racing, but I found it fascinating to watch these men casting their weekly fortunes on the roll of two ivory cubicles with black dots. But the Sunday dice game was regular as Mass itself.

It was not unusual to see twelve or thirteen men huddled in a tight circle, their voices carrying over the din of Sunday morning traffic. Money fluttered down as bettors wagered for or against the passer. Occasionally the dice would not roll cleanly, and the gamblers would demand a new roll. Arguments would ensue. Often the arguments erupted into fist fights. The worst of these resulted in broken noses and blackened eyes, but as money was the object, not pugilistic victory, the other participants quickly dispatched the vanquished. They wanted to gamble, to pass the time, not to fight.

The police were always passing by. To be caught by the patrol car meant a court appearance, at the least, and jail time at the most. In either event, the cops were sure to confiscate the money left at the scene to be used, of course, as evidence in the forthcoming trial. But the trials never came, and the evidence disappeared, and more time passed until the cycle began again and ended in much the same way. In either event, none of the gamblers desired a brush with the law or the loss of their weekly wages in a means other than gaming. Thus, they hired the youngsters to keep an eye out for the police. Any kid of suitable age, with good lungs and sharp eyes could play chicki. The moment the black and white patrol car was spotted, the cry of "chicki" resounded. In seconds, men evaporated to the four corners of the wind as if shot by a cannon blast. Though they pursued, the police seldom caught anyone. When they did, there was little enough evidence because the dice were always cast into the nearest sewer.

On the issue of the chicki, I am not sure about the origin of the name. I have heard it said as: chiggers the cops or chicki, or chiggi the cops, and I leave the reader free to select his own pronunciation. I could conjecture that it was a derogation of the word "chicken", meaning that the participants were afraid of being incarcerated and thus were known as chickens, but knowing the propensity of the Pacific Loafers to muscular endeavors, I am not sure anyone would wish to pursue that theory on a face-to-face basis with a longshoreman.

There is one gambling incident that is notable in my recollection and for the sake of levity and posterity I mention it here.

Across from Lena's Confectionery Store lay an old building owned by a black tailor. He did cleaning and pressing as well as alterations, and, while he had a large black clientele, he also had a fair number of whites. Unfortunately his yard seemed to be the most favored place for scattering gamblers, and more than once, his rickety fence came down as the escaping men scaled it to disappear into the alley beyond. This was a marvel in two respects. The board fence was weathered, old and slanted from frequent use by the gamblers, and the fence was a full ten feet in height. On numberless occasions, the scattering gamblers scaled the fence hard, shaking it vigorously and forcing it to bow in a most precarious manner. That it never came down before was miracle in itself. That the old man kept repairing it rather than complain to the police was an even greater miracle, but people from the streets often resolved their problems without resort to law. They seemed to know better.

Eventually, old man Roberts tired of the repairs. Time and again, he screamed at the gamblers. On several occasions he tried discussing matters reasonably and always received assurances they would not escape through his yard again. Then necessity compelled it, his yard was a convenient escape passage because, once over the fence, the men had three or four routes they could take, none of which the police could pursue unless they did so on foot. More often than not, the cops simply wanted to break up the crap game, haul off the evidence, and go about their business.

Roberts finally had enough. He bought and trained a large silver-black dog, half German shepherd/half wolf and kept it chained on the other side of the fence. The animal really did not need much in the way of training. One look at those malicious, lifeless eyes would convince anyone that this was not an animal to be trifled with. Not only did he have the appearance of a wolf, but he had the look of a predator. And he had teeth to match. On more than one occasion when someone passed by the fence, the dog bounded up from the other side, trying to reach its target. One had only to knock lightly on the battered gray boards to know the wolf-dog was on duty. He was chained so he could not escape, but with enough length to capture anything in the yard.

Inevitably one Sunday, the police cruised by and the cry of chicki exploded. The herd scattered in the direction of the fence. Two or three of them scaled it until it nearly lay parallel with the ground. Finally the fence went down. Wolf, as he was called, seized the first man to come within range and savaged him brutally, tearing clothing and skin with the indiscriminate precision of a drunken surgeon. He shook the man despite the blows that rained upon him. Then he lunged for one of the others, caught a leg and tore flesh from the calf. The police stood mutely by, watching with amused grins as the gamblers crawled away from the enraged canine, but while they didn't stop to pick up the pieces, they did take the money as evidence. After that, the dice game moved to other locations. The Loafers got smarter and rented a building where they could cordon off the front entrance and gamble to their heart's desire.

But the streets did not consist merely of stevedores and citizens. There were others who called the streets their homes. In the myriad of narrow, linear streets, the homeless rummaged through garbage cans, scraping out whatever booty they could find. It might be uneaten pizza, stale bread, half a bottle of soda. On a good night after holidays, a fortunate bum might boil the last few drops of whiskey from a discarded bottle. Darkness was his ally. The shadows, his cover. Between each house coursed the alleyways that separated the buildings. Where the bums came from, no one knew. If they had a home, it was not something we knew about. We only knew how they came into town. Some dropped off the passing freight trains. Others just wandered into town searching for a place to rest and a new crop of suckers from whom they could pander money. Still others hitched a ride off the highway and landed in lower Newark.

They scoured the garbage cans, searching for anything of value. In the evening hours they situated themselves along the busy streets where movie crowds filtered into the boisterous streets.

"Hey brother, can you spot me a dollar for some food? I ain't eaten in three days."

"If I give you something, are you going to drink it away?"

"I swear on my mother. She was Catholic. I was an alter boy too. Served at the nine o' clock Mass every Sunday."

"And how'd you get where you are?"

"Mister, I ain't going to lie to you. I got a drinking problem, but I ain't had a drink in a week. The cops caught me and dried me out. They took all my money. Fed me some stale bread and old coffee and turned me out broke and homeless. I swear on my mother I'll buy some food."

And the sucker dug into his pocket and, in a fit of generosity, handed the bum two or three dollars. Then bowing his head as he backed away, the vagrant slobbered a departing commentary. "God bless you, mister." Then to the lady, "Lady, you got a nice man there. I'll bet he treats you real good."

But the women recoiled at the sight of these toothless, life-beaten figures, hunched over from fatigue and abuse, emaciated from starvation and drink, unkempt and smelling like yesterday's garbage. And if you stared into the eyes of these men, there was therein a message of defeat. Who knew where they came from or how they came to such desolation? Who knew what forces of life pounded them into such demise? Their eyes were sad and sullen. They stared with pleading vacancy as if there were nothing behind them but a mindless semblance of what once had been a human being. In this modern age they call them the homeless, and they feed and cloth them, pander to their habits, pay them for failure and reward them with a special place in society. But we knew them only as bums, misfits, men who gave up on life and abandoned their pride. Men who begged and stole and ruffled through trash cans in order to survive. We knew them as bums, as derelicts, as the wastrels of society and, despite our scorn, we made ourselves feel honorable and generous by slipping them dollars on which they soused themselves with cheap whiskey and lay vomiting in the streets.

I remember them well, lying in alleys or in front of the flop house they could not afford to sleep in. Occasionally there would be a police car with an overhead light rotating around and around like a bloody eye glowing in the night sky. Then the ambulance would come, adding its own eerie dome to light up the walkways. Police might mill nervously about, pretending they were not awed and frightened by the death before them and there, still as death itself, lay the bum who had finally found peace in his final drunk. Most of them sat up against the wall, feeling darkness overtaking them, and then gradually slumped left or right until they lay curled in a tight, stiff coil as if they had been frozen and then dropped there.

Sadder yet were the women, for they were neither bums, nor prostitutes, nor whores. They lined the bars shortly after noon, hungry for that first drink, warding off the shakes and the chills. Whatever money they earned or stole the night before had to be coaxed through the early hours until the men staggered in from their begging. The drinking, then, began in earnest for there was fresh money to bolster the habit. The women sat there, sipping their drinks, clutching them as if afraid someone might steal them. And they came in all sizes and shapes, some blond, some brunette, some with tar-black hair, the tall and the short, the thin and the buxom, the attractive and the plain, all lined up at the bar like a Venus fly trap waiting for the next fool to come along.

Long into the evening they drank, staggered off to the bathroom, returned to the bar. And then, the men, still viable, still able, gulped down a last drink, and the two of them retired to the nearest alley. Sometimes they returned. Other times they did not. Those that returned showed evidence of their indiscretion. They sojourned at the bar again, and they drank again until one or the other or both of them nodded off to sleep. The bouncers then escorted them to the sidewalk, and they wobbled down the street to wherever they could rest undisturbed.

I was friendly with one of them, perhaps more aristocratic that most of the others. Her name was Edie, and she was, perhaps, on a good day the small side of thirty. She had curly brown hair that hung around her ears as if plastered there and a round, cherubic face beset with luminous, hazel eyes. Yes, Edie was well filled out, solid breast, robust legs, prominent hips that curved into her upper thighs. She always wore high heels that tightened the muscles of her legs, and it occurred to me that she could thrust high up into a man and give him a real thrill.

Although Edie was a true prostitute, she did have a male friend who contracted with her for most of the time. It was no secret that I desired her. It was no secret that Edie had a maternal instinct that protected me from myself. She permitted me to buy her drinks until her Lew would show up and then she belonged to him. Nor did we discuss the prospect of a bed time tryst because Edie was determined to guide me away from temptation. More than desiring her, I liked Edie. I felt protective toward her. In those days I dreamed of riding off into the sunset with the woman who only had eyes for me. I understood nothing about motherhood. If I had, I might have understood Edie's protective instincts toward me. I know now that a mother's love is so terribly strong that she will lay down her life for her child. I also learned that her husband is a dead man if he thinks she will do the same for him. It's not the fault of women that this is so. It is as nature and God designed it. A woman may say she loves you but her heart belongs to a child . . . not just hers . . . but any child. I am not cynical on the point. I do not begrudge motherhood the benefit of their love. I wish my own mother had demonstrated her love more, and perhaps my education would not have begun and ended in the streets. I adopted Edie as my mother because I had none. No matter what she was, Edie cared. She cared about me. If I told her I wanted to be a writer, she encouraged me. If I told her I'd never get a girl because I was short, fat and ugly, she reminded me that I was cute and cuddly, that I was not really interested in bedding down with her so much as having a friend. Sad that I sought a woman of the streets to be a mother, but my own mother was cold and emotionless.

The streets taught me that I needed a mother. The streets taught me something else, too. They taught me how to survive, how to gauge a person's loyalty and trust, how to determine when one may safely turn his or her back. If I sound a bit skeptical, it is because I have been too trusting and my back is full of wounds. But I also survived because of the hurts life dealt me. And if I am strong and full of vigor and if I take hold of life and live it to its full, it is because of my street diploma that I am what I am. I am streetwise. Thus, I cherished Edie, but I never bedded down with her. I often wonder what it would have been like. Alas, I shall never know. Edie adopted me as her child, and she was not bedding down with her child . . . at any price.

Thus it was that Edie protected me. She guided me. She nurtured me. Somehow in that love-struck nineteen-year-old, she saw some talent, some prospect of success. I think she saw in me the ability for me to rise above myself and to become something better. She did not wish me to be a man. She wished me to be something better. She adopted me as her child. She paced her drinking so that she never became intoxicated in my presence. She feared that the whiskey might alter her protective course. But we spoke of many things, and, most of all, she loved when I recited poetry. The romantic poetry of Keats, Shelley, Dickenson regaled her senses. She applauded and I bowed. And then she'd place a loving hand on my face and whisper:

"If you were ten years older and not so smart, I'd take you to bed. But you have to finish school. Get out of rat holes like this."

In that touch I felt the humanness of a street woman, and I knew she was a person. I knew that prostitutes had feelings, and I knew that in her very own strange way, Edie loved me. Not as a man, but as a person.

"You'll have a few broken hearts in your lifetime," she would say. "Be something. Make something of yourself and no one can take it away from you. Me? I'll drink and do my thing, and one day they'll find me curled up in my bed, cold and stiff. But you, Russell, you're smart and you'll be someone. See if I'm not right."

I saw Edie at the Club 421, a dingy little bar where all the nothings spent their days and nights, and guys like me, who were under the legal age, went because Freddie tended to look the other way on age. But it came crashing down one day when I walked into the bar for a quick look to see who was in. Edie was sitting at a rear seat. Her face was pallid, her hair unkempt as if she'd just got out of bed. It was just turning ten a.m., and she was trembling so hard she could hardly sit on the stool. The way she was whispering to Freddie told me it was adult conversation.

I stood along side her. Put my hand on her shoulder. She smiled and looked away. I motioned Freddie to bring her a drink on me. She smiled again.

"You're sick," I said. "I'm taking you to the hospital."

"I've already been. It's just that time of the month."

"But you're shaking like a wet dog."

"Lew's coming. He'll know what to do."

"Edie, I know something's wrong."

"I had some bad food last night and I've got my period."

I felt very grown up because I knew what a period was. I signaled Freddie to bring us both a drink and laid a fiver on the table.

"You don't have to buy me drinks, Russ. You're a nice kid. You need to save your money and finish your school."

"I will, Edie, but right now Lew isn't here. I'd like to take care of you."

She shook again, her shoulders heaving and trembling. I looked down at the floor to spare her embarrassment, and there was blood flowing down her legs and onto the floor.

"Christ, you're bleeding. I'm calling the hospital."

"No." Then she looked at Freddie. "Get him off my back, Freddie. I don't want to hurt the kid."

"What the hell is going on?" I jabbed.

She spun around and nearly fell off the stool. Her face drained even more, and she slumped into my arms.

"Edie, we're friends, right?"

"Right, kid."

"If it were me bleeding, wouldn't you do something about it?"

"Yeah, kid, I would. But this is adult stuff so don't make me give you a lesson in life."

"You couldn't do that."

"No?" She righted herself on the stool and swilled down her drink. She held the glass to her lips long after the whiskey was gone and turned her dull and sullen eyes toward the mirror. I found myself staring into that mirror and into her eyes, watched as she slammed the whiskey glass down on the bar. She tried lighting a cigarette but she could hold neither the cigarette nor the lighter steady enough to do so. I positioned the butt between her lips, waited until it steadied long enough to light it, and did so. She inhaled a long puff and let the smoke curl out through her nose.

"I'm not sick," she said. "I aborted a kid, understand? The quack that did the job screwed it up, and I'm bleeding like a cut artery. They couldn't stop the bleeding, and I couldn't go to the hospital. Abortion is illegal. I did the next best thing. I got high on booze and drugs."

She saw my shocked expression staring back at her in the mirror. "That's right, kid. Your golden idol is a slut. An alcoholic and a drug addict."

"It doesn't make me any less your friend," I offered, the fright registering on my face.

"It doesn't make me any less your friend either. Do me a favor. A big favor."

"Anything."

"Promise?"

"Scout's honor." I smiled, hoping to help in some way. I felt so powerless watching her hurt that way.

"Get out of the 421 Club right now. Get out and never come back. People like me don't need your kind of help. " She slumped forward on the bar. Freddie brought an ice pack and laid it on her neck.

"Edie, I can't leave you this way."

"Kid, let me do one decent thing in my life. Let me do this. Then when I close my eyes for the final time, I can say I did one lousy, stinking thing right in my life. I saved a kid from going the wrong way."

I gagged on my words and couldn't say them. Freddie said them for me.

"Get out, kid. This is no place for you. You're not even twenty, and you got no right to be in here. Get out before I call the cops." He shoved my bar money back across the distance. "Take this with you. The last drinks were on Freddie. Now go do something with your life."

Stunned, I walked out the door of the 421. I thought of all the things I should have done and then came to understand why I could do none of them. We are all helpless in life. Some times more so than others. There are those who would condemn her and those who would cast the first stone, but what I saw in Edie was a lifetime of compassion, of regret, of pain, of one step after the other and down into the precipice of departure.

From time to time I revisited the 421, but I never saw Edie again. There is still a soft spot in my heart for her. When I think of her now, I pray for her, pray for the prostitute who cared enough about me to shove me out the door. Many men can boast that a woman is hooked on them, but few can boast that a prostitute cared beyond the pale of sexual indulgence. My money would never have been any good to her. Whatever her life, I could only see the good in her. Whatever my faults, she could only see the good in me. My love would not have fulfilled her because she had to escape . . . and the only escape she could find was in the hope that she could steer a single, worthwhile individual into the light. But the other women at the bars were not like Edie. They were hard core alcoholics, rummies, female bums and panderers. They were forty-year-old ladies in sixty–year-old bodies, and one day was no different than the next and never would be.

To be a bum was to risk derision or worse. The cops tended to hassle the homeless, drag them into waiting police cars, shove them into waiting prison cells and let them lay until they were sober enough to bow before the bar of justice. They made pitiable figures, standing disheveled and rumpled before the bench, facing a judge who troubled not to even look at them. They were less than human. Men who had fallen off the wagon, fallen off the float of life, and no one cared about them. They could not afford the luxury of a shave or a hair cut, and their eyes were gaunt and hollow. So they stood before the bench, caring not whether they lived or died, anxious only for that next shot of whiskey and hoping that the next drink would be their last.

They used to speak of tremens and hallucinations, but these men were beyond that. They were hopeless, futile. Friends and relatives had long since ceased to care. Wives and children shunned them. Even the social workers and the clergy who tried to salvage some vestige of their souls discounted them as beyond salvation. They stumbled before the judge and answered only when spoken to. Most of them dared not even raise their eyes for the shame of their failure was heaviest upon them. The judge passed sentence. It was always the same. Committed to the psychiatric wards for rehabilitation from alcoholism, they could only look forward to the "drying out" period when they savored no liquor for many weeks. When done, they were loosed upon the streets where the cycle commenced again.

Some of them were mere vagrants, too. They did not drink to excess but lived a life free from the conventions of society. They searched the same garbage cans, but they did so in order to survive. They hopped the freight trains, hid from the yard police, begged enough money for a meal, sat around cozy campfires with other hoboes. They shared what they had including their stories, and when the pickings grew slim, they hustled another freight train and traveled to distant states where the kind of heart donated money and food to the caravan of wanderers that preyed upon them.

I am given to understand that during the Great Depression, many of these hoboes even worked for their keep, knocking on strange doors, asking for a meal, or a day's work, or even a dry place to sleep. And sometimes I might pass them, curled up on park benches, covered with newspaper to keep them warm, or huddled up against a tree, hoping to keep out of the downpours that soaked them to the skin. They were ragged men, hardened, coarse faces, brillo-like hair, scraggly beards, lost souls without a home, without a life.

But even a hobo was accorded priority status over the fags that inhabited Penn Station. Even in the 40s and 50s they perused the toilets, looking for other homosexuals. They were not politicians and priests or bishops or leaders, then. Their secrets were covert; their identities shielded. They did not openly espouse themselves as "gay" nor did they admit to the perverted existence they pursued. On the contrary, to be a fag raised awesome consequences once they were discovered. They were perverted and viewed as such. Unclean. Immoral. Less than men and not quite women. It was common practice to punch them around just for sport. The more serious guys tossed them in the path of an oncoming subway or threw them off balconies. A good portion of floaters found adrift in the bay were probably homosexuals.

There was no compassion or any remorse. To dispose of a faggot was to rid the world of something evil, inconsistent with morality, inconsistent with God's law. They were neither protected by hate crime laws nor by government officials in high places. They were protected by no one. The city sheltered its people. It sheltered the gays who clung to low cast bars and hole-in-the-wall taverns. Like vermin hiding in the woodwork, they hid in places decent people seldom visited. Someone turned a rock over and sent them scattering to the next dark place. They scurried about from one bar to another. Meeting places changed as old ones were discovered. When they were discovered, the toughs who pursued them pummeled them into unconsciousness. No punishment was too unkind. No wound too severe. Even those who did not participate harbored no sympathy for them.

The fag sought out his own kind to perform perverted acts of sex. The bums led a more simple life. They were drunks and alcoholics. Some, even drug users. Most had been drinking many years. They had but a simple goal. Panhandle enough money to feed their habit; then, find a flop house where they could sleep off a good drunk. Most had no need of food, and, if they did not die of cirrhosis of the liver, they died of malnutrition. Many a drunk I took for a sandwich, who waited until I was gone, then brought it back and turned it in for whatever he could salvage. The profit went for booze. None of them were sad people, and few deserved any compassion or understanding. They were failures. People who spurned life and secreted themselves in lonely, dark alleys to sleep away the night, to mark one less day.

If one were streetwise, he avoided the bums. He made no eye contact with them for to do so was to be doomed. If he heard the familiar refrain: "Hey, pal. I ain't et in two days. Can you spare a quarter?" and he stared into their eyes, he was destined to feed their habit. They were persuasive and pitiable. They were the poor of which Christ spoke. No decent man could turn away. Sometimes, looking at them, they all seemed familiar. Grizzled, drawn faces, graying hair, slicked straight back or sometimes tussled and uncombed, bloodshot eyes, and the weary look of someone who wants to die but is afraid to do so. If you halted, hesitated, they had you. They lied with an effectiveness born of necessity. That quarter was a drink of cheap booze, a fix they needed. They'd lie, cheat, steal, even grovel just to get it.

War lords no older than twenty compelled them to kneel and bark like dogs or crawl on their bellies for a dollar. They'd sing a tune. Recite an old nursery rhyme. Hop on one foot. Say the Lord's Prayer. All for the sake of money that would bring them a slug of rye. But even among God's fallen there are exceptions. They do not rise above their addiction but they shine in spite of it. I met such a man once. He didn't appear to be an alcoholic. The man stood six feet tall, tawny hair with hazel eyes. He wore a tweed suit, shined black shoes. Even the magenta tie and white, starched shirt characterized him as a man of distinction and, hardly, a bum.

He caught my eye as he approached the Thunderbird Lounge, another of my nefarious haunts. Normally I would not have given him a second glance but his manner of dress was out of character for a bum, and, therefore, he seemed conspicuous. He fixed me with eyes that smiled, warm, inquisitive sentiments. I knew better than to make eye contact with a stranger but even then, his appearance enticed me.

"You're wondering what a well-dressed bum is doing here?" He pointed his finger as if it were a gun. "Got ya, didn't I?"

And he did. He had me. "Well, yeah, we don't often see a suit and tie around here. Are you lost?"

"Depends on how you mean 'lost'." He smiled, gesturing with open palms. "You look like a nice kid. Do you work?"

"Work and go to school."

"Good. Good. School is good. You need education." He paused, swaying just a bit. "And you work!"

I almost resented the questioning. "What do you do?"

"When I'm right, I write for a living. Short articles. Nothing much but it makes a living for me. Truth is, I'm between jobs right now. Got a batch of rejection slips." He hesitated. "From the awed look on your face, you like to write too."

I nodded

"Ever submit anything?" He stepped toward the lounge door.

"Just some greeting card verses. They turned me down." My eyes hit the ground. It was tough admitting failure, and here was a guy who actually sold articles. He glanced around then and, for the first time, seemed distraught. "Look kid. I'm a writer. Sometimes I even sell an article. So let me level with you. I'm alcoholic. A well dressed bum. I quote Shakespeare and Tennyson, and I do it so I can get that lousy drink. I wake up in the morning, and I despise myself for my weakness. I swear I won't touch another drop. I go to Mass and

Communion, and I swear before God I won't take another drink. It's always the same though. I shake. I hurt. I see the burgeoning world around me and I detest what I see. It's like looking in a mirror and seeing a monster staring back and realizing that the monster is you. I write. But I don't make a living at it. If you have any sense, you won't write for money. Write for pleasure or bows or praise but, Christ, don't try making a living at it."

I was spellbound by this man. Utterly fascinated that a man so distinguished would speak to me so compellingly. I had money and hearing him out was worth a few drinks at the bar.

"I'm out to hustle you for a few drinks. Maybe some food. See, I'm a fraud. I'll be anything you want me to be as long as I get a drink out of you. I write. Last thing I sold was three years ago. Sometimes I edit for the *Newark Evening News*. Mostly I tutor little kids for a few extra bucks. See, I'm too honest to be anything but a bum."

We stepped inside and took a table near the back room, away from the flow of traffic. Only the rest room lay beyond as the evening poker game was not in session and the bar deserted.

He sat quietly as the first drink arrived. Then, he spouted.

> *"But such a tide as moving seems asleep,*
> *Too full for sound and foam,*
> *When that which drew from out the boundless deep,*
> *Turns again home."*

His voice had a lull to it, tranquilizing and restful like the cadence of the sea waves upon the shore.

"That's Tennyson, 'Crossing the Bar.' I had to memorize that in grammar school," I parried.

"Sunset and evening star,
And one clear call for me!
And may there be no moaning of the bar,
When I put out to sea."

"I told you I know that poem." My chest puffed full with pride.

He cocked his head and displayed an impish smile. When he did so, he did not appear a man in his early 40s but a child who sprang from a leprechaun.

"Who is your favorite poet?" he asked.

I hesitated. There were many poets I wished to emulate. Men who selected the only possible word, just the right mournful thought. Men capable of imbuing a deep, symbolic meaning to words beyond most human comprehension. "Matthew Arnold, perhaps. 'Dover Beach.' It's the only thing he wrote I really enjoyed. Never understood it all."

He near leapt alive from the seat. "Surely. You have to know. It's so obvious. He was speaking about his own hopes and dreams. He'd once had faith so strong, so well rooted. But life disillusioned him. Pummeled him. Then in his later years, he understood. Life holds nothing for us but pain and hurt. There is no escape but death. We don't even know why we are here. Yes, yes, that was it. Can't you see it? The depth? The passion?" In his exuberance, his eyes glanced at the empty glass before him.

I was fascinated by the man. My college education was not beginning in school, but there in a dingy bar, ill-lighted and smelling of mold and whiskey. "Gabe," I hailed. "Bring us the rest of the bottle."

How could this erudite man be a drunk, a common bum? How could he fall to the spell of drink? I drank but I hated the stuff and only drank to be one of the boys. But this man had substance. How could he have fallen from grace? The bottle arrived, more than half full and with it, the helpless glance of the bartender as if to say: "Russell, the guy is a bum, and you're feeding him drinks." But Gabe said nothing, merely set the bottle before the writer and went.

The author tilted the bottle and filled his shot glass. He savored the drink as though it were his last. "You want to know how it got like this. Am I married? Do I have children? Have I ever stopped drinking?" His eyes were bleary and half closed. But his thoughts were not closed nor were they bleary. He was steeped in thought and remained silent for a long time.

"How does any man get to where destiny brings him? He slips a step at a time. A social drink at a party. A drink to kill pain. A drink, then, to turn the mind from some emotional hurt or some fear. A drink to escape. Then, it's a drink for the taste. A drink for the urge. A drink for the need. One day he finds himself with nothing in the house and no money for purchase. He asks a kindly stranger and he obliges. It all becomes a blur." He ceased the dialogue, as if pausing before the next line. He raised his arm, pointing a finger at the ceiling. "Life's but a walking shadow; a poor player that struts and frets his hour upon the stage and, then, is heard no more." The last words were almost muttered rather than spoken. "Truth is I write a little but don't sell much. I worked as an administrative assistant at the Board of Education. They had a job opening that would have put me in the big time. So I danced the dance. Social events. Political meetings. Ass-kissing all the big wigs. The minorities are coming in to their own so you line up with them. In the end, the minority guy gets the position. I get a pat on the back."

"I guess that would tee anybody off." I raised my shot glass and sipped a little more. He swallowed his down as if the memory had to be blotted out. I poured another for him, not quite understanding why I fed his habit and, yet, not wanting this man to leave. I felt mesmerized by his knowledge. I hoped some of it might rub off. "Married?"

"Yes. I am married. God knows why. Can I tell you how often she has carried me up the front steps so the neighbors would not see me crawling like a worm across their lawns? Can I tell you how often I failed at sex in a drunken stupor? Can I tell you why she tolerates all this in the name of love?" He swigged down another drink. "No!" he exclaimed, raising his voice. "Neither can I tell you why I permit her to endure this disgrace, this abuse, in the name of love!" Then, to himself, "Will I ever have any peace in my life? Or will I forever be tormented by the pain of a wretched existence?"

I sipped my own rye, let the glass slide down my lip. "Kids?"

"Alas." He delivered the line well. "No children, God be praised. Can a misfit such as myself be sire to a living being?" He began sobbing softly. "If I had any real courage, I'd do her a favor and wipe myself off the face of the earth. But the only eraser is suicide. 'Ah, but in that sleep. Perchance to dream. Ay, that's the rub.'" He dropped his head as if bowing for the audience.

"Every man has value," I offered.

"'And therefore, never send to know for whom the bell tolls. It tolls for thee.'"

"For whom the bell tolls? John Donne, Scottish poet," I volunteered.

"You enjoy literature. Ah, you're a romantic. Why else do you befriend a drunk? Ply him with his weakness and steal the wisdom of his years." He offered his hand in a shake of comradeship. It was then I noticed the years had not dealt kindly to him. A mere few drinks, and he was sinking into the mire of insensibility.

"You're a nice kid. Good hearted. I guess you know I'm just bumming drinks off you. Flat broke and nowhere to go. A lie for every drink. If I go home, I have to face my wife. Her eyes, her face, all the hurt, all the broken promises. All there when she looks at me. Then we talk until the morning hours. You know what I see in her eyes?"

"Contempt? Pity?"

He shook his head, swallowed again and set the glass down.

"Love. Damn it to hell, she kills me with her love. I stare into those innocent, loving eyes, and I hate her for forgiving me. Why? I ask myself, why? What drives her to stay? To be so loving? So patient? Why the hell doesn't she just go? Let me wallow in self pity and drink until my guts split open."

"Love. Can't explain it to you but that's what it is," I said.

His hands began to tremble. "The shakes. Oh God, not the shakes. I get the tremens. Bad sometimes. Dark figures dragging me into this pit, and the muck is inching up toward my face. I tighten my mouth and struggle to swim but my arms are paralyzed. Then it's up to my nose. I'm holding my breath so the muck doesn't clog my nose, but I feel it slithering up my nostrils like a worm. My air expires. I have to breathe. I know if I breathe, the crap will block air and smother me. But I can't hold out. I need the air. I suck in a breath. The mud oozes into my nostrils, jams my throat shut. I just keeping swallowing but there isn't any air. Oh God, not the tremens."

He grasped the bottle and took a long pull. I banged the table with my own glass. He startled, then look straight at me and he was sane again.

"Thanks, kid. I was starting to slip. It will happen later. They'll find me in the streets and take me to Bellevue for observation. They'll dry me out and enroll me in a program. For a time I'll stop drinking because I'll have to. But it won't matter. I'll drink again as soon as they release me. They never keep me too long. Too many other drunks. All they can do is dry you out, treat you for two or three weeks and turn you loose."

"I guess I'll never understand why guys drink that way. I get sick when I drink too much. Is it something chemical? Or maybe something in your childhood? I mean, you're a bright man, educated. Why do it if it causes hallucinations?"

He sat back in his seat and pondered the question. "Pour me another drink while I think about that," he hissed, knowing full well the bottle was empty. I bought a small pint and brought it to him like an obedient servant.

"Do you want the truth or do you want some bullshit that maybe you can help me? I can do either. "

"No sense in lying. If you don't want help, you don't want it."

"I want help. I just can't stop drinking to get it." He paused. "As for intelligence, there is no relation between intelligence and emotional stability. Sure, I'm smart. Educated. Taking stress, rejection? That's another song. I drink to escape. Then, I have to escape from the drink. Around and around and around the circle. Sometimes I meet a nice guy, somebody like you, and I wish I could let him help me. But I've got enough broken promises behind me to match every bottle I ever uncorked. I'm past that. On a collision course with Death and I know it. I wake up thinking, maybe today I'm lucky and I'm dead. But I never am, kid. I'm always alive. Ready for another day." He halted. "Hey, let's talk about you. What do you do for a living?"

"Work at a major bakery as a GBW," I answered.

"GBW?"

"General Bakery Worker. Any crap job that happens to be open, they assign to me. Sweep floors. Work on the ovens.

Clean machines. Unload boxcars. Dump flour. General bakery worker earning $5.13 an hour and working with the dregs of civilization. The other night I walked out in the parking lot and saw two guys banging a pregnant woman. Can you beat that for brass?"

"Shocked you?"

"I'm naïve. Stupid, maybe. I came up in an Italian/Sicilian family. We have high ideals about women. They're the vessels of life. So, yeah, it shocked me."

He lapsed into silence and drifted off for a short time. For some time he'd been holding an unlit cigarette, and it dropped to the floor. I moved around and picked it up for him.

"Wush going on here?" he barked. When he gazed at me, his eyes were distant, and he showed no recognition at all. He snatched the cigarette to his mouth. I lit it for him, watched him drag away at it. Whatever we had been talking about was far from his recollection, and we slipped into silence. When the silence became uncomfortable for me, I roused him by jostling the table.

"Sorry. I'm a little bit tipsy."

"Coffee?" I asked. "It may sober you up a little."

He laughed. "Another untruth. A drunk who drinks coffee is merely a drunk who is wide awake. Caffeine has no effect on how quickly the body metabolizes alcohol. I learned that after my second drunk driving offense."

"How do you get around?"

He slapped his legs and held up his right hand in the gesture of a hitchhiker, the thumb pointing in the proposed direction of travel.

"I can drive you home," I volunteered.

"I am home," he muttered. Then declared, "Why? What do you care if I get home? Are you one of those do-gooders? Think you're going to reform the drunk?"

"Ah, I can't reform myself let alone someone else. Anyway, it's better than walking," I quipped. "You never said what kind of articles you write."

"What articles?" he slurred.

"You said you write articles for magazines."

"You want to write, don't you? Write that best seller. *Gone with the Wind, Four Feathers, Man Who Would Be King.* Fess up now, man. You're all stoked up with dreams of fame and notoriety. Write the great novel and the world glitters. Book signings. Movie contracts. Like the conquering Roman general, you stride victorious into Rome. But all glory is fleeting." He sobered a little, then went on. "It's all bullshit, kid. There is no glory, and your chances of writing anything that sells more than four hundred copies are improbable. Not because you're not a good writer. Everybody's a good writer. That's just the damn problem. You want to be a member of the fourth estate, don't you?"

"I told you that before," I sparked.

"And the rejection? Can you tolerate that? The editing? Can you tolerate some self-made, little high school twerp tearing the guts out of your art? Love's labor lost! Can you endure the landlord pounding on the door for unpaid rents while the rejection slips pour in? If you cannot suffer the slings and arrows of outrageous fortune, man . . . find something steady that pays." His voice faded a little, then rose again. "For God's sake, do something else if you can't bear rejection." He avoided the dismay on my face and steadied himself to pour another drink. Some of it sloshed over the rim and coursed down the glass. "A waste of good whiskey," he lamented. He shoved his chair suddenly backwards. "I've got to pee," he said as he staggered from the table.

"Rest room is to the right," I submitted.

He turned and rendered a lordly bow, sweeping his hand as if it were his hat. It was a mocking gesture. Was he ridiculing me or thanking me for the direction?

Gabe seized the opportunity and stepped near me. "Pal, what the hell are you doing? Spending good money on this rummy. He's a bum. A four flusher. He's making a mark out of you."

To be streetwise, one must never be a mark, must never be humiliated by someone smarter than himself. I was not being savvy. I was being a mark. This man was entertaining me for his evening's drinks, and I was letting him. "I'm just passing time. I've got the night to kill. And the guy's educated. He knows about writing. I'm learning something from him."

"The guy's a bum. Never sober enough to walk straight, let alone write anything."

"Ever been in here before?" I asked.

"I never seen him before, but they're all alike. This one is just dressed better. So he's a high-classed bum. Save your money and tell him to take a hike." Gabe had grown grumpy with age. His rounded face portended drooping cheeks and deep ridges near the hair line. He always wore a starched shirt with bow tie that accented his stubby neck. His charcoal pants had never seen pressing.

"I know you mean well, Gabe. I don't get much time off. Let me buy the guy a few drinks and see if I can learn anything."

He shrugged and stalked off, then returned with a quarter bottle of rye. "This is on the house. Just don't give him any money, hear?"

"Got it!" I smiled, and noted the whiskey was the cheaper variety he sold to drunks when quality didn't matter any more.

The muse returned, his tie loosened along with his collar button.

"What's a young guy like you doing in here anyway? This is a rat hole. You'll never meet any girls here. Even a drunk can smell the toilet a block away."

"I never meet any ladies anyway. Short, stocky men aren't in season just yet."

"Feelings of inferiority about your height? Right?"

"Something like that. I've tried my hand at women. Not much luck. First time I fell head over heels. I was supposed to meet her at a local hang out. She never showed. Later that night a couple of my buddies told me they had a girl and would I drive them around while they screwed her. Even suggested I might get some of the action. Well, I picked them up and watched them stripping this girl in the back seat of my car. I didn't see her clearly at first. All I needed was to hear her voice, asking them not to tear her clothing. Guess who it was?" I sipped some of my own drink. There was no one in the bar but Gabe and ourselves. I was free to talk. "Seems like every time I find a girl, I'm just not the type. Can't blame them. Who wants a guy with his belly hanging over his belt?"

"Whoosh! You've had some bad breaks, kid. The girl in the back seat. Maybe you should have just gone in the back with her. At least you'd have something to show for it. But you know, you aren't all that bad looking. And looks don't matter anyway. Look at me. A drunk. A bum. My wife would knock your eyes out. Hey, tell me, have you ever seen a guy and a girl and wondered how he got her? I mean a guy who is nothing to look at who has this beautiful woman on his arm?"

"Sure. I've seen that lots of times. Some of the mob guys have women like that, but they've got money, position. "

"Do you think he goes around knocking himself to hell? He's got confidence. He knows that there is a woman out there somewhere who has the hots for a gorilla. Maybe it's his build.

Maybe she likes hairy men. Maybe he's a savage in the bedroom. You have to change your attitude, kid. It will dampen your entire approach."

"You got a name, mister?"

"Dirk. Call me Dirk."

"What makes *you* an authority on women?" My anger thrust him into sobriety.

"Sorry. I thought maybe I could bolster you a little. Confidence. Believe in yourself." He hung his head and stared at the table. His glass was empty, but he didn't pour.

I felt a little guilty about rattling him. "Look . . . I was at this amusement park. Fifteen. Never noticed girls before but suddenly there's this girl in the swimming pool with my friend, Carmen. Carmen is pretty good looking. I guess it's the first time I ever noticed a girl. She was attractive, and suddenly I thought I'd like to be kissing her. There I was floating in the water like a hippopotamus, my breast hanging down like a woman's tits. She asked me how old I was, and I lied and said seventeen. I thought I was really being cool, and she was attracted to me. But she whispered something in Carmen's ear and they laughed. She wasn't attracted. She was ridiculing me. And it's never been much different for me since. I go to bed nights debating whether a girl has an interest in me. Even when I convince myself they have, I'm wrong. So don't tell me about that special girl who is out there waiting. I've heard it all before."

He nodded solemnly. "Sure you have. Know what's wrong?"

I glanced away, annoyed.

"The girls in your age bracket are all gaga over the good looking, Joe-College type. Right now, that's what they're after. Give them a couple of years, friend, and they'll be looking for someone solid, someone romantic, steady, reliable. A guy who treats them like gold and has a little challenge in his life. They date Joe-College, but they marry the guy with substance and a future, not looks."

"Maybe." I met his eyes again.

"No maybe about it. Five years from now they'll be throwing rocks at Joe-College and you'll be the man. See if I'm not right."

I shrugged because I didn't believe him. He pulled himself upright from his slouch and stared into my eyes. "Tell me what you write?"

"Adventure mostly. Wrote a story called 'Spots in the Snow.' It's set in Korea during the conflict. A couple of rookies are out on patrol when they see spots of blood on the snow. They're following the spots when they see two gooks coming toward them, hands held high in the air as if surrendering. The sergeant is a skeptic, and he wants to gun them down. The private is arguing to give them a chance to give up. When the Koreans are twenty yards away, the front guy bends over, and there's this automatic tied to his back. The other guy steps forward, grabs the gun and cuts loose. The private goes down. The sergeant is new to Korea, but he's seen combat before, and he dives into the ground. Up comes his weapon, and he sprays the goons. They buck back from the impact like limp little dolls. The story ends with him saying that whenever a soldier sees spots in the snow, he needs to be on his guard."

"Nice story. It has potential. Fiction is hard to sell. I'd have to read it to see how you handled character, plot. I'm not much on stream of consciousness either. How many times did you rewrite it?"

"Twice, maybe three times."

"Fifty rewrites isn't too much. The more you write it, the better it gets." He lowered his glass and shoved it away from him as if it suddenly burst into flames. "Know the secret to every good writer?"

"Rewriting?" I asked.

"A good editor. No good writer can function without a good editor. You may hate the bastard, swear at him, call him names, threaten to maim him, but in the end the skunk is right, and you need him like you need your arms, because without him, you have no arms."

"Are you telling me that guys like Robert Louis Stevenson, Rudyard Kipling, Hemmingway, Faulkner, that guys like that had editors?"

"Every last one of them. In fact, Kipling self-published some of his own works because he disagreed with his publishers and editors. Faulkner drank like a fish and always fell off the wagon when his editor started cutting his work. Writers get ground up in their work, and they lose themselves. The editor keeps him straight. He cuts out the excess. Corrects the grammar. Sharpens the plot and the characters." He pulled the shot glass toward him, then pushed it slowly away, as if resolving to quit, to find himself, to kick the habit.

"So, tell me something you've written," I asked, sipping my own shot of rye.

"My best piece was called 'In the Mountain High.' I wrote it for Argosy magazine."

"What was it about?"

"I took the theme of a guy stranded on a mountain top and how he hears the wind blow, and it sounds like the voice of the mountain. I wove it around a theme that he and his wife separated, and he can't see his boys anymore because she has custody, and he can only have them for one month a year because of his outdoor job. He travels a lot to different countries, and, as he sits on the mountain waiting for the storm to stop, he thinks about what each child looked and acted like the last time he saw them. That's where the theme comes in because he sees his kids growing in leaps and bounds, not continuously like a father should. So each time he sees one of them it's like that voice of the mountain howling out of the darkness. It was a great article. Editors loved it. One of them even wanted to hire me for a full time column about the emotional side of outdoorsmen and how they related to their families."

"So did you take it?"

He pulled the glass nearer to him, bent down to sip off the brim so it didn't spill, and then upended the glass.

"No."

"You didn't take it?"

"Lost my nerve. That article was first rate stuff. I couldn't duplicate it. The damn thing just came out of the blue, hit me right between the eyes and spewed out like molten gold. I couldn't have done it again in a million years but it read like silk. Smooth transitions and insights. Just the right words. I cried every time I read it. But I knew I'd never be able to do it again."

"So what then?"

"I had an appointment for the next week, and they wanted another article from me. I tried, kid. I really tried. Don't know how many pages I rapped out of the typewriter. I'd read it back, and it was crap. I was forcing it. You can't force good writing. It's just there. All the writing schools tell you just to write. Write every day. Even if you don't like what you write, just do it. It doesn't work that way for some of us. It didn't work that way for me." His eyes were welled with pain, tiny droplets of it tracing down along the nose and careening off his upper lip. He shook his head slowly as he relived the life-turning experience.

"The editor called me four or five times. I made excuse after excuse. Finally I sent him an article. Pure garbage. He didn't call any more. I sent him a few more articles and called him twice. He never returned my calls. That's what writing did for me, kid. It broke my hump."

I turned away in silence and reach out to grasp his arm. It felt thin and devoid of muscle as if there were only the suit jacket and no substance. We both spoke little after that, just hoisting drink after drink until Gabe announced the two a.m. closing time. There was depth to this literate man. We had spoken of literature and life, about his failure at writing. Mostly he spoke of his addiction to alcohol as if it were a merit badge for some accomplishment. I asked him why he just didn't stop, and he told me that life brings with it a cross to bear. Liquor was his. And he was his wife's crucifixion.

We spoke of his wife again. Would she be wondering where he was? What was she doing with her time? Did she worry about him when he was out drinking? Did she work? Did he have a photo? We spoke of hobbies. His was drinking. Mine was race horses. If he didn't live off his writing, what did he make a living at? Where did he come from? Where was he going?

I spoke of cherished days at Monmouth Race Track when everything seemed to go right and how a timid friend cost me ten thousand dollars. I was on a winning streak, and I selected the daily double as well as the next nine winners. All I got was a hundred thirty-five bucks. He doubted my friend had been scared. And he voiced my own suspicion that my good buddy, Joe, simply pocketed the rest. We were just sampling my stormy relationship with an over-domineering mother when Gabe sounded the closing call again. The drunk hurried down the last of the bottle almost like Katherine Hepburn finished off her tea in the *African Queen* and then stood up, shaky, but able to walk. I asked him when he'd be willing to review my writings. He never answered. His eyes were yellowed and distant as if I were not even present. I touched him on the arm and brought him back to reality.

"I'll be around tomorrow," I offered. "Day off. Nothing to do. We could talk more about writing."

I was hoping to meet him again. For a drunk, he made sense. He filled a longing to learn about things my own parents had badly neglected. I was twenty-two. I knew nothing. He spoke of going through the mood and told me that one day the chemistry in my body would go haywire, and I'd shake to the very core. It had happened to him except he never pulled out and used alcohol to cloak the fear. When it happened, he told me, my entire existence would shutter to a stop. I'd be afraid to be alone. Consider suicide. Question my sanity. I'd look to God for comfort, and, when that didn't help, I'd turn to the occult, the mysteries beyond life, perhaps even alcohol. He wouldn't meet my eyes when he spoke.

"Tomorrow?" I questioned.

"It's a date," he replied and averted his eyes again. "I like talking to you, and you're not stingy with the booze. Bring something you've written. Believe in yourself. You've got a lot to offer." He hesitated by the front door, pushed it open and staggered outside. Moments later, when I shoved through the same door, he was gone.

I stopped into Gabe's several times the next day. I always got the same smug I-told-you-so look. I wanted that man to show up. Perhaps he was right that I wanted to redeem him. Perhaps he was right that something in him was worth salvaging. He seemed worthwhile. I appointed myself his savior.

In the future that lay ahead of me, I did reclaim some lives. I did save people from hurt and harm. Not enough to make a difference, perhaps, but there were divorces I stopped because I could reconcile difference. And there were young kids I kept off the streets who might have turned bad. In the end, perhaps, it made no difference at all because I couldn't emancipate the drunk from his nemesis.

Why did that trouble me so? I think because I recognized myself in that drunk. Saw the seeds of my own destruction. The failure hung heavily on me, and failure was to become a way of life as it does when one ages. We see failure in everything we do—even if it is not so. We emerge from the shell, take life by the throat and defy all the rules. We win. We struggle. We surmount battles. And just when we get boastful, we find ourselves aging, afraid and incapable. What was once taken for granted, we can no longer count upon. We fail and we determine not to fail again, but we do. We fail until failure becomes a way of life that we accept. And that is when we are dying. Because when we are no longer able to succeed, we become like that educated bum, that drunk, who had grown afraid of too many tomorrows. I could not redeem him, and I knew when I met him that a day would come when I could not redeem myself either.

All this I learned from the drunk at the tavern, a solitary drunk who quoted literature and poetry, who lived from drink to drink. In my own time, I turned to alcohol to run from those who hurt me. I drank because I required a love that others could not give me. I became much worse than the drunk in the tavern, and I do not know how often he crossed my mind as I swilled down a shot of bourbon and followed it with two or three pills. I was miserable and a man without a remedy. The women in my life came and went because of it. They hid behind their jobs or behind their children and grandchildren. I was scorned, abandoned, with but a single pair of friends to sustain me. I turned to God and even He could not help me. And in the end, woman after woman abandoned me for her children and her sanity, and I had become worse than the educated bum. And who can blame them? I had become the educated bum.

I waited for the drunk the next evening. He never showed. I surmised Gabe wanted to say something as he watched me jump every time the door opened but he kept silent. It was difficult stretching out drinks until closing, and, somehow, I kept hoping this man would appear and teach me more about life. If nothing else, he quoted literature and poetry I'd never heard before. Each time the door opened, I thought it might be him. I wondered why the offer of free drinks did not entice him. Perhaps, he worked a bar only so long and moved on. Perhaps, he was lying stoned somewhere out there in the streets. No matter. He never showed and I never saw him again. The well-dressed drunk entered and departed my life as quickly as did the money I spent on his drinks. What he offered was a vision of my own future and, at any price, it was worth what I spent. If nothing else, in becoming streetwise, I learned that not every man can be helped. Not even myself.

I always felt sadness for the well-dressed bum. His life seemed a waste, spent on cheap booze, idle nights wherever he could mooch drinks. He must have suffered unkind men who shoved him away or kicked him into the gutter. I know if he had returned I might have gazed into his crystal ball and seen other fates about to befall me. I thought I was learning about his life, his weakness, but in reality I was learning about my own. And it did me no good. No good at all.

But Down Neck abounded with stories, among them three brothers affiliated with my mob friends: Turk who ran drugs,

Cisco who recruited and pimped prostitutes, and Joe Hook who ran numbers for the mob as a sideline.

We called him Hook because he had a beak like a parrot, bent at an angle that made his nose appear like a small hook and a light, indistinct mustache that looked like baby hair. He could have been Middle Eastern, but he wasn't. He was Italian. Hook was average height with Mediterranean eyes and hair slicked straight back in thin, black streaks. Swarthy skin and narrow facial features. He collected the day's betting money from the local bars and pool halls and delivered it to the mob banks and tellers that counted the day's receipts.

He spoke mostly through his nose, rapidly and with a slight slur. At nineteen, Joe's life was simple and direct. He also worked in a mill factory five and a half days a week and earned a handsome paycheck for his efforts. On Friday night, he sat in a local bar scoffing down Four Roses whiskey and staggering home at closing time. By Saturday night, he was in full bloom, drinking up the last of his pay. On Sunday, he was near broke and borrowed money to finish out the weekend drinking. That his father was a bartender who raised him on a bar stool probably did not help. Hook always paid the money back. And he always borrowed it again on Sunday night. How he avoided drink the remainder of the week always puzzled me, but he was always sober. Not that he would refuse a free drink. He just confined his drinking to off work hours.

Sometimes I accompanied Hook to the bars. It was entertaining to see him as he made drinking an art. For the first hour, the barkeep couldn't pour fast enough. As he became inebriated, his drinking slowed as if he had attained a certain state and no longer needed to hurry. By the evening end, he was totally drunk, often went wild and became unruly and was escorted out of the bar. He promptly went looking for other bars, most of which were closing when he arrived.

It was not that Hook was stupid. He was intelligent and interesting, but he was sullen, depressed and addicted to liquor. His life, in my life, would not have been noteworthy, but, in the course of events, his brother, Cisco, discovered a runaway girl of fifteen whose family had been abusive. She had left home and wandered the streets until she came into the Down Neck area. She was a buxom blond of easy virtue so Cisco had no problem accumulating condoms in the rear ashtrays of his car. In fact, she resided in Cisco's car for several days. We brought her food and drink. One might say that we worshipped her as if she were a queen. And that is what we called her . . . the Queen. But pandering to a queen does not always get one into the bedroom. We brought her snacks and little items of delight, a pair of earrings, myriads of Cokes. We brought her clean clothing and a used bomber jacket. She had no need for underpants or brassieres since they were off more than they were on.

Whenever I saw her, she looked as if she had just gotten out of bed, as if she had just finished screwing. I believe that Cisco shared the young lady with his brother, Turk, an ex-military man who had served in Germany and could recite the most wonderful pornographic poetry like the Ring Dang Do. Turk was more notable because his upper teeth were perfectly level as if they were false teeth, but they were not. Unlike Cisco and Joe, who ran numbers for the mob, Turk used drugs. In those days Vicks made an inhaler, and Turk would break open the plastic container and chew the cotton wad. Vicks was really used to break up nasal congestion, but he said it contained Benzedrine, which gave him a high. I don't know if it did or not, but it smelled like hell and I couldn't envision chewing it. I often wondered if the Queen had problems making love to someone who smelled like medication.

This is not to say that Joe didn't have affection for the Queen. He was enamored, spellbound and in love. Unfortunately, even whores have a threshold, and she had no particular affection for Hook. Hook, on the other hand, was prepared to marry her once she turned of age. In the meantime he'd settle for sex, none of which was forthcoming.

When Cisco returned to work, he could not keep the young lady in his car. It was impractical to do so. So, he told his grandmother a sad story about this poor little girl, abandoned by her parents who needed a home and had to be protected from Hook who was hotly pursuing her affections. Since Cisco had an angelic face and amazingly deceptive, blue eyes, his grandmother bought the story and allowed the girl to reside with her. This worked out as a very favorable situation for Cisco, whose cherubic, baby-face belied his real intentions. He escorted the young lady away from his grandmother with falsehoods about special movies and church dances (he hadn't been in church since baptism) took the young lady to a motel, ravished her and then, returned her minus his sexual pleasure. Either grandma was stupid or she favored Cisco over either of his brothers.

The blond slept in the downstairs bedroom. Its window fronted on the street and stood next to the front porch. One could climb in the window from the top landing. The grandmother slept in the next room to the girl. One Saturday evening, I accompanied Hook on one of his drunks. He became more unruly than usual, and we found ourselves on the street where his grandmother lived. "I'm goin' to see that bitch," he snarled.

"Your grandmother ain't going to like it, Joe. Come on, let's find another bar somewhere. Maybe pick up a couple of broads."

"I'm in love with that bitch. She's put out for Cisco and Turk. What's wrong with me? I'll tear that ratty skirt off her and bust her head wide open," he snarled. In all the time I'd known him, Joe Hook had been calm, facile. He seldom raised his voice to me, even when intoxicated. But he was raving and threatening, and no amount of persuasion would deter him from his course. We reached his grandmother's house. Like most Down Neck homes, it was a narrow, two-story wood frame home, upper and lower floor, adjoining the house next door with no walkway in between. The plan was for him to tap on the window, gain admission and bed down with blondie. That was his plan. It wasn't the Queen's.

His tap raised more than the blond whore inside. It woke his grandmother as well. For a woman in her 80s, she was amazing fit. Short, stocky, well proportioned. Her face contained an ominous scowl as she listened to Joe's contrived story. He pretended, at one a.m., he had come to visit. She disbelieved his drunken tale and shut the door in his face. We visited a nearby bar where he imbibed more liquor, lacing each drink with a dozen swear words for his beloved's guardian. I spent the time trying to talk him out of his foolishness. One plan after another was discussed. I always found some flaw, hoping to deter him. In the end, we returned to the grandmother's house. He tapped on the window and the girl opened the sash. She refused to admit him or to come out, but his grandmother did not. She appeared like a summer squall, broom in hand and profanity on her aged lips. She swung the broom with the vengeance of the Angel Michael, striking Hook on the head and shoulders. He threatened to bust her greasy head. Not only was she not deterred, his profanity raised her ire to a murderous pitch. She continued swinging, even harder. For a woman mere four-feet eleven, she was spectacular in her assault. The broom whished through the air like a sword, striking the cheek, then the neck, then the head until I thought the handle would shatter into pieces. I managed to pull him off the porch and away from the swinging broom. He was still swearing at his grandmother when I led him away and the door slammed.

"I gonna call the cops you drunken bum," she screamed, and I was amazed at the might of her voice.

Next to the house was a factory. I recall it well because the building had small pane windows stretching its entire length. I stood horrified as Hook punched in every single window. His knuckles were covered with blood. At each punch, he swore an oath to kill his grandmother and bash the blond. He picked up a pallet and threw it through the upper windows. Glass shattered like rain drops. We were awash in splinters. A police car squealed up to the curb, doors slammed, men leapt from the vehicle. They pinned Joe and me up against the wall. I was fortunate one of them recognized me from his beat and accepted my suggestion to ask the grandmother if I had caused any problem. She gazed at me for an indefinite time and then signaled to the officer. "He was pulling Hook away. He no cause any trouble here. He try to take him away but he no go." She pointed to Joe. "He a bum. No good. His brother, Cisco, he good boy. Respectful, no drink. But this one," she shoved her finger into Joe's chest, "he no good. You take him to jail. Let him stay there."

Age had wizened her and the wrinkles on her face bespoke the typical difficult life of an old woman, and yet, there was an aristocracy of age present, as if one should bow in her presence because she was royalty. I searched the face of one so belligerent. She had known hard times, come up through the Depression, raised her son and daughter, never knowing where the next meal came from or how much it would be. She lived off the scraps at the farmer's market and rummaged in marshy fields to find wood enough to burn in her stove. Somehow, as the nation had turned back to prosperity, her fortunes changed with it, and she now owned her own two-story frame house near an industrial zone.

She harbored and protected the girl because she had a respect for womanhood that her grandsons did not. Despite her wisdom and her years, she was taken in by Cisco and detested Hook. It occurred to me that Joe was very much like his father, Joe Sr., because the father worked as a bartender and was seldom home at night. One wondered how this could spring forth from a woman whose bedroom was littered with statues of Jesus crucified and the Blessed Virgin Mary, and always, like all the old Italian women, a candle burning before each one, a rosary draped over the statue of Christ and the smell of incense lingering on the musty, brown air.

The blond, of course, had disappeared. No good letting the cops know a runaway was sitting at the base of the fracas. I often wondered whose car she resided in after that. They booked Joe for disturbing the peace and being drunk and disorderly. He pleaded to the lesser charge, paid a fine and was released. Once he was released, Cisco looked him up and punched his face into bloody little welts for screwing up a very convenient deal. I assumed from that altercation that Cisco never located the girl again.

I never understood what drove Hook. He was only nineteen. He was as streetwise as any of us. But at nineteen he was an alcoholic. There was a sadness in Hook's weakness. One saw it in his eyes. They were deep and dark and behind them was the soul of a young man who lost himself and wandered through life with no direction. Ten years later, I was in law school and returned to Down Neck to visit some of my old buddies. It was Sunday night, and, as I walked by the Blue Dahlia, I heard drunken laughter with a familiar tone. It was Hook. Still drunk. Still broke. He staggered out of the bar and nearly into my arms. He recognized me instantly and asked to borrow ten dollars. I had no doubt he'd repay but the chances of seeing him again were slight. I handed him the money and begged off having a drink with him. If Joe is still alive today, I've no doubt he spends his pay on Friday, Saturday and Sunday in a bar and is broke by Monday. But that is the fascination of the streets. Those who are streetwise learn from such experiences and survive even if it's in a bar. The streets are jungles. One professional hunter coined a phrase. 'That's Africa for you. Everything bites.' I could coin a similar phrase. 'That's Newark. Everything fights.'

There is a sadness in the streets. Yes, there is humor, but there is also sadness. The players are sometimes people who are hurting. Hurting so badly they destroy themselves in attempting to escape the inevitable. We are all creatures of fate. No matter how we twist and turn, we are inevitably bound to face our destiny. It is in such moments that we know who and what we really are. I found such a moment when I was twenty. Her name was Rosalie . . . and since she may still be alive, I cannot mention her last name. But it was one time when I turned to the mob, and they refused to help. It was business, you see, and business comes second to no one.

After having been asked to leave two private prep schools, I was enrolled in a slockish, second-rate school in Newark that was distinguished only by the fact that it accepted just about anyone who could pay the tuition. In fact, the school was so inept, they were not even accredited, and one had to take state examinations in order to obtain recognition of the credits. I think the teachers were the dregs of society who could not find employment elsewhere and settled into the hallowed walls of mediocrity. It's main claim was that it catered to recipients of the G.I. bill who could attend school on the government. In those days we fought wars, not police actions, and soldiers were entitled to benefits. So, they went to school and the government paid their tuition, and the teachers saw to it that they received adequate grades in order to continue the government subsidy.

The school was privy to every drop out and misfit the world countenanced. I was one of them. I had been sliced from one school for academic indifference and from another for selling fireworks on the main campus. At age sixteen, I was out-earning my father. One might say I was the hub of every illegal activity at the school, from spiking the party punch with gin to selling test questions and answers to the underprivileged. The school thought of me as a rogue, but I fancied myself more a Robin Hood, stealing from the rich and giving to the poor. By age nineteen, I was out of business and working at the A & P Bakery in Newark. My illegal activities had been cut off by school authorities, and I had quit school and was hoofing around the streets. Although I was officially graduated from high school, I still visited my friends as Newark Preparatory.

One such glorious spring afternoon, I loaded a bunch of kids into my car, and we took off for the Jersey shore where we lounged around on the beaches and enjoyed hot dogs at Max's Boardwalk Restaurant. I often drove the kids around the area and we had a rollicking good time. Since gas was only seventeen cents per gallon, this was not a difficult thing to do. My favorite haunt was driving Chet Jaslowicki around Perth Amboy, hunting up girls or seeing which bars would serve underage males. But on that fine spring day, my life took a turn that would lead me into the streets and damn near into jail because on that day I sequestered five young people. We drove down to the Jersey shore. Ate pizza by the slice. We walked along the sands of Long Branch. We kidded, joked and fooled around as kids of that age often did. But eventually it came time for everyone to return home. One by one, I dropped the kids off until there were but two of us remaining . . . myself and Rosalie.

"I'm not going home," she said adamantly. "I'm running away."

I stared at her as if I were seeing her for the first time. She stood five-feet-six, stocky and sensuous, and had the rust-colored hair of the Irish. I looked at her rounded face and peered into the wide green eyes that accentuated her statement. They were deadly serious. But the thought that someone would not return home startled me. My home had always been secure and safe for me. Though my mother and I disagreed on everything, I still had a modicum of freedom and security there. Why would a person not wish to return home?

"Running away?"

"I mean, I am not going home. Drop me anywhere." She riveted my eyes with hers and did not waver. Rosalie was serious. She was not going home. And I didn't know what to do with her because I *had* to go home.

"Anywhere. Just take me to Paterson and leave me on a street corner."

"I can't do that!"

"Why not?"

"Because you're not a prostitute to be dumped on the streets. All kind of things could happen to you."

"Like what?"

"Kidnapping. Rape. Murder. Hey, a million things."

"I can take care of myself. Besides, I *am* a hooker."

"Well, I'm not dropping you on any street corner. I was brought up better."

"That is just the point. You were. Know what my life is like?"

I huddled down in my seat. "No, tell me about it."

"My mother is blind so she cannot get around. I even have to take her to the bathroom. My sister is retarded, and my mother can't care for her. So I get the job. I have to change her crappy diapers. We don't even get enough money from the state to live on, so I have to go out nights and earn. To escape, I buy a few drugs, but not with money. I buy with trade because I can't part with the money. I'm fifteen, but I'm fifty. I tired of it, and I ain't going back."

"Well, I am not treating you like a prostitute, and I'm not dropping you anywhere but home."

"I'm not going home. And I am a hooker."

"Fifteen? And you're a hooker?" I was incredulous.

"Yeah, and I take drugs too."

"Sure."

"I do." She pulled out some small packets from her purse. "I do work the streets at night. How else do I get any money?"

"Sure, sure. I'm not buying that."

"Lay ten bucks in my lap and I'll show you." She fixed me dead-on with her eyes and there was something sensuous and cunning in them. "Just tell me what you like."

"Quit it! I don't like that kind of talk. You're a nice girl, and you got a bum break at home. Your family needs you, Rosalie. You got a retarded sister. How you gonna feel if you aren't there to take care of her?"

"I'm through taking care of that little misfit. She ought to be put away." For the first time she turned her head and gazed out the car window. "Now drop me off somewhere in Paterson."

"No deal."

"What then?"

"Suppose you come home with me. Spend the night. I'll move you into my bedroom and sleep downstairs. Tomorrow we can talk more about it. I don't go to work until four p.m."

"What's your family going to say?"

"My mom won't like it, but she'll not like me leaving you on the streets either."

"You live in Newark?"

"Down Neck."

It was seven o'clock. We drove to my house. I went in first and explained the situation to my mother. Like always, she was very understanding. The girl could stay for one day and then . . . out. To her credit, she did offer Rosalie an evening meal with us, but she said little to the girl, and her hot glances told me she was less than pleased with her wearisome son.

I ushered Rosalie up to my bedroom on the third floor as if she were a queen. I'd never had anyone stay over, and I was shocked that mom let me get away with it. I had no ulterior motive with Rosalie. I was truly concerned for her welfare. To me, it was inconceivable that anyone so young would just abandon her home. We spent two hours in my bedroom with the door open so mom's frequent visits revealed no hanky-panky going on.

"You didn't mean that about being a hooker, did you?"

She smiled with sad, dull eyes and shook her head. "I'm not a virgin."

"What's that mean?"

"Russell, you are soooooo naïve. How old are you?"

"Nineteen."

"And you've never slept with a woman, have you?"

"Who says?"

"You do."

She was laying in bed, the covers drawn over her body and her breasts peeking out from the blanket.

"I never said that."

"Sure you did. You've got reformer written all over your face. Go out and save the world and save poor Rosalie too. Only you can't because long before I met you, I was already doing drugs and hooking for bucks and drugs."

"Sure."

"Don't believe me. I'll prove it." She tossed the covers away from her and hiked up her slip. I gawked as she displayed white, thick thighs that bowed into the crevice of her privates.

"Well, it's yours if you want it."

"With the door open and my mother downstairs?" I was stammering the last words, tongue-tied. She had me and I knew it.

She tossed her head back and laughed, and it was good to see her happy even if it was at my expense. Then, her face grew compassionate, and she slid her hand to my cheeks. "Don't ever change, Russell. Most guys are scum, but you're my white knight."

"Yeah, too shy to take you up on your offer."

"That's what makes you special."

I stood up and pulled the covers up to her chest again. Before I straightened, she grasped my shirt and pulled me down to her. Her lips touched mine, and she kissed me soft, then harder, then harder yet. I felt the blood pulsing through my body, but I knew the kiss meant nothing to her. It was as if she were saying thank you with her lips, but the gratitude was momentary, and she felt nothing else for me.

"You're the only friend I've got, and I won't bring you down. Tomorrow you take me back to Paterson. I need to get some work." She leaned back against the pillow, and her eyes went dim.

We had breakfast courtesy of my mother who stood watch during the night. She was grumpy without her rest and said little during the meal. When the meal was finished, Rosalie got up and started washing dishes. For a moment, I knew what it felt like to be married, and I suddenly wondered if I could fall in love with this girl of the streets. Was she really a hooker at fifteen? Was she really running away from home?

I didn't have to report to work until four p.m. We lit into my car, and I drove aimlessly around, heading out to the highway where there was space and some quiet. The open road always held a fascination for me as if there were something new unfolding past every curve, and every rise was an adventure, though nothing was there except the open road. But this time, I wasn't alone, and it felt good to have company.

"I wrote a letter to you last night." I handed it to her, and she shoved it into a small, leather purse.

"I'll read it later."

"Sure."

"I will."

"Okay."

"No one ever wrote me a love letter before."

"I write letters all the time."

"It's not gushy, is it?"

I blushed and shook my head. "No, it's one of those 'let's save Rosalie' letters."

She twittered and for the moment, she seemed her age, as if the hard years rolled away, and she *was* fifteen again.

"Are you trying to save me?" she asked.

"Not 'save', just keep you from making a mistake, I guess."

"Why?"

"It's what I do. I help people. I can't help myself, but I can help others so I do it."

"You can't help me. All you can do is get dirty."

I looked away into the traffic that swirled up around us and swept into the vortex of other traffic. "I just think you have a lot going for you. Too much to throw your life away on drugs and sex."

"I don't have anything going for me. I'll bang away for any guy who pays the price. I'll pop pills to forget my life. One day, some guy will bust my head and kill me or I'll scarf up one pill too many, and they'll find me dead stiff in some hallway."

"God, have you got an attitude! It doesn't have to be that way at all."

"No?"

"Hey, you're a swell looking girl, and you're not stupid. You meet a nice guy, get married, have a flock of kids, drive them in the station wagon to school. Sundays you all have a big dinner and watch football . . ."

"I don't like sports."

"Well, then you watch something on television with your husband and your kids."

I motored toward the Club 421. Time was running low, and I had to get to work. I didn't quite know what to do with Rosalie, and I knew I couldn't bring her back home. The 421 Club was the only other home I knew.

We walked into the dim light of that sleazy recluse. We could have been in a cave for all the light that filtered in. Freddie, the bartender, looked up at me. Edie wasn't there, but a girl from Texas, Shirley, walked over to greet us. I had spent a lot of time buying Shirley drinks, and I motioned Freddie to set up a round for the two of us. I asked Rosalie what she wanted.

"Water."

I introduced Rosalie to Shirley and took the woman aside.

"I need to have you watch this kid," I said.

"Is she your girl?"

"A friend."

She nodded understandingly and looked at Rosalie again.

"I work the graveyard shift, and I've got nowhere to keep her. Can you watch her until I get off at twelve?"

"Yeah, I can watch her."

"She had breakfast but no lunch." I handed her a ten dollar bill. "Drinks and lunch are on me."

She nodded again.

"I'll pick this kid up at midnight when I'm off. Don't let her go and don't let anything happen to her."

"You sure she's not your girl?"

"She's running away from a bad thing at home. I'm trying to keep her straight."

We returned to Rosalie who hadn't touched her water but who seemed comfortable sitting at the bar.

"I've got to go to work now. I'll be back here at midnight to pick you up."

She nodded, but said nothing.

"Rosalie, we need to talk some more. Don't take off on me."

"I won't," she said, staring at the bottles behind the bar.

"Promise?"

She turned and faced me, a little admiration in her eyes. "I promise. I'll be right here."

And Shirley smiled and sat alongside Rosalie. "Don't worry, kid. Shirley will keep the wolves away."

Sure, I thought. Maybe she will at that.

But she didn't. When I returned that night, Freddie's partner was behind the bar, and he knew nothing about Rosalie. Shirley was gone. Freddie was gone. Rosalie was gone as well. I drank until closing time at two a.m. and drove around the streets looking for the girl I had abandoned. I thought of all the things I should have done and bashed myself for trusting the bar woman from Texas. Whatever I had been thinking, I should have taken off from work . . . yet, I didn't know what I could have done differently.

Freddie could not officially open until twelve p.m., but he was always there cleaning and making ready for the afternoon trade an hour before. I stopped in and sat at the bar.

"Can't serve yet," he rasped, laying his half-burned cigarette in the ashtray. I watched the smoke curl up in the mirror behind the bar and nodded my understanding.

"I'm not looking for a drink. What happened to the girl I left yesterday?"

"The little Irish girl?"

"Yeah, Freddie. I left her with Shirley and she was gone last night."

"She went with *la puttana*. They met a couple of mob guys last night, and they left about eleven."

"Where?" I asked.

"What?"

"Where'd they go?"

He shrugged. "I can't keep track of things like that. We had a full crowd. My partner had to come in. That's all I know."

I was frantic. I had left a young girl alone in a bar because I couldn't take her home again and now she was gone. I felt responsible. I left the bar and drove around the streets. They had Saturday classes so I stopped into the school and asked guys if they had seen Rosalie. No one had.

I returned to the bar. There was a Puerto Rican guy sitting there trying to explain in Spanish that he wanted a beer. I ordered in Spanish. *Dos cervazas.* I impressed even myself. We struck a sudden camaraderie, and before I knew it, the waters of drunkenness were swirling around the two of us and we were lit. My friend, Edie, was sitting at the far end of the bar. I staggered over and asked her if she had seen Rosalie. Her voice dropped to a low whisper.

"She's around the corner. That yellow building on East Kinney. Shirley took her last night. She's a hooker, Russell. Leave her be."

"But I'm responsible for her."

"She knows what she's doing. Believe me. That girl knows how to work."

I pulled away and rejoined my amigo.

"They took my *novena*," I said.

"Your girlfriend," he repeated in Spanish. "They take your girlfriend."

"She's around the corner with another man."

He pounded his fist on the table. "We have one more drink and then we get her."

I felt charged with superiority. I had amassed an army. An army of one, perhaps, but an army none the less. We finished our courage drink and stumbled out the door. I walked down the basement steps and pounded on the door. A big guy answered.

"I want to see Rosalie. I'm a friend."

He said nothing but left and shut the door. I waited. Rosalie came. She was dressed in a kimono, looking as if she had spent the night in bed.

"Time to go, kid," I smiled.

"I can't leave right now," she said.

"Better if we did. Now come on or I'll drag you out of there."

"Let me get dressed."

"Five minutes or I'm coming in."

She laughed and shut the door.

Ten minutes passed. No Rosalie. I pounded on the door again. No answer. My friend and I pushed the door open and walked into a gloom so intense it hurt my eyes. The quiet was belligerent, as if daring us to enter. It smelled dank and mold-ridden as if it had been a hundred years since someone opened the vault and entered. I wondered how anyone could live there.

The gloom deepened as I trod down the hallway. My eyes had not yet adjusted to the murkiness, but I felt uneasy, as if something were stalking me, waiting in ambush.

I was about to turn and say something to the patrol behind me when something smashed into my stomach. I went down. And when down, I doubled up in pain. I started to rise, gasping for breath, when something struck me in the face. I stumbled backwards. Then, the thing in the darkness was on me, punching my ears, jabbing my chin, whacking me from side to side until I fell into a deeper blackness, and all the sounds of my execution were lost and faded. Down and down into nausea I went. I could hear myself heaving. Down and down into the blackness. Then everything was quiet.

At some point, my eyes fluttered open. I was lying in the gutter in front of the apartment. My soldier had fallen next to me. His mouth was bloodied; his nose twisted at an odd angle, and his head was crimson with blood. There was a huge welt across his face as if he had been struck with a chain. But I had fared no better. When I peered at myself in the window of a parked car, my mouth was bleeding and my chin was red and swollen. My right eye was tightly shut and puffed, my nose flattened. There was dirt grounded into my cheeks. It must have been a hell of a battle . . . one-side . . . and my army and I had lost.

We both staggered upwards and brushed ourselves off. When I looked at the building, the door was open and there was no one inside. Youth is one-quarter intellect and three-quarters fool so we entered the building again, searching for my lost Lenore. We searched through the rooms. Dismal bedrooms in lock-step together as if it were a factory for prostitution. Smoky rooms where the musty smell of sperm saturated the air, and the events of the previous evening were all too apparent. Rosalie was gone. So was everyone else. My hope for saving her was gone too.

I sobered up at home and cleaned the bloodied wounds that characterized me as having been in a losing fight. I went to see my grandfather's *paisan*, a local mobster who held sway over every illegal operation in Newark. He laughed when he saw me.

"Somebody didn't like you," he laughed.

"I was trying to save a young girl."

"I think she is in better condition than you, eh?"

"I think so," I laughed, though it hurt to smile. He listened with a sympathetic gleam in his eyes, soft, caring, almost fatherly. When I had done, he gazed directly into my eyes and nodded. There was a smirk on his lips, but his eyes were deadly.

"Leave it alone, Russell. It's business. This young *putan* is trouble. She ratted on every guy who touched her. She stooled on the bartenders, the landlords, the girl who fed her drugs. She would have ratted on you too, but they had your letter and that saved you. I respect you, Russell. You are decent and honest. A real *pezzanovante*. But this is business. She's property now, and she belongs to someone. I cannot interfere. It's business." And that was all he would say.

And business was good. For over the weekend I had been agonizing over Rosalie and searching for her, the mob enlisted her as a staff prostitute, and she had slept with no less than twenty-one men, some of whom went to jail because Rosalie was a minor. I remember a detective questioning me in such a sweet, lilting voice that I almost confessed to something I didn't do. It was as if I wanted to confess because he was so compassionate and understanding.

"Now, Russell," he looked at me with kind, deceptive eyes, "did you have intercourse with Rosalie?" His voice dropped, and his kindly eyes met me squarely.

"No, sir. I was trying to help her." I lowered my voice so no one else would hear. "I've never been to bed with a girl, sir. Never." He smiled at that, and his eyes were laughing. I wanted to punch him out. Was it a sin to be a virgin?

He pulled out the letter I had written, a letter extolling the virtues of a good life, a letter giving her hope about the future if she just hung tough, a letter telling her I was her friend and would never violate her trust, a letter telling her to be a good daughter and sister, a letter that now seemed to be exonerating me from this awful crime that would have sent me to prison for twenty years.

"I read your letter to Rosalie." He snuffed his cigarette into a nearby sand bucket and stared into my eyes. I wondered what his own eyes had seen. Murdered victims? Rape victims? Robberies? Accidents? He seemed old and fatigued, his jowls sagging beneath a rugged jaw. He had the sad face of one who has seen too many atrocities to be affected by them any longer.

"It was a waste of time, huh?" I asked.

"It was a very sincere letter."

"I really wanted to help."

"She took a lot of people down with her. The bartenders are in trouble. Shirley is in trouble. This kid isn't kidding around. She was mainstreaming heroin. Hooking all over Paterson. Cops over there pulled her in several times. She's bad people, Russell. Walk away and forget it." I nodded, and he motioned me that the interview was over. I signed my statement and left.

When I think back on how close I came to disaster, I shutter. Yet, my interest in Rosalie was never sexual. I genuinely wanted to help her. And it was a time I understood that, where business was concerned, the mob I dealt with for minor favors would be of no assistance to me where the dollar was concerned. From Rosalie, I learned the kind of man I was to become. Honorable. Loyal. Compassionate. From a common hooker, I learned I was head and shoulders above the men who had taken advantage of her. If I could have saved her from that kind of life, I would have. And despite whatever other poor opinions of myself I have, I was proud that I was a better man than most, that sex was not worth the satisfaction gained, that it was eminently more gratifying to help someone rather than to shove her under. And who knows, after all, that when they are counting points up there in that great burial place in the sky, someone may find a white mark near the black ones and credit me with trying to save some hapless soul.

I saw Rosalie again at the Alcoholic Beverage Commission where she was testifying against Freddie and his partner about getting drinks at the Club 421. She was sitting two rows behind me, looking demure and precocious and paying avid attention to the proceedings. I asked the female custodian if I could talk to her, and she suggested it would be better if I didn't. Nor did Rosalie appear anxious to speak with me. Perhaps she was still high on drugs, or drying out, or her life had turned hard and cold. Perhaps she realized what a dumbbell I was. Or perhaps she blamed me for leaving her in a bar while I went to work.

She took the stand and was sworn. They went through the usual routine of ensuring that she understood the nature of the proceedings and her rights. As she took the stand, her skirt swept away from her leg, and it was as sensuous and appealing as it had always been. I wondered, then, what made me different. I wondered why I had not seen her as a sexual object to be conquered. I wondered what would have happened if I *had* seen her that way. I thought about my letter and how it had saved me by being truthful and honest. I wondered if it had any impact on Rosalie. I wondered why I found the need to "save" people and why I had not just dropped her off on a street corner. But that answer was before me. It was because I care.

I often wonder if Rosalie ended as she predicted. Did some guy high on drugs slit her throat or beat her into oblivion? Or did she shoot one needle too many and go cold and stiff in a dark hallway? Those are the things we never know. But I sometimes believe that when we go to Hell, we see all our mistakes, and we relive them again and again. And when we go to Hell, we see how our actions would have played out had we chosen a different path.

These were the stories of the city, my city. It was not like any other city in the nation. It was different. It had a heartbeat of its own and a life of its own. Though I have been away from it for some forty odd years, I doubt it is much different now. Only the players have changed.

So it is the city in which I was reared. Part of my life. Part of me. Each story, each life I met was like a guiding rod, shuffling and channeling me like a mouse negotiating a maze. I speak of the city, the streets and the people because they are eternal and because they will survive me. I write of them because they "are" me and because they should not be forgotten.

Chapter Two

◆

The Men I Knew: The Mob

That the streets are hard is a lesson not easily learned. Three boys, lolling an afternoon away, tossing firecrackers into the air. In no particular hurry because they had nothing to do. In the streets, there is always something to do. Sometimes, it is to avoid danger. One moment we were carelessly making noises on a summer-drenched cobblestone street, and the next we were confronting death.

It was a snub nosed .38 small, compact, ugly, capable of belching death, grasped tightly in the hand of a drunken detective who, bleary and red-eyed, had charged from the Chestnut Street Tavern into the streets where we had been carelessly tossing firecrackers. Shouting and cursing, the drunken detective lined us up like tin soldiers against a sooty, red brick factory wall, his finger tightening on the trigger of that little black object that precariously swung from boy to boy. The tavern was owned by a mobster. We knew him as Pete C or Pistola or even The Pistol, and this

COP WALL–This is the wall where a drunken detective chased us down and held Red, Johnny and me at gun point. Had Pete not rescued us, I really don't know if I'd be writing books.

drunk came running out of the building and held us against the wall.

"Don't move. Get against the wall. Against it. All the way."

We shimmed up against the wall, wondering what the hell had happened. On my right was Little Red, huddled against the wall, bleached from fear, and standing on the left of me was John Roach, the black boy from down the street. I was frozen in the middle. It's not like in the movies where the hero suddenly leaps for the gun, wrestles it away and subdues his attacker. Not like that at all. In the streets of Newark, there were no such heroes, and death was a fact of life, whether it occurred on the docks with the crushing of a union worker, or with the gunning down of some informant, a welsher or a rival hood muscling into someone else's turf. But that day it was me who was lined up, facing death, for nothing more than a boyish prank of exploding firecrackers.

How could death come so soon? I asked myself over and over. I was riding high on life, earning big money, free of my parents for the first time. How could fate so suddenly turn the tables and put me in harm's path?

I had earned my living from the time I was eleven, when I pulled a red wagon around to the factories and sold drinks and cakes to the workers on their breaks and lunches. My dad sold me the items at his cost. I kept the sodas in a red metal cooler and made the rounds from factory to factory. Because the workers had little time to reach the nearest confectionery store, it was worth their while to pay me extra for the sodas. Later, I started hauling sandwiches and made a good profit on those as well. By the time I was thirteen, I had abandoned the delivery business for a more lucrative line of work . . . selling fireworks.

I connected with a prize fighter with connections at the Port of New York Authority. He was able to purchase cases of fireworks for a paltry sum, so he and I formed a partnership, with Del supplying the raw materials and Russell establishing a distribution system. There was a large market for fireworks in New Jersey, primarily because they were illegal. Make something illegal, tell people you can't have something, and it becomes more attractive to them. Freighters came into the Port of New York and Newark at least once a week and sometimes more often. One of the cargoes they carried were fireworks, and they could be purchased cheaply. Since Del was attending school with me, he was a logical partner with his connections at the Port. I graduated St. James Grammar School with the naïve attitude of a virgin, but it didn't take long for Del to convert me to a teen-age racketeer.

Del was a Golden Glove competitor who was lean and tight. He stood about five feet seven inches and had narrow eyes that stalked a man like quarry. But I didn't meet Del in school. I met him through Pete because Pete was a sponsor for the Golden Gloves competitions.

Around that time, I graduated grammar school and entered St. Benedict's Academy where I was able to double or triple the price of my goods and sell them in school. I lasted a year in St. Benedict's, was asked to leave and was enrolled in Seton Hall Preparatory where I lasted for two years. And they were lucrative years, indeed, for the boys at Seton Hall were much richer than the boys at St. Benedict's and our profits soared. If anyone complained, I reported their indiscretion to Del who paid them a visit and discussed our differences. I always admired Del. In fact, I regarded him somewhat as an artist. He had a straight jab that jerked his adversary's head straight back and an uppercut that was swift and arcing like a sweeping scimitar. He was also a gentleman, often picking his opponent up after he had decimated him and helping to steady him. His persuasiveness often resolved the problem without repetition. In fact, they often became even better customers than before. Fireworks christened me into the ranks of profiteering. There were weeks when Del and I split more than a thousand dollars in profits.

And fireworks were in demand throughout the year. Boys will be pranksters, and fireworks are part of the prank. So there were times when I actually loaned my father money because I was earning substantially more per week than he was. But my little prank of lighting some of the profits and tossing them in the air backfired on one luminous sunlit day. There we were, three boys lined up against a wall, waiting for execution by a drunk.

The cop had come charging out of the bar, waving his gun and chasing us down the street. Because we did not know who he was, we simply stood in awe, thinking him an unruly drunk with a big mouth. But he had a mouth and a gun and a badge as well. I found myself staring into the cold, steel barrel of his .38, fearing the news accounts would read: *Fifteen year old resident cut down by brave detective.* There are times when bravery compels us to do nothing. My objective in life was to rise above my circumstances, to succeed in business and life and to live long enough to do all three. To do that, I had to survive.

I stared at the man with the gun. There was no light in his eyes, as if he had a windowless soul and nothing within, a mindless void oblivious that he held three frightened kids at gunpoint. They were narrowed, blood-shot eyes, blurred with drink and fierce with anger. The more you stare at the man holding a gun on you, the more you see how terribly drunk and mindless he is. The more you understand how, in seconds, this man has a power, a power to extinguish your life for nothing more than a prank. He thought we had been firing guns. In his drunken stupor his mind surmised danger, a danger his profession warned him could snuff out his own life.

The gun wavered over each of us, to me, at my gut, then to Red, then to Roach, then back to me again. The detective was standing only five feet away. Perhaps enough time to jump him when the gun moved to the last boy. What then? Who was I to challenge a trained police officer? And one with a gun? How sensitive was the trigger? I'd heard of cops who had the trigger so light a straw could set it off. Rumor? Perhaps. Right then, an inebriated cop held me hostage against the wall, and the siege seemed endless. I kept waiting for the sound and wondered if I'd feel the bullet first, then hear the roar. I'd seen men shot in the movies. I wondered if I would fall the same way. Would it hurt? Would it burn? How long would it take to die? Dumb thoughts. Stupid thoughts.

We dared not move. Not an inch. Even our breath seemed to cooperate by remaining in limbo; even a blink seemed to threaten existence. He defied us to talk. So we stood, quietly, containing our fear, controlling our shakes and hoping for rescue. It is said one's life flashes before him just as he is about to die. I have never had that experience though I have faced death many more times than by the hand of a drunken sot. What gained prominence in my mind was that just a week before, Jamsie L, an icon of the neighborhood, a pinnacle of mob affiliation, had been returning from a clandestine meeting with the Essex County Prosecutor when he was gunned down.

Jamsie got a little education, and through the mob, earned a position as Principal of the local high school. The school had bulging sides, that is, new migrants into the area were filling it to over-capacity, and an annex was needed. The State Board of Education funded the construction with over 1.2 million bucks. I saw the cement foundation laid, and over a two year period, some cinder block went up around the foundation but the building was never completed. The State commenced an investigation into where the funds had gone since Jamsie claimed more money was needed. They called it an over-write.

Jamsie was summoned to the Prosecutor's office. In fact, he was summoned a number of times which was a favorite trick of the law enforcement people because it notioned the Mob that one was in cahoots with the law and giving information. Why else would he be down there all that much? The obvious conclusion was that he was cooperating with the fuzz. And that may have been true, and it may not have been true but the Mob, just like the Government, takes no prisoners, and Jamsie was a liability since the project money was gone and those who funneled it into their own pockets were at risk. So Jamsie was targeted for extinction, a breed of one, signaled to be executed.

He alighted from his vehicle one moonlit night, after just returning from another session with the Prosecutor and heard, perhaps, a familiar voice calling him. It was enough to halt him mid-track. Too late to realize, he had halted for his own demise. The shots were muffled, too. Pft, pft, pft, pause, pft, pft. The subdued ring of a small caliber .22 worked like an artist's brush in the hands of a professional hit man. Three, then four, then five small holes opened up in Jamsie's forehead, neat, round and cylinder-like. He had cried for his wife. Called to her for help even as the first shot struck him. He had turned after the shots had found their home. He was a big man, a strong man, grown sturdy from work on the docks, from street fighting and an internal toughness that grew in the streets of Newark. But even this big man was not so big he could not be killed. Even he was not so big he did not call for his wife to aid him. So he sagged to the ground and then the final Pft, pft, one in each eye, to seal the contract, and Jamsie was dead.

I grew up with Jamsie. He was older, tougher than me. When he strode from his house, we all looked admiringly at him because he was a king. We were just kids. He'd snug his suit jacket under his open collar and slick back his wavy, ebony hair, and we all knew he was meeting a date and that things would happen that we could only read about in magazines and dirty books. Before the Godfather, there were guys like Jamsie. I saw him when he went after a guy who flirted with his sister. The guy just whistled at her. No touching. No rape. Nothing more than a pass. And Jamsie caught him eating an apple as he nonchalantly sauntered out of my dad's grocery store. And then the apple was rolling along the street, while the wise guy was lying in the gutter with blood streaming between his teeth and huge welts around his ears and cheeks.

Then Jamsie stood over him.

"Stay away from my sister, pimp." He breathed, not even slightly winded. Another kick to the head. "Away," he grunted.

We all shook with fear at his ferocity. That was Jamsie, and we were frightened by him. But Jamsie smoothed back his hair and rubbed his thick Italian jowls. The passer remained quiet. Unmoving. Jamsie strolled away as calmly as if he had merely been passing time.

And that was racing through my mind as the .38 snubbie passed from me to Red to Roach and back again. *Should I jump him? Take the risk?* He looked strong enough to take all three of us. Drunk like he was, the gun would probably go off. Who would it hit? Me? Roach? Maybe little Red? Stand dead still. Don't friggin' move. Breathe and invite a bullet. Christ! Over a few firecrackers. So we stood. And we stood. Watching the gun move back and forth between us, trying to be brave and daring nothing until it was over.

I do not think I would have lived if Pete C had not come to our rescue. It was Pete's bar, and he was the local Mafioso. He had been plying Cookie, the cop, with drinks all afternoon because Cookie was on his payroll. Feed the Irish booze and they leave your booking operation alone. Give him a winner from a fixed race once in a while, and the cop forgets he has a badge. The saying was: He was the best cop money could buy.

They may speak of killers and mobsters with disdain. I cannot so speak. It was Pete who took Cookie away, got him to holster his gun, still screaming epithets at us, still lusting to spill our blood in the streets. He calmed him and then calmed him again because drink had clouded his brain. Nothing seeped through. Finally Pete got him away and signaled us to scram. That was his word. "Scram."

And scram we did.

There was new spring in our steps away from Pistol Pete's that day and yet, the further we paced, the braver we became. But when one is fifteen, the world of reality and the world of which we dream are very seldom the same. So we boasted and we became brave. Brave because the danger was past. Brave because it was unmanly not to be brave.

"I was about to jump that big mother," Roach said. Always the impetuous one. Roach was black, sinewy and handsome. He had quick hands. He jumped rather than moved. He was a good kid, just arrogant. He sounded full of bravado but that was the fear speaking. He was scared like the rest of us. Too many of his brethren had ended up hanging from trees or pumped full of shot shells. Then Roach was spouting how many things we could have done if we knew that drunken cop was going to jump us. Roach, ballplayer, strong, mouthy. His family lived down the block, good Baptist people who attended services. I remember the kids dressed in their Sunday finest and Johnny grimacing as his mother dragged him along to an all day session at the store front church around the corner. He always wore a white shirt, open collar, except on Sundays when his mother made him wear a tie. I remember him too because his mother said that one day the whites would be slaves because they had enslaved the blacks. I don't think that ever happened, but she believed it.

Roach played ball so he was part of the team. Even went for try-outs at the Newark Bears which was the farm team for the New York Yankees. He should have made it, too, except in those days they just did not hire blacks to play for the majors. Jackie Robinson was yet to come. Blacks had their own farm teams, their own league, and Johnny Roach could have been a big ballplayer. But he had other ideas.

He had a lot of good qualities but he could be gross, one of those guys whose entire personality was tied up between his legs.

And he'd hold his stomach all the way to the corner, turn, then he'd make a motion like he was boxing someone and yell, "Blip, blip, hey man I'm fast. Blip in the stomach. Blip, blip in the jaw. Got ya man." And he'd run off laughing. I remember Roach later on in life too. Up the block from my house stood decaying, old, roach-infested tenement houses, long rows of dilapidated buildings with rotted fronts and sagging wood porches. And in these roach littered palaces, the madam plied the wares of her whores and served hooch whiskey on holidays and even after hours when liquor could not legally be served. She kept a bottle of colorless moonshine underneath her kitchen sink. Liquid fire that plummeted to the pit of your stomach and flamed when it landed. And there were whores lying in various positions around the beds and couches, tight, short dresses that they slowly hiked above their knees to display their thighs. Some of them were damned attractive too. And coquettish as well.

Ten bucks bought a room and two throws. But I never did. Something about those girls spelled trouble. From the time I was old enough to understand her broken English, my grandmother admonished me to make my grandfather proud. I bore his name. The name of centuries of ancestors. My belief in that pride kept me from harm's way again and again. So when the girls cajoled and prodded, I smiled and ignored them. I went there because I campaigned for Democrats who controlled the black vote. So my Negro friend took me there for a quick drink on Election Day and then we motored blacks to the polls to vote . . . and vote . . . and vote. Voter fraud is not an invention of the 21st Century. It's been going on since men concocted the vote. Probably since the days of Rome, though I've no evidence to support that.

It was not difficult to vote on multiple occasions. Just around an hour before the polls closed, the challengers would check the list to see who had not been in as yet. Being a small district, we often knew why some had not come into vote. It was a simple matter to have someone come in and sign for that person and cast the vote. When things became so flagrantly one-sided that no Republican dared compete in my district, voting seven or eight times was not unusual. Every vote counted because it sent a message to the opposition that read: Don't even try.

Roach was at the bordello sometimes. Too often. One girl in particular held his fancy. Her name was Jolin. I was twenty-two then and in law school so politics was a potential career for me. I'd see him from time to time, pull my Chrysler to the curb so we could chew the fat. We didn't spend a lot of time talking but we spoke about the things that mattered. We spoke about the future and where we hoped to be. We spoke of young days, boxball and the Yankees. Playing tennis across the concrete slabs in front of my house. And kick-the-can. We spoke of buying three sweet potatoes for a nickel and cooking them in the gutters with whatever paper and wood we could find. We spoke of his baseball career and why he never pursued it. But Johnny was black. Blacks didn't have the same opportunities. They knew their place because they only had one place. This was long before civil rights and the sixties, when things changed. So Johnny was snagged in a job and the moonshine and the whore he loved.

I guess I can't blame Johnny for his life style. His father had died when he was very young. His mother worked two jobs cleaning house and doing laundry for the rich. His brothers and sisters were pretty much left on their own. It wasn't that there was discrimination in Newark. The difference between blacks and whites was just an accepted thing. They were poor and lived in slum houses, and the whites had money and decent jobs and lived well. It was inevitable that the kids were on the streets, and Johnny was no exception. No matter how religious his mother was, Johnny was a child of the streets. He would live that way and die that way.

Then I didn't see Roach for a while, but I saw him one last time coming home from school. I motored past the old tenement. Usually that time of day it was quiet. But that day there were police cars and an ambulance in front of the place. I pulled over to investigate. After all, the building was only a block from my home, and it was the very same house that Johnny frequented and where I solicited votes.

A man was face down on the porch and the remarkable thing about him was that the back of his white, open-collared shirt was stained bright with red blood. I had seen that kind of shirt before, and it was not common to see such a thing.

"What happened?" I asked a crimson-faced cop, who stood there looking compassionless.

"Got his throat slit." Then he whispered, "You know these Black Irish. Messing around with some guy's girl. Got into a scrap with her boyfriend and belted him on the button. The guy pulled a razor, and the kid raced on down the stairs. Guy caught him right at the door and pulled his head back by the hair. Slit his throat. Did you know him?"

"Don't know." I felt weak when I said that. The shirt looked all too familiar.

The cop jerked the head back, exposing a raw, gaping wound that penetrated into the arteries. I thought the head would come right off. And there, eyes closed, lips twisted in a dumb smile, was Roach, and he was cold and lifeless and all the arrogance was gone out of him. I did not know that Johnny would end up with his life oozing out of him on a filthy porch. Perhaps it would have been better if the drunken cop had shot him. It had to be a better death than he suffered.

But the day the cop jammed us against the factory wall and held us hostage, Roach was boasting how he'd hit the cop here and then there, blip, blip, then wham in the jaw and down, eight, nine, ten. So I let him brag. After all, seven years later he'd be lying on a rotted porch with his blood spilling between the boards and staining his Sunday white shirt. "I would take that cop out for sure, right Russ?"

"Yeah," I agreed. "I'd like to go back and ace that sucker. Who the hell does he think he is? Shove that gun up his left nostril and punch the trigger." Then Roach looked at Red, but Red was pale and quiet. He was ready to cry. His face drew into a pallid little knot and his freckles twitched and jumped. He was built slightly and narrow with an elongated face and electric eyes that beamed with inquiry when we teased him. The remarkable thing about Red was that his nose was always runny. Not both nostrils, just the right one. He always seemed to have a cold, and his nose always seemed runny. Other than that there wasn't much else remarkable about him except he was a very timid kid. Until then, I hadn't noticed him shaking. Really trembling as if he were having a stroke. I tried to coax him out of the shock, but he was scared witless.

"Yeah, I was watching to see which way the gun went," I said. "I figured to jump him when he went far right with it. I figured to grab his hand and pull the gun down until you two guys could jump in." I was trying to bolster Red's courage, but he did not lighten. He stiffened and jerked straight up, then welled over and started puking. There was no food coming out just fluid, some of it dribbling down his chin in tiny rivulets, and his eyes rolled back in his head until he went down.

He regained consciousness, looking foolishly at us as if his reputation for cowardice might be spread throughout the Down Neck area, and he might never again hang with the big boys. But we were not inclined to mock him. There was always something different about Little Red. His clothes were old and worn, but clean. He never seemed to gain any weight. When others were headed home to have lunch or dinner, Red just waited around for all of us to return. I remember that day because we almost got shot just for tossing firecrackers to celebrate the 4th. But I also remember

PETE'S BAR–This is the modern version of Pete's Corner Bar. The original had yellow brick and thick plate glass window squares.

it because that day I discovered that Red's family was on welfare and toward the end of the month, they had no money left for food.

"Hey, I never saw a guy vomit water before. What the hell did you have for lunch?"

"Nothing." He wiped the spittle off his chin and started crying.

"Red, no lie. What did you have for breakfast?"

Never said a word. Just shrugged.

"Hey, I'm talking to you. When'd you eat last?"

"I don' know. I don' get very hungry. About two days ago, I guess. Ma needed medicine for Gooch. We can't always eat when she buys medicine. I guess it was a couple of days ago. I can't always remember that kind of stuff."

"Are you kidding me? Two days? You went two days with no food."

"I don' mind. Gooch needs the pill. He gets these things, seizures. Gets spasms and jerks all over and his eyes roll up in his head, then he passes out. Then we have to keep a spoon in his mouth to hold down his tongue so he don' swallow it. It's okay. I don' eat much anyway."

"Lift up your shirt," I snapped.

"Huh?" he squeaked.

"Lift up your shirt. I want to see something."

He pulled the wrinkled, thin shirt up over his face.

"Crap, look at those ribs. Hell man, you aren't hungry. You're starved."

"I always been wiry. Don' eat much."

"Bull. Red. Come on!"

I turned and started for Pete's tavern.

"Where we goin'?"

"Chestnut Bar."

"Nnnnnooooooo. Not goin. That cop will gun us for sure."

"You need something to eat, and Pete's always good for a touch. I'll do the talking."

He looked so mournful, standing there, facing his fears and denying his hunger, I could have carried him there. Little Red had always been frail. We just thought he was skinny. He had to be Irish because he had those brown freckles on his face and that Irish red hair that curled straight up on his head. No one ever questioned the why of it. We just accepted him as he was. We never even knew where he lived. Never saw his apartment. He just appeared one day and was one of us. He had a brother, Gooch, oval faced, thin hair, droopy eyes, that duh kind of look about him. He bore the brunt of all our jokes because he was slightly retarded. Put a pair of dice in his hands, and God looked out for him. I was there the day Gooch made thirteen straight passes and not just sevens and elevens either. Gooch shot little fours and big nines, all hard numbers to tally.

But he suffered epileptic fits and sometimes went spastic right while we were talking to him. We just knew the family was poor, and Gooch wasn't "right", but after all, he was one of us. Gooch wasn't afraid of anything. He was too dumb to be scared. But Red, he was slight, hyper and gullible. It didn't take much to shake him. And he was shaken by the incident. That skinny kid was being hijacked by fear, and he had not the strength to run from it or to confront it. I needed to pull him out of himself.

Pete's tavern was at the very corner of the block, with the entrance at the exact angle of the corner. One could see inside, to the bar. Toward the near corner, there were assorted tables, and two back rooms with thin curtains barring the entrance. Assorted liquors and whiskies lined up on the shelf behind the bar like so many soldiers waiting to pull duty. Beer flowed from the taps. It spouted and fumed air and beer into the glass below. Outside the tavern beat the heart of a complex and noble city. Inside, the world was small and secure and distant.

Pete himself was undramatic. Pan-faced, deep-socketed eyes, black orbs, thin black hair laid back against his head. He had the fatherly look of a priest when he addressed you. His trousers were black and neatly pressed and his tan shirt an open-collared sport type. He wore brown, unassuming shoes. In point, Pete was a very ordinary looking man, barely touching fifty, married, two sons, one useless and doting, and the other smart enough to be groomed for leadership.

There are leaders and there are leaders. Chenzo was a born leader and inherited mob business when Pete decided to retire. Pasquale, on the other hand, basked in the light of his father's glory and had Chenzo to cover for him when he screwed up. Eventually his father gave him half of Long Branch, including the amusement park section of it, but Pat never did much and was never introduced into the business. To say he was a screw up left much to explanation. Pat was one of those guys you could like and dislike all at the same time. He acted like a big shot, directing his father's men to perform menial tasks for him. When he laughed it was a false laugh, not from within but from somewhere in his ego where he thought himself a very important man. On the other hand, he had a nice side when he wasn't pretending to be what he wasn't. And he desperately wanted to be his father's right hand man—except he wasn't—he couldn't. Not in a million years.

Every mob guy must make his bones by performing some feat of daring. In most cases, it's just a simple mob hit. The fledgling moves in, rubs someone out, and he is inducted into the family as a soldier. It's like Confirmation in the Catholic Church except no one is going to heaven. No one was going to assign a hit to Pasquale. He had to make his bones another way if he was going to make them at all.

Pete controlled the Boardwalk in Long Branch along the beach front. Millions of bucks in property value not to mention the amusement games, pizza fronts, hot dog stands and kid's rides. One particular vendor was smitten with the gambling bug and got into Pete for some pretty heavy money. The caper was assigned to Pasquale, twenty-two at the time. He seemed more Irish than Italian, tall, slender, a squarish face bejeweled with somber, hazel eyes. He was handsome, and he let the girls know it. At times, he carried himself with an air of royalty, except he was disregarded by anyone in the mob who had any common sense. His line was great with the girls, and, because he drove a 1950 Olds 98, they all believed his stories about his high station in the mob. No true solider would ever have spoken of such matters, and his indiscretions were overlooked mainly because he was Pete's son and because he really knew none of their intimate business.

Because he entreated his father for some respect from the other members of the family, he was given a simple task, namely, to torch the business place of the indebted gambler. This was not a difficult assignment. The building overlooked the beach and was accessible by the boardwalk. One had only to stroll up to the front of the building, set the incendiary switch and toss the fire bomb onto the roof, a distance perhaps of fifteen feet. Each store was marked with the name of the business. It was not a difficult task because the area was well lit, and the police seldom patrolled at night. A common misunderstanding about the mob is that the boss enjoys taking out gamblers and borrowers who do not pay. In fact, there is little profit in exterminating tardy payers, and object lessons, such as breaking ribs or jaws, often achieve much more than eradicating them. Thus, Pasquale was assigned the task of burning down the man's business. It was his watered-down manner of making his bones.

Along the Boardwalk and next to the business of the reluctant gambler was an infamous hot dog stand that still has roots in the area. I recall the place because the owner was Jewish, and he had photograph on photograph of famous actors and actresses who had visited his California restaurant. It was my spring tradition to visit the vender as soon as he opened for the season. Pete himself was often a diner there. Unfortunately, this kosher palace of delicious delight was located next door to the vender who owed money. Not only did Pasquale use the wrong kind of incendiary—one concocted to make a small, controlled burn—but he tossed it onto the wrong roof—the roof of the popular hot dog stand. Thus did an icon of the Boardwalk find its hot dogs very well done and out of business. The gambler's place was untouched, but he did get the message. Eventually, the icon rebuilt his hot dog eatery far, far from the Boardwalk and any chance of mishap by a misdirected fire bomb. He must have lost thousands of dollars in business having to move his location, but it was safer than demise at the hands of an incompetent would-be mobster.

To say that Pete was livid over the episode is mild retort. As understanding and patient as he was with others, he had little patience for Pasquale and promptly banished him to Calabria for two years. Pasquale, of course, visioned himself as on-the-run when, in fact, his father simply exiled him because of his filial embarrassment. It was this I was thinking of when we arrived at Pete's saloon because it occurred to me I had not seen Pasquale for some time.

The cop was gone. And when I spoke to Pete, he told Red to take a seat in the back room and brought a plate of sandwiches out to him. Imagine, a mob boss waiting on a starving kid! That is never shown in the movies. I watched Red nibble methodically on his food, forcing down each morsel. Pete just shook his head. We watched as he stuffed some of the food into his shirt. Pete saw him but said nothing. Then, embarrassed, Red grinned and said: "For later."

Pete saw me shaking, all my bravado simply show and nothing more. He swung around to the bar and grabbed a bottle of Four Roses whiskey. In those days, Four Roses was a lower-priced rye whiskey. When bourbon became more profitable, Four Roses became a bourbon whiskey. He shoved a shot glass in front of me and poured. "You take a drink. It's no fun having a guy stick a gun in your face."

"I'm all right, Pete. Really."

He pushed the glass closer. "Take the drink," he said, his eyes piercing my own as if he saw into the fear of my very soul. The one thing I learned about the mob guys was that they had a way of penetrating your very thoughts. They knew when you were bluffing and when you were straight. It's like a learned behavior or maybe an instinct, but Pete knew that I was scared rabid. He wouldn't embarrass me by saying that. Bravery is much regarded within the mob circles. It was one thing to be afraid, and another, to show it so, I could take the drink and still preserve my honor.

I dumped the whiskey down my throat and felt the fire coursing new courage into my soul. Another drink and I was ready to tackle that cop and beat his bloody head to fragments. For years after, my nightmares consisted of turning the gun into his ear and pulling the trigger. But for the moment, at fifteen, I was thankful the cop was home sleeping off another drunk. Nor have I ever revealed the truth of this matter until now, when I am too old and weary to care any more. So I took the third drink and let it settle my shaken nerves.

"Thanks, Pete. I guess I was thirsty." But he knew I meant that I had been scared at the thought of death, and he merely nodded. Then, he turned, his face serious, almost menacing.

"Russie, do me a favor." It was not really a request. Pete did not make requests. He commanded respect and knew how to use his authority.

"Sure, Pete"

"I'll feed your friends. You go down to the Blue Dahlia and ask for Jamesie Lou. Know him?"

"Sure. He does the bookin' at the bar around that area."

"Take him this note. He'll give you something to bring back to me. An envelope. Understand, kid?"

"Sure. He gives me an envelope to bring to you. Got it, Pete."

I started for the door when his voice halted me. He had a peculiar smile on his face. "Russie, there will be five grand in the envelope. Don't make any side trips."

"Five . . . ." I choked. "No side trips." I began to shake again.

The Blue Dahlia was the local bar, mostly patronized by the blacks who lived in the area. Quiet enough except on Friday and Saturday nights when fights broke out and sometimes shots broke the noisy din. On Saturday nights we'd sit on my front porch, waiting to see the action. Mostly knife fights where somebody got stabbed or slashed, but one night a short guy, about my five-foot height, took on a monster of six foot. I remember the fight because I rooted for the little guy, but he took an awful beating. The big guy got him down, then caved him with a garbage can and lugging and winded went back to the bar. The little guy called him out again. This time he had a table leg with the bolt sticking out of the thick end. He swatted the big guy, and he went down, more from drunkenness than the shock of the blow. That made him mad. He stormed up and all over the little guy, wrested the table leg away from him and proceeded to turn him into turnip soup. The big guy just kept hitting the little guy in the chest with that bolt. And the little guy just whumped up in the air each time he was hit. Sometimes the big guy stopped exerting himself and just stood there. By the time the cops got there, the little guy was half dead. Some old Negro lady came out of the bar and poured a beer bottle full of water over his head. Then she returned to the bar, came out with another supply of water and dumped it on him. This went on until the emergency squad came. The guy was either dead of his wounds or of pneumonia from all the water dumped on him. I never knew what happened to the big guy. They handcuffed him and stuffed him in the cop car, and that was the last of it. So the Dahlia was not a place where whites went, though, it was safe enough in the daylight hours. Time or two, I was invited for a drink ... and accepted. But that day, I just retrieved the envelope and returned to Pete's, shaking at each block I walked and looking over my shoulder for the robbers I just knew were behind me.

When I arrived, Pete handed me a C note and patted me on the back. "That's a hundred," he said.

"Pete, I don't want this. You and my grandfather were compadres. He wouldn't like the idea."

He pierced me with dark, mesmeric eyes and commanded my attention as only authority can do. "Russie, if you are going to be a mouthpiece, you learn to accept money for what you do. Your grandfather was proud of you. If he was still around, he'd be the first to tell you a good Sicilian never refuses money or a deal. So you take the money. Put it toward your school. When you get into law school, you come to Pete for help. We got to stick together. You know the Micks and the Feds, they hate the Italians. Call us Wops and Dagoes. They'll bust our operations and hound us into jail, but they'll never touch the competition because they know we respect the rules. The others don't. We got

Haitians, Jamaicans and Chinks selling drugs. That we don't do. But they'll bust us and look the other way with the rest. No justice. We got to show them we can amount to something. Something they can't slam in jail. So you take the money. Make something of yourself. Go to school. Learn. Become a damn lawyer and beat the rats in their own courtrooms. Got me? And one day, just maybe, you do something for Pete, uh?"

"Yeah, Pete. I understand. My grandmother scolds me all the time. 'Keep out of trouble. Stay away from bad company. Carry your grandfather's name with pride.' I made myself a promise. I'm second generation, and my parents are average people. I am getting out of Newark. When I do, it will be because I succeeded. No matter who I know they will never push me into trouble. Promise."

"Can't let them put the Sicilians down." He said this with diligence and pride, and though his family came from Calabria, his origins were rooted in Sicilian culture.

He insisted I eat, gave us all a glass of wine and told Little Red that he was under orders from the Boss to see Pete any time he needed a meal. That Pete was able to serve liquor to minors was a small vestige of his power over bureaucrats. In all the years I knew him not a single agent from the Alcoholic Beverage Commission ever came to his establishment. They didn't want to be seen in his company. So he fed us and served us wine and, later, even gave Red and his brother Gooch work playing chicki for the back room poker game on Saturday night. It was good money for them because the local cops wanted payoffs to run the games, and once in a while a new kid in uniform wanted to make a name for himself. It wasn't that Pete couldn't fix things with the judges because he could. It was just inconvenient so he'd rather pay a chicki. Sicilians have a thing about not wanting to burn up any favors unless they really need one. He didn't really have to pay anyone to be chicki though. There was a code Down Neck that says no one rats on you, and no one deals with the cops. So even if you weren't paid to play chicki you did it anyway just to thwart the cops.

We finished our meal, and Pete dismissed us when a runner came in looking frazzled and concerned. The runner was Fat Toddy, a four hundred pound hulk of flab and muscle sitting under a head twice as large as a mule. Fats, as he was also called, did not walk. He lumbered like a gargantuan ship wallowing at sea. His thick arms were bloated and matched only by his thighs which jiggled as he oozed from place to place. Yet, for all his size he was amazingly agile when breaking someone's skull. His favorite tactic was kneeling on a guy until his ribs cracked. I mean, the guy was big.

Fats always wore a blue serge suit, black tie, plain silver tie clasp and deep, dark glasses as if he were in mourning for anyone he called upon. But despite his efforts to appear sedate and conservative, he resembled a circus fat man in conventional clothing. He huffed a message into Pete's ear, then gasped as he awaited reply. This was a man completely loyal to Pete because he did not have the brain power to be disloyal. Because of his brawn and loyalty, Pete stashed him on the payroll, granting him assorted assignments that were simple enough for a child to handle. Nothing complicated. Fat Toddy could not cope with anything that required more than minimal thinking.

I first had understood the depth of his witlessness a few years earlier than the cop incident when Fat Toddy was assigned to escort an honored guest on a flight to Miami. The honored guest was to be executed if his explanation to the fathers did not match their expectations. Due to his ponderous size, the ticket agent informed Fats he needed two tickets because he could not fit in a single seat. Toddy took offense from the statement and hauled the agent over the counter, proceeded then to do what he did best, namely bash the agent to the floor and kneel on him until he heard the sternum cracking.

Five cops and three security guards later, Fat Toddy was in custody, and the honored guest was running as fast as he could from the airport. This was a guy slated to meet his doom and he just disappeared. At least, for six months anyway. They finally found him.

Immediately on being bailed out, Fats snared another flight to Miami, paid for the two tickets and proceeded to search for the missing guest. He never found him. That was a job left to the Miami mob.

Pete didn't know whether to be amused or angry, but even though he learned a lesson, he sometimes forgot about Toddy's limited capabilities. So when he whispered into Pete's ear, it could only mean a problem of some kind.

We stayed long enough to know that whatever news Toddy brought was not good news at all. From that news was to unfold one of those mob business deals that not only went completely astray but topped the humor columns for months after.

Fats was assigned the task of dispatching a certain welsher named Mario Ponzo. Said Mario had accumulated a tab of lost bets totaling some $21,000.00. Among mobsters this kind of debt is unpardonable, and the interest of ten per cent per week becomes so unwieldy that it is impossible for anyone to repay. So Toddy was dispatched, not to persuade the recalcitrant gambler to pay what thou owest, but to draw immediate attention to the fact that people who welsh on their gambling debts do not survive to speak the tale. Mario was known to have a keepsake diamond ring worth a considerable fortune. It was a gift from his father, and he would never part with it. So when Fats shook Mario down trying to get the ring, Mario swallowed it. Nonplused by this quick action, Fat Toddy was stymied. He had been assigned to obtain money or the diamond and Mario had swallowed it.

Fats was accompanied by Zeke Sabronski, an up-and-coming boxer and part-time bone cruncher. At least, he was until a weighted boxing glove stove in the side of his head and finished his career. But Zeke still looked like a heavyweight boxer, tall and straight, hawkish face, flattened ears, a deviated nose that dished inward and accented his boyish, green eyes. Unlike Fats, he wore a cotton, turtle neck sport shirt with two pockets and narrow ridges down the front. His huge hands hung down like meat cleavers, almost as if he had no fingers. Zeke was probably ten points higher on the I.Q. test but not a Nobel Prize winner either. Zeke suggested that they retrieve the diamond by means of surgery. But Ponzo was still alive. That was remedied easily enough. Fats kneeled on him, trying to force the diamond up.

In dispatching Mr. Ponzo, Toddy decided to be somewhat innovative, and while Zeke hammer-locked the tardy gambler, Fats shoved the nozzle of a power washer into his mouth and plugged four thousand pounds per square inches of water into the open cavity. It has been conjectured that he was trying to flush the diamond out somehow so he could deliver it to the Don.

Needless to say, that much water pressure blew the man's lungs out and made a very messy scene. But it did not flush out the diamond. Fats and Zeke carted the body to a local meat factory where they thought to shove the corpse into a meat grinder and turn it into hamburger. Zeke suggested that the diamond would be ground up as well as the body. They left the building, returning to the Don for further instructions. His instruction was very clear: "Get me the money or the diamond. I don't care how."

They returned to the crime scene only to find that the police had discovered the Ponzo body and dumped it at a local mortician. They were about to right their wrong when the assistant mortician arrived on his shift to embalm the most recent corpse and prepare it for the wake. Since he had been on vacation, he had not the slightest idea who was to be embalmed but was told there was only one viewing.

Now Mr. Ponzo was a thin and wiry man while he lived, sallow faced, with a prominent beak and a sunless, pallid color that made him look the part of a recent corpse. The power washer episode left him even more sunken and pallid, but he still held on to the diamond with the tenacity of death itself. He was not quite stiff when the mortician began his work, dusting the face with make-up to alter his pale appearance, then injecting the fluids that would preserve his body long enough for burial. This was not exactly prescribed protocol for a mortician, but he was in a hurry and wanted to finish early. The wake would go on as scheduled. Even if it was the wrong corpse. So Mr. Ponzo was prepared and placed in the coffin.

There are no two funeral acts quite alike. Every widow is an individual. There were those who fainted over the coffin; those who passed out before they reached the casket; those who attempted to dive in with the deceased; and others who were more sedate and simply stood shocked and numb. Then there were those widows who strolled nonchalantly down the aisle, knelt in prayer by the funeral bier and spat upon the deceased.

The mortician, however, was not quite prepared for Mrs. B's scene though he had seen many Italian funerals. For when Mrs. Battaglia gazed into the face of the shrunken corpse of Mario Ponzo lying in state in the rosewood coffin for which she had paid $7,000, she did none of the things a sorrowing widow would do. First, her huge corpulence floated to earth in one resounding thud that shook the floor and rattled the coffin. Then she emitted a guttural scream ranging from a low, sorrowful wail to the angry screech of C above high C. When the howl reached beyond human toleration, she made a grunting sound signaling that she wished to be helped up. Then, having regained her footing with the aid of seven mourners, she grasped the mortician by the tie and promptly dragged him over to the coffin where she commenced to drag him into the coffin. In a moment of respite, she spat upon what should have been her late husband, accusing the embalmer of engineering the deception, even though he was nowhere present when the switch occurred. She had never seen a man dehydrated by a power washer and did not believe the man in the coffin was her husband.

When Pete discovered what occurred, he threatened to have Fat Toddy and Zeke roasted in his pizza oven and demanded that they retrieve the deceased. He wanted that diamond. No one—dead or alive—was cheating him of his due. They didn't know how they'd get a body that was on exhibit. Still, neither man intended challenging the boss, and they headed for Bilondi's Funeral Home as hastily as traffic would allow.

They arrived in the funeral home in time to hear some of the continuing altercation between the overweight widow and the slender, but fearful mortician, Bo Bilondi, who was at a loss to explain what had occurred and was unable to make amends because he was constantly being pummeled by Mrs. Battaglia. Amidst the crowd were moans of anguish as well as fearful threats of bodily harm to the mortician, who was still held by the tie and being shaken vigorously by the infuriated Mrs. B. The shock of the mourners was augmented when two unseemly gentlemen barged into the funeral parlor pointing shotguns at the bewildered bereaved. Mrs. Battaglia promptly fainted, again thumping the floor and straining its capacity. Her supporters punched their hands skyward and stood rigid. The mortician, having already suffered the outrage of a scandalized widow, simply slunk to the floor and asked to be shot.

Zeke yanked the corpse from its resting place and slung it over his broad shoulder while Fats menaced the family with his shot gun. It took some doing for Zeke to tote a stiff body while backing out of a funeral parlor filled with chairs. Each time he banged the hapless corpse into a chair or door jamb, the shocked occupants moaned at the disrespect. There was a chorus of ooohhhhs and ahhhhhs with assorted swear words muttered as well. In moments, Fats and Zeke were backing out of the parlor, impeded not only by the corpse and their unfamiliarity with the funeral home, but also by their shotguns still pointed at the motionless relatives. For good measure, Zeke banged the corpse against the door jamb one more time before exiting. The occupants were too stunned to move and proceeded to fan Mrs. Battaglia before they summoned the police. The entire scene had the grotesque and surreal color of an abstract painting.

In a matter of moments, two gunmen had hijacked a body from the funeral home and sped off, leaving the wake in total disarray. Mrs. Battaglia, recovered from her dismay, seized the mortician by his tie and dragged him to the empty casket.

"If you no bury my 'usband, you give me my money back, you crook."

The police, of course, thought some children were playing telephone jokes and refused to respond for more than two hours. After all, who would steal a corpse? By that time, Bo Bilondi had managed to escape the clutches of the angered widow and wall himself in one of the downstairs embalming rooms. Mrs. Battaglia continued pounding on the door, cursing him in two languages. Fats and Zeke retrieved the diamond (I will not describe how) and dumped Mario in the Newark meadows where the muck promptly swallowed him. The story was so incredulous that the family pleaded with the police to keep it from the newspapers. Thus, the headline that would have read, THE SNATCHING OF THE CORPSE, never made it to the copy room. It was as if it never happened.

I often wondered what conversation Pete and Fats were having and how it would turn out. No matter what Toddy did wrong, Pete had a liking for him and refused to fire him. But since they were engaged in whispered conversation with furtive glances in our direction, we left and walked to my parent's grocery store in the Polish section of Newark. The gun incident was still fresh in our minds, but the bragging, which is the right of all those who survive such incidents, ceased. On that day the incident would end. We did not speak more of it. We all knew the other was lying about their bravery, and we were not fools enough to actually jump a cop, though the thought really did occur to me. We spoke no more of it because in the telling our deed would grow bolder and bolder until there was no resemblance to the truth. These days when I think of it, I encounter a wave of sweat sweeping over my forehead, and I hear the gun blast as a bullet rips toward me. I see myself on a slab in the morgue, lifeless and cold. We were young, then, and perhaps more foolish. Perhaps, more fortunate than wise. And perhaps, more fortunate than we had a right to be. We all agreed though, that if a union mobster named Pistol Pete had not come to the rescue, at least one of us would have died that day.

Pete was right about me returning a favor. By then, he was affiliated with the international labor unions. Some years later, I repaid a favor of him saving my life from that drunken cop. I finished college and law school, passed the Bar and opened a practice. I had not seen Pete for many years. He was in his 60s when I saw him again, more stately and refined than the young Pete I had known. Time had not hurt him much. He still had his hair, parted and combed straight back, a little thinner, a lot whiter but full and robust. It wasn't jagged and ruffled the way some old people get. Perhaps he had gained a little weight, but he was more distinguished as if time had mellowed his features and his build. He still spoke clearly. He still observed the ritual of extending his hand so I could kiss the four carat diamond he wore. The wispy, innocuous smile he donned for the public he met still graced his thin lips. Perhaps the eyes dulled a little and his movements were not quite so quick or deliberate but he was still Pistola and he still carried himself with dignity. He still spoke with that slight Down Neck slang that made his Italian sound dignified.

ALIA STREETS–On the streets of Alia, walked my revered grandparents. There is still a Rosolino Vassallo living in the town.

"*Buon giorno,* counselor," he crooned. "I don't see you much any more." And he mustered a slight hunch of his shoulders as if to signify his disappointment at the absence.

"Pete, I may not see you, but I never forgot."

He shrugged. Looked around the office as if appraising everything he saw and yet, not really seeing it at all but he had a purpose to his visit.

"Sit, please," I said, motioning to the couch, rather than using my desk which would have separated us and placed him in a subservient position.

"You're still respectful, Russie. Always were." He removed his overcoat and slid gracefully into the leather couch. "Nice. Doing well?"

"Well," I replied. "Somehow it seems my practice grew almost immediately. I seemed to find many longshoremen and union men becoming clients. Accident cases, Worker's Comp., traffic violations, real estate closings. The Unions provide a lot of work. I must have an angel who is a Democrat."

He snickered. His eyes lightened just a touch as he hunched forward to enjoy the joke and share another.

I nodded knowingly, as if acknowledging that it was his friendship which feathered my nest.

"*E tuo famiglia?*" The fact that he was speaking Italian to someone who did not totally understand the language indicated he was calling upon our common heritage, our Sicilian blood. People just never did that without a reason. He was American born and seldom resorted to Italian.

I knew that he and my grandfather hailed from Sicily, probably came from a town much like Alia, with the countryside littered with rocky promontories and caves. They had to bring the mules and horses into their homes at night to avoid their being stolen. They etched out a living from the hard land, and, when they foresaw a future with more than back-breaking labor, they immigrated into America and, later in years, joined forces in the family business. So as he continued speaking, a word of Italian here and there, I knew he was not making a social call.

"A boy and a girl. Everyone is fine." I hesitated a moment, searching his face for some clue as to his visit, but men such as Pete did not give clues. They gave orders and he wasn't ready to speak just yet so I continued the conversation. "And your boys, Chenzo and Pasquale?"

"Chenzo is good. His kids are grown now. You used to baby-sit his son. He needs no baby-sitter now. He's sixteen.

Tall. And Pasquale?" He reflected, searching for the right words, a helpless smile stealing over his face. "I pray one day he will grow up. Maybe. Maybe never."

"Pat's all right, Pete. He's just different. Always liked him."

He shifted impatiently, waved his hand to change the topic.

"Counselor, I need your services." Then he bent closer to me, not wishing to be heard, though there was no one there except the two of us. "I know you worked for the insurance company. You negotiated a lot, uh? A lot of experience negotiating?"

"It was my specialty." He already knew the answers but this was protocol, making conversation while probing for my receptivity to his proposition.

"Joe P told me how you got his older sister off the shoplifting charge. She's getting on in years. *Essa pazzo.* Losing her mind." He rotated his finger near his forehead, signifying insanity. "Lifting goods at the clothing stores, what was she thinking?" He became restless. I let the conversation continue.

"I did what I could to help her."

"Did he pay you?"

"He paid me. And he did me another favor."

"Make sure he pays you. Joe's a cheap bastard."

"He treated me just fine," I concluded.

"You know I have some interest in Las Vegas. Not much. Just a little place here, a casino there."

In point of fact, I had visited the casino and stayed as his guest. I signified I knew of his interest there. I said nothing more. Pete had a way of signaling when he wanted no interruption.

"I think the time will come when the State Gambling Commission will clean house. What do you think?"

"It's not important what I think. It's what you need me to do," I cajoled.

"But I value your opinion," he groaned, the impatience in his voice signaling he wanted an answer. And it was always a dance. A dance of wit. Speaking the right words. Understanding the signal correctly. It wasn't that Pete didn't know the answer. He did. But he asked to gain the thinking of other minds, someone who might see the one thing he had missed.

"I do. I think the Feds are coming up with new ways to prosecute and stamp out La Cosa Nostra, and some of the non-Sicilian rats are squealing for their bed and board. It's not like it used to be."

"And they will find our legitimate businesses and harass us more. The states will follow suit. Even when you pay now, they turn against you." Sadness welled in his eyes, a hint of earlier days when silence was the law and death the penalty if you broke it. "So, what would you do if you had these interests?"

"Depends on whether you want to stay in the same line of investment."

He nodded assent. "It's easy money though they steal a lot, the employees. They take bread from the mouths of my children." This was an old Sicilian saying. Often it was prefatory to the elimination of a rival faction cutting over the borders of someone else's turf.

"I'd branch into other areas, foreign areas. Places where they have gambling, offshore," I suggested.

"I like that. Off-shore investment." He laughed. "Great! You got a head on you."

But I knew he already knew so I continued. "I would think about Aruba. It's right off the coast of Florida, and the government is friendly. An underdeveloped place is Caracas. I'd stay out of Asia. I don't like the way the Chinese are rattling their sabers. Too much risk there."

"You spent time in Venezuela, eh?" he asked, knowing the answer.

"I have a friend there. We owned time share in Aruba. Luis. He invited me to La Guaira, stayed at his condo. He has many friends in government there, but the bolivar is a little unstable right now. No matter what happens, though, people will gamble. The country doesn't need tourism because of their oil fields. The high and mighty of the social 400 earns enough money with their own investments to make any casino profitable."

Then came the punch line. The reason for his visit. The reason for his careful questioning.

"You would go there? Work out something for the purchase of a casino? No limit on what you spend to buy it. No limit on what you need for yourself."

"I need to repay a generous man who helped me stay out of trouble, who took a gun out of my belly, who put bread into the mouths of my children by sending me business. I'll accept my expenses. Anything else is repayment for all your kindness."

For the first time that day, our eyes met. This was an emperor in his declining years. Still feisty. Still alert. Still preserving his empire. Reverting to the culture from which he sprang. And he was turning to me to help him preserve it. A great honor. But one I could not mention to anyone else.

"You honor me," I continued.

The discussion ended by making travel plans on my behalf. I telephoned Luis and expressed a desire to visit. As always, he was receptive to have a guest. Two days after my discussion with Pete, I was transported in his private limousine to a small airport not far from my home, and several hours later, I was in Venezuela. I did not even clear Customs and Immigration. I was just landed on an airfield and met by another vehicle.

Caracas was a city that truly sprawled. Major highways. Common traffic. From the nearby mountains, one can see a halo of pollution smothering the city, yet, up high, where the elite live, the air is clear and sharp. The social and business structure of Venezuela harbors sharp divisions of those who have and those who have not. As we passed through a tunnel, I saw people carrying water buckets from a lower spring to the switchbacks leading to the top. The entire mountain was composed of dirt that was penetrable only on foot. The driver spoke enough English to be comprehensible, and I fancied myself possessing enough Spanish to sound well-traveled.

The driver's eyes met mine as he glanced in the rear view mirror. "Peons." He hissed derisively. "They live on the mountain in those shacks."

Looking again, I saw bare shelters composed of cardboard frames, some with corrugated metal roofs. A strong wind might easily level them.

"Is that where they live?"

"Si," he issued, from the side of his mouth. "Each year we have the floods, the big rains. The mud comes down the mountain. The huts at the top slide down the sides and are covered. When it is done there are many dead, but the people at the bottom escape because they see it coming."

"And then?" I questioned, my eyes still gazing at the grassless mountain whizzing by.

"The peons on the bottom move up the mountain, and they build new huts. Until the next time."

"They build new huts? Even though the people at the top are buried under mud when the rains come?"

He nodded assent. "It is great prestige for the peon to live up higher. They have no *come se dice? Banos . . .*"

"Bathrooms?"

"*Si. Sanitario.* Toilets. " He heaved a pensive sigh. "They relieve themselves outside. The waste goes down the mountain. In summer, it smells very bad. So the peasants at the bottom want to move up."

"*Muy malo*," I added, feeling smug at my knowledge of his language.

He fell silent then. I resumed my survey of the city. I noted along the way a good number of broken traffic signals and asked the driver if the kids were really that bad. He advised me that the lights were broken for the glass. The glass was then brought to jewelers who cut and polished it, passing the glass off as amber, ruby and emerald, selling it to tourists and out-of-towners. I made mental note not to buy any souvenir jewelry.

We passed through the historic section where the government buildings were located. Like most European cities, there were huge and impressive monuments, fountains with glittering, glaring night lights, houses that were stark white with orange tile roofs, towering glass buildings as well as the aged monuments, most of which were dedicated to Simon Bolivar, the national hero of South America. Most of it was Spanish motif, black wrought iron gates and fences, brilliant white stucco walls with arches, the Spanish courtyards with walkways and plants and trees.

I contacted Luis and met with him for dinner. His English was passably good except he could not say the word "angry", always mispronouncing it "hongry". We often laughed when he told me his second wife, Solonye, was very "hongry" with him and threw him out of the bedroom for getting drunk.

Luis was typically Venezuelan, dark, curling wavy hair, thick glasses with heavy tortoise frames, masculine cheeks which creased when he laughed. He had brown, Spanish eyes, a twinkle that belied his intelligence, and for as much as he drank, he was relatively well-built. His notion of breakfast was Buchanan Scotch and water. He was usually drunk by three and sick by seven. And drinking again, at nine. We ate dinner each evening around ten o' clock at his country club. It was a palatial Spanish building, built around a central courtyard with a centered fountain, a long outdoor corridor that overlooked the interior patio and well-lit rooms. The restaurant and bar were arranged so that one could dine inside or outside and still see the yard or choose a seat where they could see the ocean and the dazzling moon that rose up over the horizon. Wicker seats lined the corridor while inside great chandeliers brightened the dining area. There were game rooms and television rooms. They enjoyed their own spa. Members could not gain membership unless they played golf or owned a yacht. They were approved by a panel which reviewed their credentials, and they had to have the vouching of at least two members. No one valued at less than five million was admitted. The club house was part of the Yacht and Golf Club, and the members were so exclusive that the President of Venezuela had to obtain permission to have an affair there.

We dined on some of the best red snapper I have ever tasted, steamed in a large brassier of aluminum foil, marinated and circled by potatoes and onions, drenched in a tangy sauce that sucked the moisture out of my mouth. The wine was imported, though. Luis stuck to his scotch and water. As I recall, it was a moonlit night, perfect for romance, though I saw few women at the club house. Not because they were not permitted but simply because they had other social events to attend.

I offered to pay for a round of drinks, but the bartender could not even understand what I was offering. No money passes hands in the club. Everything is billed to the member so I was unable to buy a single thing in the lounge, but I lacked for nothing as Luis was a generous host. We drank the night away until he became sick for the second time that day and regurgitated most of his meal and then settled enough to have more Buchanan. Waiters were not called. They were summoned with a clapping of the hands or a loud whistle, the like of which I had never seen before. It was the custom, Luis explained. From the appearance of the waiter's face, it was the patron's custom, not his. They worked until the last member was escorted to his vehicle. Then they retired to their hovels, some of them perhaps, to the mountain of mud. The month before, one of them had disappeared near a condo in La Guaira, the victim of a jaguar since the complex was constructed right at the end of a National Park. And there was no Worker's Compensation for the family. He was simply listed as missing, and another waiter replaced him.

For all his drinking, Luis remained lucid and very capable of discussing business. He forged his own construction company and ingratiated himself with the Government to the extent he built low-cost housing for the minority. I heard him one day arguing with a government official on the telephone. When he hung up, he was outraged that they should ask him to build a low-cost housing project at a contract figure of one million U.S. dollars. He could not possibly do this without losing money just to move the equipment there. In the end, he consented, though on condition that he received first bidding opportunity on a modern office building estimated at 20 million U.S.

When he heard what I was looking for and who wanted it, Luis told me we would be the wiser to build our own casino rather than buying one.

"All of them," he wheezed, "are old. They need repair. Air conditioning. Good rooms. Like Las Vegas. The entertainment here is so/so. If your friends let me build, I will obtain all the permits, even the casino permit. But we can also renovate one I will show you."

"You can do this?" I sounded incredulous. I had no idea he was connected that well.

"Absolutely," he boasted.

"I need to know this will succeed, Luis. My clients are not nice people when things go wrong. *Comprende*?"

"I understand who you are working for. No problem."

Two evenings later, we visited a downtown Casino, and I understood why he was recommending a new building. Sure, he'd make a profit on it, perhaps even purchase some interest in it, but if Pete wanted something to replace his Vegas interest, he needed something spectacular. From the outside, it appeared no more than an ordinary hotel. We entered the lobby and had to hunt for the casino. When we found it, the room was large, filled with stagnant air and sparsely populated. No one circulated with free drinks. There were no waitresses in short skirts. No buffets to entice customers. Only a single restaurant in the entire place and a coffee shop that closed at 11 a.m. But Luis was right. It was something that could be salvaged.

The swimming pool was outside, illuminated by green, yellow and red lights. The hallways leading to the rooms were narrow and confining. Dull carpets, badly worn, dim lights, sticky locks. The rooms were dingy and uninviting and appeared more a hostel for prostitutes and johns than rooms in a fancy hotel. We inspected the outside. We viewed the gaming rooms and facilities. They had a small gift shop but nothing worthy of any note. Personnel were friendly but not overly well trained. The hotel clerk did not know how to cash a Traveler's check. The single waitress at the bar seemed as if she'd been handling johns all day and was too weary to serve drinks. The entire atmosphere of the Casino could have been summed up in two words: GO AWAY!

Luis and I discussed possible changes. It was suggested that Pete visit Luis when he had some architectural plans to show. He would draw one plan showing a renovated building and a second plan showing a completely new building. I again impressed him with the seriousness of making commitments. Luis assured me that once the plans were approved, everything would go smoothly. And he was correct. There were no problems. Everyone received some of the pie. For a time, I felt very personally involved and highly important to Pete, as though I had been indoctrinated into mob politics without the need to make my bones. The big man requested my presence for dinner and asked my frank impressions about everything. He wanted to know about government stability. Who the "big" people were? Possibility of revolution? How strong the government was? He wanted to know about crime in the streets.

On that issue, I told him that all the influential people lived in superior homes high above Caracas, and all their homes were surrounded by wrought iron. Gardens, front walks, garages, doors, windows, all walled in by wrought iron to keep the thieves and kidnappers out. The kidnappers were no amateurs. They didn't send ransom notes. Just a finger or an ear with a price demand and where to deliver.

Muggings and purse snatching were more commonplace than in New York. One night, I recalled, Luis took me to a special restaurant in downtown Caracas. The parking lots were full because traffic is a problem in the city. In fact, they had an odd/even license plate system and cops checking the feeds to make certain you weren't in town with an odd numbered plate when you needed an even number plate for that day. So, Luis had to park on the street near the restaurant.

From the shadows of a building, a tall, lithe young man stepped out and spoke with Luis. Now, Luis had three safety devices on his vehicle to prevent theft. A bar for the steering wheel, an audio alarm if someone broke into the car, and a shut-off valve on the gas line so the vehicle could be driven only as far as the gas in the fuel line permitted. Still, he handed the young man some money and pointed to his vehicle. When I asked him what was going on, he advised me the man was a parking lot attendant, and, for a small sum, he protected Luis's car from damage and theft.

Road blocks were another thing I spoke of. Passports had to be carried everywhere. Even inter-city flights could not be booked without a passport. On the day I had arrived, two political prisoners had been shot trying to escape their guards. How far they expected to get with handcuffs and manacles was always a mystery to me, but the driver didn't seem to think it unusual.

All of this Pete listened to avidly, not interrupting, not interjecting any comments. He was seeking knowledge and listening was his key asset. Nothing more was said when I concluded. He inquired about where to reach Luis and asked if I could arrange a personal meeting between them. Candidly, I was offended when I was not included in the meeting but it was Pete's way of telling me that my function was at an end. I could ask a return favor but I was not included in family business. After he and Pete met personally, Luis built a palace of mirrors and stages, bars and bedrooms, games of chance, far more elaborate than anything existing there.

On the other hand, Pete was well pleased with the investment. He invited me to an exclusive opening night party announcing the construction of a new casino. Even the Venezuelan military showed up for the affair. It bothered me that in the face of adverse information about the country, he was still willing to pour millions of dollars into an investment that could wind up like Cuba. But Pete was, by far, not a stupid man. If he was investing his money in something, it was a sure bet he had things working for him. All bosses operated with the theory that one hand knows not what the other is doing. I am sure there were other people working on investments for Pete and in the same country. I was not his sole messenger in Venezuela. That was almost his trademark. However, I was never made to feel unimportant. On the contrary, Pete praised me to everyone he introduced me to, and I was astonished at the high ranking officials he knew. So I went to the party, feeling somewhat shunned about being cut off, but basking with self-glory at still holding his favor.

I received the same royal treatment with limousines and private flights as I did while arranging the transaction. More than once, Pete strolled to my table, clapped his arm around my shoulder and told me what an effective job I had done. The praise was to defuse any hurt feelings I might have. It impressed me that Pete would have made a capable politician. In fact, all the family heads could have been multimillionaires in legitimate businesses had they not chosen the underworld. It was their way; their choice. Pete was no different. He understood business and he understood people. Those loyal to him were well rewarded, for within the mob, loyalty is primary.

For my loyalty, he placed me at a table with very important Venezuelan officials and their wives, people reeking with money and influence. The wives, of course, were all interested in American dancing, including the twist and, lousy dancer that I was, my night was filled with the aggrandizement of thinking that alcohol made me a better dancer than I really was. The single girls applauded my dancing skills and literally formed a line to dance with me. For a five feet two inch, slightly rotund man who thinks little enough of himself, this was an ego booster beyond contrast. In any event, the women sought my company and invited me to social events occurring around the world, one of which was to honor a returning matador who had retired from the bull ring because he had been gored.

I met him at an event so tightly-controlled that even relatives needed a special invitation to attend. And thus, I met my first bullfighter. The matador was everything you expect a bullfighter to be. Tall, lithe, slender, shapely, his back arched, his shoulders straight, his stomach tucked in from the tight bands he wore when he fought. His every move was graceful and artistic, and he was articulate and learned. He spoke Castilian Spanish beautifully and was gracious when I fouled up the language. He attracted the attention of the most beautiful women in the room so I understood what bravery and masculinity can accomplish in a roomful of lovely women. Still, we spoke of many things including art, literature and even law but, when I raised the topic of bullfighting, he changed the subject as if it was too painful to recall all the bulls he had killed. There is an old adage in *Espana*: one who bets on the bull is a fool.

While I was talking to the matador, Pete brought one of the headliners with him. He had hired him to sing and to draw other Hollywood stars to the evening event. Pete brought him to my table. He didn't introduce me. Rather, the star acted as if we were old friends. The women swooned at the headliner's good looks and clung to me like flies to sugar when they thought I knew him well. I guess they thought something might rub off. The headliner glanced around the table, assessing the ladies sitting there, then turned his attention full to me.

"Russ," he uttered. "It's great seeing you again. Pete told me a lot about your work. You did a great job setting all this up. Really first rate. Hey, we have to have lunch or dinner. Call me! You know the number." He smiled at the young women, his blue eyes oozing adoration and charm. He swung his arm around me and squeezed. I felt as if I had known him all my life. I was not even a fan of his but he inspired me that night, and I never forgot the experience. In moments, he was on the stage, captivating his audience. Of course, we never had lunch or dinner or anything else, but he put me on a high in front of important people, and, for several years thereafter, I made numerous trips to Caracas and was richly entertained by influential people. The President of one of the big three in Brazil engaged my services to invest funds for him in the United States, and, on several occasions, I visited his ranchero. Others thought about dabbling in the movie market, wanting to produce films in Venezuela. All that flowed from a movie star coming to my table and acting as if he had known me forever.

After the star left, I was an even bigger hit with the ladies, some of whom were single. They wanted to know when the star and I had met. Half shot with Dom Perignon, I exaggerated that he and I went back a very long time, that I had represented his theatrical agent and that we often partied together when he was in New York. I had to admire the manner in which Pete handled things. He must have surmised my hurt feelings about being cut out, and, not wishing to make an enemy, he uplifted me to the heights of egotism. Bright man.

In South America, I learned the true meaning of democracy. In a democracy, the corruption starts at the top. Pay the big man and everyone below him falls into line. Work permits appear. No labor problems. Contract times are extended. Money overrides are met with smiles instead of frowns. In other governmental forms, each bureaucrat is a sovereign unto himself. One pays as he goes, negotiates a price that may be far less or more than another bureaucrat, and the same smooth operations occur. Each price is determined only by the greed of that particular bureaucrat. The top man doesn't know what the guy on the bottom is doing and vice versa.

The thought occurs that laying the groundwork for this investment was done in three visits to Caracas. In the movies, much fanfare occurs about women brought in to entertain the guests. No one ever offered and I never asked. Nor did Pete. This was business. Serious business. Cash millions flowed in briefcases and luggage to finance more building construction. And it is an odd sensation to carry a large sum of money in a brief case headed for Luis or one of his associates.

We ate well. We enjoyed the luxury of the Club. I had my own condo in La Guaira. I was invited to social events and private homes. New friends flew me to Maracaibo where I visited the oil fields and spent time on the Lake. Another Spanish gentleman invited me aboard his 110 foot, aluminum yacht, and we spent the day sailing to the Margarita Islands.

I met two classes of Venezuelans: the elite and the new rich. I found the lower classes to be very macho, their children full of brio (spirit) and totally undisciplined. What mama said didn't mean a thing and the more spirited the kid was, the better his father liked it. With the elite, their children were educated in foreign nations, and money solved any problems that arose. I thoroughly enjoyed the upper-classed people there and totally detested the machoistic classes in the lower echelon. But like all good things, the curtain of my revelry was about to ring down.

In a matter of months, Luis had completed construction and obtained government permission for gambling and the sale of alcoholic beverages. He obtained everything including liquor permits, gained numerous exceptions to existing laws and handed Pete the keys to the palace.

Opening night, for me, was a repetition of my evening at the announcement party. The entire building glittered like brilliant sunlight. The whir of roulette wheels whizzed and clicked along with a sound of merriment that seeped through the walls and streamed out into the pavilions that adorned the grounds. Fountains danced with light while musicians strolled the walks, playing requests. Center stage had one great act after another. There was no cheap wine and no off-brand liquor. Every meal was gourmet as was the buffet. There was a hum to that success. The hum of money, of profit, of accomplishing something vital. Before the building had been constructed, I thought of the initial stages, the simple meeting of a friend from Venezuela and where it had led. I thought of viewing the beach front where the new Casino would be constructed and how, while Luis and I were sizing up the feasibility of the land for building, a young girl tugged off her bathing top, exposing rather incumbent breasts, and slid on a tank top. Then, noting us watching her, she lifted the top again for another gape at her breasts. And she was, yes, generously endowed. Where she stood, then, was to be the foyer of the great monument. It was only sand and rock and sea spray back then, but it would rise into something elaborate. And there would be other breasts there, show girls, singers, strippers, prostitutes, wives, girlfriends, all sparkling in the stunning array of their various professions. Croupiers from Las Vegas would be in attendance as would the muscle men, the security, the bouncers. They would be there too. They all crammed together in the monument Pete constructed. A United Nations of races, creeds and colors and all dazzled by the gold and the gambling that awaited them there. And when I saw it completed, it was blinding lights and uniformed doormen, leggy young ladies in short, revealing skirts. It was a glass monument where none had stood, and, that night, the moon lifted itself over the black ocean and reflected the lights of the Casino Grande.

As to what Pete did with his holdings in Vegas, I cannot attest. And I am not at liberty to say how my expenses were paid or my services rewarded. I will say that Pete was as generous as he had always been. If I visited the casino, I was always directed to one certain blackjack dealer. I never seemed to lose, though, I was very careful not to make a hog of myself.

In the future, Luis and I also did some business. I learned that Latin America can be very grateful to its friends. The Venezuelan government was having inflation problems similar to Argentina. It was suspected they were going to devaluate the bolivar. Luis telephoned and asked if I'd like to visit his country club. That was his key to telling me he needed my services. The government proposed a four-fold plan for devaluing the bolivar. My memory is not completely clear on how they proposed to do it, but the value of the bolivar was to be linked to the kind of item purchased. If the item was a luxury item purchased outside the country, the bolivar's worth was only twenty-five per cent of its actual value. If the item was medical services, health care, or burial services, the bolivar was worth full value. Gambling dollars were worth full dollar because they were attracting a good tourist following and, of course, whatever the tourist purchased was given full value on the bolivar. There were even street venders speculating in the U.S. dollar who gave better rates than the banks.

It would have been simple enough for Luis to place his money in Swiss or U.S. banks, but he had friends in government, and such a move would have aroused suspicion that he did not fully support the government. Whatever had to be done, it had to be quiet and attract no notice. We structured a mortgage company founded in Venezuela that would make international loans. We then established nearly sixty foreign corporations, ranging from the U.S. to the Caribbean, Singapore, Spain, Portugal, which applied for loans from the Venezuelan Company. Funds were transferred from Luis's personal accounts into the mortgage company, Cosmopolitan Mortgage Association, and then disbursed as loans to the foreign corporations. In actuality, the money was transferred from the foreign corporation into Luis's investments and savings accounts in Switzerland, Austria and the Netherlands. Not only was Luis a happy man but I earned substantial fees as a result of the scheme.

Men such as Pistol Pete are like magnets. They attract money no matter what they invest in because they simply "will" their way to success. Pete started with me as his first building block, then Luis, then Luis's contacts until he constructed a virtual pyramid. Along with his success, he enlarged the wealth of those who invested their loyalty in him. As he matured, he matured in business too. Youthful brashness gave way to the suave and the cunning of age.

This was the older, more sedate Pistol Pete. Wisdom replaced anxiety. Business superseded territorial expansion. An older Pistol Pete was settled, more ingenious, more aware of sophisticated finances. He diversified his investments from nation to nation and spread his money into upcoming ventures. Many of the income sources which produced his vast fortunes dried up with changing times and events. The state lottery replaced much of the booking operations. Horse racing dates were nearly year round and races were more difficult to control because of vying factions. Alcohol was legal, and drugs were becoming the more profitable venture. The older Pete changed with the ebb of changing tides. He invested in vacation resorts, condominiums and time share, off-shore banking, off-shore gambling, oil wells, silver mines, shipping companies. The extent of his empire will never really be unfolded, nor will the extent of his wealth. That was the older, wiser Pete.

The younger Pete controlled the booking and numbers operations for the whole of Newark. His local saloon was merely an extension of his former occupation. Pete had been a bootlegger, bringing in quality merchandise from Canada, and, in some respects, he was still a bootlegger, trafficking in prostitution, illegal and stolen booze and booking bets. He had a hand in anything that would turn rumor into cash. He was more sophisticated than the average rum runner. In fact, during Prohibition, Pete established three layers of corporate structure. The first tier catered to the high and mighty, the money people, people of influence. They drank the best Canadian whiskey, smuggled into small inlets and coves off the Jersey or Delaware shores, and sold at high prices to the very wealthy at speakeasies or for home consumption. The next level was bath tub gin so-called because it was made in private homes, often in the bathtub, and then sold to mob collectors who paid the brewer and bottled the stuff in official looking bottles. This was the average man's drink and cost substantially less. And the third level was rotgut liquor, consisting of bootleg moonshine diluted with swish. Hard liquor, called swish, was squeezed or boiled out of the wooden casks to make a less enhanced whiskey. The wood absorbed some of the brew and remains. When the barrel was soaked with a moderate amount of water, the water drew the alcohol out of the wood. Hence, swish. This was for the hardiest and hardcore drinkers. Pete never played with wood grain alcohol. Too many people going blind from the stuff. If he vouched for something, at least, it wouldn't kill you.

It was rumored that the saloon had several escape passages that led away from the bar and into various outlets but this was never confirmed. When Prohibition ended, he had merely to obtain a liquor license through his political connections, and he had a legitimate business. It did not stop the illegal activities though. Only provided a valid front for them. It was said that Pete had a loan sharking operation and even printed and promulgated his own lending rules:

> Lending day is Friday. Interest or vigorish is payable the following Friday. Vigorish is ten percent of the loan amount and does not reduce the principal loan. So if you borrow $1,000, the interest is $100.00, and you still owe the $1,000.00. Repayment day is Friday. No reduction for early payments.

I am sure he owned houses of prostitution as well, but they were more covert, and he never offered services to the young guys. On occasion, a gasoline truck would be hijacked. I always knew when this occurred as Pete would have me fill my tank up at his personal gas station. It was my good fortune that on the one occasion when Sammy the Squash hijacked a load of diesel fuel, in error, that I had a full tank and required no fuel. But very high echelon mobsters were having their cars serviced when the vehicles sputtered to a stop, choked with the wrong kind of fuel. To rectify the error, the gas dealer pumped the diesel/gasoline solution out of the ground tank into a local sewer where it clogged the entire system. Two days later, an itinerant drunk dropped a lighted cigarette into the sewer and promptly found his way to alcoholic heaven with the greatest high he'd every experienced. It was months before they found all the pieces. And Newark was ablaze again.

Perhaps, the most lucrative of Pete's enterprises was the gun rental business. His operation stocked a multiplicity of weapons, everything from handguns and shotguns to machine guns, hand grenades and bazookas. The going price was a $1,000 a week or completion of the job, whichever came first. Of course, references had to be furnished before a gun was rented, but the operation was thorough and efficient. I have often laughed at the so called "anti-gun experts" who believe that restricting gun ownership by law-abiding citizens will reduce the number of guns on the street. There will always be crime. There will always be weapons to commit crimes with. All the restrictive laws accomplish is to raise the price on rented guns.

If a felon wanted to pull a heist or bump somebody off, he contacted an intermediary who, in turn, contacted Pete's organization (never Pete directly). The transaction was arranged. The deposit made (usually $5,000) and the gun loaned. Upon completion of the contract, the gun was returned, and the deposit refunded less the $1,000 fee. There were no records. The serial numbers were filed or altered. The barrels changed so the ballistics were useless. The weapon was forwarded to another division or sold in a foreign country. There was no manner in which authorities could trace the weapon. In a way, Pete was the first advocate of gun control. He controlled the purchase and rental of guns and controlled the entire operation, including the sale of special ammunition designed to knock someone down on the first tap.

Yet another enterprise was contraband. Cases of items "fell off the truck" at the Port of New York. Watches. Jewelry. Optics. Furs. The items were quickly hustled for sale in parking lots, ball fields, parks and public areas for a fraction of their original cost, the proceeds of which were funneled into Pete's Personal Retirement Pension. On one occasion, one of Pete's less-endowed drivers heisted the wrong truck. It was supposed to contain fur capes and coats, one of which Pete had promised to his wife. Unfortunately, the driver heisted a load of lady's girdles and received a swift clout in the head from Pete. He could not stash the stuff and risk being caught with something he could not move in a hurry so Pete told the driver to get rid of the merchandise. He did. Ignoring protocol and bills of lading, he drove to the local department store, had store employees unload the girdles onto their loading dock and departed, leaving the store manager to wonder where the items had come from and what he was expected to do with unordered items. Pete got a laugh every Sunday when they ran sales in the *Newark News* advertising girdles at discount prices. His wife eventually got the fur coat when the correct truck was heisted. There was a very ritzy fur shop in New York where the goods were disbursed. Famous labels at very low prices.

When I wanted a fur coat for my future wife, I was directed to the exclusive shop in New York. There was no hassle in getting to view a number of lovely coats from full length to shortie. One in particular struck my fancy. I was told to visit a satellite shop, and there I purchased the coat at a fraction of its original price.

Control of the unions also meant control of the trucking industry, and contraband was common among union leaders. Whether or not that still exists today, I do not know since I have been away from the area for a number of years. I do know that union leaders of the bakery where I worked were indicted and found guilty of embezzlement. So much for the sanctity of unionizing and banding together for more job benefits and security!

If the N.J. mob was anything, it was discreet and low key. It didn't carry the same fanfare as New York or Chicago. Because it was a small state, it tended toward less violence and notoriety. Perhaps it was easier to control the politics because it was a less populated state. There were mob bosses like Pistol Pete who controlled certain segments of mob activities, and there were other factions that controlled the wharves and the dock unions. It was, in fact, the men who controlled the docks who dominated much of the implementation of mob activities. If one dominated the unions, he controlled not only the money, but the contraband that entered the country. It was through the various ship arrivals that the union bosses obtained stolen goods, but they also amassed huge sums of money from union dues and direct payoffs.

A single family headed the local Longshoreman's Union. Superman, Pottsie, and Vito Calasurdo lived right around the corner from me until the two older brothers married. Vito was around my age, perhaps a year younger. Superman was the eldest and Pottsie, the middle kid. I seldom saw the father or mother, but I did know Vito and Pottsie pretty well.

From the ground up, Superman held a prominent place in the union. He had worked as a longshoreman for many years, and, in his forties, he was selected to run for president of the association and won. Holding such a position placed him in control of large numbers of voting members from the union. He had but to mention the candidate that most favored legislation in favor of the union, and his membership cast their vote for the chosen candidate. Some of them cast more votes than one. Such chicanery was not unknown in Newark.

They didn't call him Superman for nothing. He was medium height, square, brawny build, black curly hair that attracted more women than his wife approved of. I remember him well because he had boxed in his earlier years and made a formidable adversary. An incident that highlighted his physical strength occurred one Sunday morning when a local child of eight was crossing the street. She had been sent to the corner luncheonette for some tobacco products and stepped in front of a moving vehicle. Fortunately, the vehicle was just pulling away from the curb so it was traveling slowly when it struck her. Unfortunately, it did not propel her forward, but traveled over her so she became jammed under the front bumper. The weight of the vehicle seemed pitched downward, and she just could not be extracted without lifting the vehicle.

Someone suggested jacking the vehicle up, but others feared that doing so, the vehicle might slip off the jack and severely injure the child. At that point, Superman arrived. Without hesitation, he gripped the front bumper and squatted so his legs would bear the brunt of the weight. And slowly, that vehicle lifted off the ground. Three of us pulled the frightened child to safety, and Superman eased the vehicle down. He made sure that the child was well. That was his first act. Then, he promptly grabbed the driver of the vehicle and knocked his head into the front door of the car until blood flowed down the man's nose and face. Superman had a thing for kids. I think his wife lost their first child, and ever since that time, he went nuts if anyone hurt a kid. No one messed with Superman. He was king of the mountain.

He was also king of local unions that worked under Pete. From a clandestine tavern at the lower end of Newark, Superman dispensed his rulings and judgments. He not only ruled the union, but he sometimes supervised the men on the docks. He alone decided who worked on a steady basis for, each time a ship sailed into port, the workers met at the union hall to shape up. The term shape-up meant to appear for assignment on each ship. There were men who operated the heavy machinery, fork lifts and cranes. There were men who worked the ship holds. There were men who loaded the goods into nets and secured them to the lifts. There were men who unloaded the nets and wheeled the goods into the warehouses. Some of them carried baling hooks. All of them wore safety gloves. If someone complained about the work, the pay or the hours, he found himself reporting to the union hall day after day without assignment. In time he couldn't afford to pay his union dues, and his membership was revoked. There wasn't any trial. No opportunity to discuss matters. Troublemakers were just booted out. Those who accepted increased dues, or voting for the political machine, or any personal assignments, such as delivering contraband somewhere, found the rewards great. In a time when other men were making five dollars per hour on construction work, dock workers could make as much as eighteen dollars per hour when the ships were in. Often, they worked double and triple time shifts at phenomenal pay.

I have been asked how the union boss knew if a worker voted for the "right" man. I can tell you that from personal experience because I worked the political streets for many years. Every district had a list of its voters. Being familiar with the neighborhood, I knew every Democrat and Republican in the district. There was no secret as to a man's political affiliation. If he wanted to vote in the primary, he had to declare his party affiliation. He could change his vote in the general election, but he had to declare himself. As a practical matter, few men did change their vote. There were approximately six hundred voters in my ward. I first eliminated the Republicans which narrowed the list down somewhat. (There were approximately forty Republican voters in our district.) Then, I coursed through the list, marking the known Democrats. The remaining people were independents, and often, some of them voted and others did not.

When the machines were read and the voting count tallied, I knew, give or take one or two voters, who had voted for our candidates. It was just simple arithmetic. Our district usually brought in about five hundred and ninety votes. Forty of those would be Republicans, and they voted for their candidate. If my count came in around five hundred and forty, I knew most of our people had voted for the machine candidate. Toward the end of the day, usually around seven p.m., I'd check the list to see if all our people had voted. There were always some who were either out of town or ill. They always made a spectacular last minute appearance to cast their vote, and their signature always seemed to vary from the last time they voted. The judges who monitored the voting registers and even most of the challengers were all Democrats. Most of them had urinary problems and had to visit the bathroom on multiple occasions often when voting was occurring. This occurred right after the signature was entered and they handed you your voting number. These people suffered the same kind of urinary problem when the vote was being tallied.

Why didn't the Republican challengers object to the practice? Most of them were there for the pay. They knew the

STRINGS & RUSS–Photograph of "Strings" and me, probably around 1952. Strings played the guitar, was withdrawn and serious, with a lightening fast temper.

Republican candidate was a decoy and had no chance of winning. Why make a fuss that would be heard by a Democratically controlled election board or decided by a Democratically appointed judge?

With this kind of power, the union boss was able to control the elections of officials. Control the politicians in a city, and you control the police and the judges. So Superman had a nice tight package working for him. Occasionally, someone would challenge Superman for the leadership. Elections were held every four years. The ballots were paper ballots, easily manipulated. And when the challenger had lost, Superman always made a show of the brotherhood by appointing the man to a special position, usually a nice cushy job. On the other hand, if the challenger was a serious contender, he found himself receiving less and less work, until, in disgust, he found some other line of work.

When we are young we know nothing of the future, nor do we contemplate it. One of the guys I hung around with was Strings Cimento. He wasn't called Strings just because he played a musical instrument. The name was pinned on him because of his build. Strings was slender, just under six feet, jet black, wavy hair that augmented his rapier-like face. He was quiet and unassuming. Nights he hung around with us, he spoke in a low voice when he spoke at all. He was known for his fury-like temper, and he was also known because he played the guitar and played it well.

I recall one evening we were watching three Puerto Rican girls that had moved in with their family across the street. Old man Memoli had his fruit market down below and rented the upstairs room. The Puerto Ricans had just moved in two days before so they had no shades on the windows. The girls, perhaps in the sixteen to nineteen range, were readying for bed and were undressing in front of the windows. As each article of clothing came off, a loud ooooohhhhhhhh rose up from the gang of us. It became so pronounced that the girls finally discovered us ogling them with the single pair of binoculars we had and apparently complained to the male family members. Out of the darkened hallway poured about five Puerto Rican boys and men, gesturing and cursing us in Spanish.

Without a word, Strings sprinted across the street, guitar in hand. He met two of the boys as they approached him and lashed them both with his guitar. Then, with the broken instrument, he battered the two fallen comrades while the remaining six of us piled into the retreating warriors. They couldn't get through the doorway fast enough, some of them actually getting wedged in the doorway.

As fate would have it, two of the girls married two of our gang that had fought that night. Squint married Pelar, and Frank married Maria. Uniquely enough the last time I saw Squint, probably twenty years later, he and his wife had moved to Florida. His brother, Frank, had rejoined the Marines, and he and Maria were living abroad.

Strings moved to Hillside but remained active on the docks. On more than one occasion he complained that the union funds were being diverted to the personal use of the union leaders. It was something both the membership and the F.B.I. suspected and, therefore, it resonated well with Strings's fellow workers when he attended meetings and demanded a review of the union's financial records. Naturally, the union leaders were not going to furnish Strings with evidence of their wrong doing. They summoned Strings to their offices and made it clear his accusations were unfounded and unwelcome . . . mostly unwelcome. He was told that, if he continued making trouble, his membership might be at risk. Bad move. Strings was not one to be threatened or intimidated. He descended from the meetings and passed the word to anxious dock workers that the union had something to hide. He started having clandestine meetings with those members of the longshoremen who held the respect of the younger members.

But he went beyond that. He contacted the F.B.I. and reported the threats and his suspicions about the financial dealings of the union. The F.B.I. concluded its own investigation and broke into the union office, armed with warrants, confiscated the union files and records, and proceeded to amass enough information to indict the union leaders, including Superman.

While this was going on, elections were imminent in the longshoreman local, and Strings became a viable candidate. Member after member pledged to support his candidacy. The union leaders were confronted with hostility and charges of corruption at the union meetings. Superman walloped a number of the more vociferous ones. Meetings were disbanded and adjourned because of the raucous caucuses, but, while the leaders were filing out, Strings and the others remained to hold meetings of their own.

Strings's next move was to contact the various ship owners and port authorities and advise them that a committee of members would determine who would fill the work details that arose as ships entered port. At first reluctant to accept Strings's authority and a new system, the ship owners discovered the extent of the membership disgruntlement when the first ship arrived in port and few workers showed up at the union hall. With no workers to unload precious cargoes, the owners had no choice but to accept the new changes. And they had to accept Strings's contentiousness.

Strings appointed a committee of six men with himself head of the committee, and they contrived a new system for selecting workers, implementing a fair system of doling out to each man an equal number of hours unloading.

All this activity, of course, was not recognized by the international union. They flatly rejected the governing body and threatened the ship owners with major strikes at all national ports within the United States. The ship owners were in total disarray, not knowing who to accept as the ultimate authority. The international union was a legally instituted organization, the umbrella under which all the smaller unions functioned. On the other hand, Strings's faction held control of the actual work force. There were so many of them, and so many of them were skilled at their jobs, there was little hope of replacing them with scabs.

This entire situation did not resonate well with the union leaders, but it resonated even worse with the mobsters who were the real power behind the unions. Although the F.B.I. was a balancing factor that hung in the background of the union dispute, unseen forces were also at work to defuse the situation. A court proceeding would take the government years to mount. The mob had other ideas on how to get quick results.

Most evenings, Superman could be found at the Jackson Street Tavern. As Newark developed, the tavern drew fewer and fewer people, but it was still able to continue operating. It was on a corner of a side street, poorly lit, with small, inconclusive windows and furnishings that dated back to the late eighteen hundreds. It was more of a take-out tavern than a place where people went to sit and drink. Mostly it was famous for its birch beer which was drawn from a single draft into home-made containers. The customer brought his own receptacle, and the owner drafted the birch beer and charged according to a loosely devised pricing system. It was a perfect place for secret union meetings, a perfect hideaway for men who wished to be private. But the very thing that made it so appealing, also made it a trap for the unwary.

The newspapers blared the news that Superman was missing. Both he and the bartender were simply gone. Some speculated that the bartender had some kind of trouble and that Superman was simply in the wrong place at the wrong time. Others rumored that Superman was the target and the bartender an innocent victim. Until this day the truth has never been revealed ... by anyone. Superman's body was discovered with two execution-style shots into the head that had resolved his election and indictment problems. The bartender was never found at all which gave rise to the rumors that he had been the original target.

I find it hard to believe that the bartender was the target. Indeed, he had some gambling problems and was known to be indebted to several local bookies. On the other hand, no self-respecting hit man would target the bar when a well-known union leader was known to frequent and stay until closing. Why not simply wait until closing and catch the barkeep going home? No, I'm convinced that Superman was the target and the bartender's death was merely a diversion. Two weeks later, Strings slipped out of his Hillside home, walked to the end of his driveway awaiting his usual ride to the union hall. The vehicle approached. He recognized it and stood waiting. The blast belched out of the rear car window and shoved Strings backward. Two blasts and the union election was resolved on both ends. The speculation held that Pete couldn't afford investigations or a warring faction for union control. His operations had expanded into a high profit drug business, and his own superiors were unduly vexed by the union war. They decided to end it in the manner of most such confrontations. The only deviation from Mafia policy was that the bodies were both found. With an older generation of Mafioso, people just disappeared. The new arm of the mob wanted the bodies to send a message. This they did, with both Strings and Superman.

In many respects, Pete was the hub, and, like all mob bosses, the spokes spanned across all lines and all endeavors. He controlled some of the unions. He enlisted the dock workers. No operation was too menial to be considered if it turned a profit. Indeed, like most Sicilians, there is a dread fear of "being" a mark and great honor in "taking" a fool to the cleaners. With taxes on cigarettes escalating, the mob smuggled contraband cigarettes in from states that did not tax them. In many cases, the cigarettes were hijacked and the profit margin one thousand per cent.

Like a lot of Italians coming to America, Pete had gained no justice from the American law. Nor were the controlling powers willing to give him decent, honest work. He started on the docks at Port Newark, but there was little chance for advancement there. Being well-built, an amateur prize fighter, Pete collected overdue payments for the local hoodlums and loan sharks. He made good money breaking ribs and busting heads. He also spent some time in the ring betting on himself when he knew he could win and sometimes throwing the fight when he had bet on the other boxer. In time, he earned enough to finance his bootlegging operation during Prohibition.

When that ended, he ran the Italian lottery and the daily numbers as well as his other enterprises. The Italian numbers were wired from ten separate provinces in Italy from the national lottery in that country. Provinces like Catania, Messina, Turin, Rome, Palermo and others held a weekly lottery in which they called ten numbers. The lottery slips in this country listed all ten provinces, and the numbers ran from left to right for each province. Those were the numbers that had been selected in that particular province for that week. How they got them to America in such a short time, I never knew. Air travel wasn't then what it is today and boats were slow. It had to be a wire service of some kind. In any event, they feasted on the greed of gamblers and the hopes and dreams of the ignorant.

The bettor could wager on three to ten numbers with the winnings increasing substantially as he selected more numbers. If the bettor selected five numbers and called all five, the odds might be one hundred fifty dollars for each ten cents he wagered. If he called all ten, the odds might be a million to one. This money was payable by the local mob, not by the Italian government, and it was a lucrative source of revenue as were the daily numbers. In all my life, I only heard stories that someone had hit all ten numbers. I don't know that anyone actually did. And in all my life of selecting and betting five numbers per province, I never collected a single dime. My reasons for betting, though, were not really to win money so much as to be a part of the thing, a part of a society where people secretly violated the law by wagering. As interesting as the Italian lottery was, it was published only once per week so most of the Blacks turned to the daily numbers here in the United States.

The daily numbers were selected from the amount of money wagered at the local race track. The gambler selected three numbers. If he wagered a nickel and won, he was paid three hundred dollars. Each day, the local newspaper would publish the total amount of money wagered at whatever New York race track was running. This was called the daily handle, and would be expressed as: Daily handle $386,490. The bettor who bet 490 (because the last four numbers were the only ones that counted) or 690, (skipping the third number from the left) would be paid at a rate of three hundred dollars for every five cents he wagered. On a one dollar bet, a gambler could win six thousand.

Did the Mob always pay off? As far as I heard, all winners were paid. Often, there was a delay in payment, perhaps hoping the lucky gambler would get reckless and bet back either on the numbers or the horses. Eventually though, the local book came through with the "bread", and the winner went off to spread a thousand dollars worth of free publicity for the policy racket. I am not a historian so I don't know why they called it the policy racket. Made it sound very official though. Policy. As if it's some kind of profession. In a way, it was. The profession of the Mob.

Of course, the mob was well aware of the daily handle as it was being tallied at the race track. If it appeared it was coming too close to a number that had a lot of action on it, they sent a local hood out to wager enough money to throw the handle off, thus making sure that the daily handle would come up for few, if any, gamblers. (The handle is what they call the total amount of money bet on all races at the open track.) Most times we searched for the handle in the *Daily News* or the *Newark Star Ledger*. We did it even if we didn't bet one of the daily numbers. It was just a thing of common interest. I'd search to see if my time clock number came up, or the number of my work locker. Things like that. On occasion I also wagered just to have some interest in the numbers.

When we hear of the Mob, we think of sinister men, pin-striped suits, blazing guns or grotesque murders. We do not think of helpful men, generous men, powerful men who gain respect and admiration by community service. When I think of men such as Pistol Pete, I recall days when, passing by his establishment, he called me inside, asked if I had eaten, and dished out bits of lobster salad. I do not hear blazing guns or see men cut down by gunfire. I hear a man telling me to stay in school. Make something of myself. Stay away from the rackets and the bums. I recall a man firm in his conviction that the Italian nationality, as a generation and culture, had to raise itself up from the gutters and become respectable. True, his manner of helping me through college and law school was unique, but it was genuine and it was real.

So how did this man of the underworld assist me in completing my education? My parents were financially unable to do so. And working full time and supporting them, I was unable to stretch to afford law school tuition. So during the summers, Pete procured me a filing job at Port Newark, two days a week with full pay. Whereas, I had beaten the pavement in the summer heat trying to get into the Port of New York warehouses, Pete simply told me where to report. No fanfare. No empty promises. There was a job there the next morning in one of the very places I had been refused. It is this kind of power that makes the Mafia so attractive. Unlike Government, which is bogged down by ignorant bureaucrats enticed by their own futile power, the Boss accomplished things with a single phone call or a single assignment.

And there were other ways of helping, too. Each summer I spent a good number of afternoons at the Monmouth Race Track. Pete had a race horse called Koko Dozo and another called Heels of Gold, neither of which was much good. But when Pete saw me at the race track, invariably, he told me to come see him just before a certain race. And the betting information he gave me was never inaccurate.

I remember he once gave me a horse called Biplane. From the racing chart there was no way that horse could win a race . . . any race. But I never doubted the information Pete gave me, and I can still see the field of horses, opening a wide gap to let Biplane come lugging through. What the horses won for me put a lot of months into the tuition I owed.

Those people who go to the racetrack occasionally witness an altercation between jockeys that erupts on the race track and, perhaps, continues into the Club House. The naïve think that something occurred on the track itself that caused the eruption. Hell, I've even seen one jockey whipping another with his riding crop to keep him from passing. But this is not the result of conscience. What is occurring on the race track is one jockey refusing to cooperate in the "fix". Perhaps, he has a bet on his own mount or just is more honest than some of the others. Those in on the "fix" will do just about anything to make it come out right, since they all have bets on the anointed horse and may also get their legs broken if they fail to please the Boss and his guests.

There were other perks in knowing the Boss. Free lunch or dinner care of Pete. Tokens to play the ski ball machines. Pete owned half of Long Branch, New Jersey, including a hole-in-the-wall restaurant called, oddly enough, Pistol Pete. Arcades, amusement park, batting cages, restaurants, he either owned them outright or leased the property to the business people who came there each summer. Spanned right along the boardwalk that fronted on the Atlantic, all the old favorites were there. Mario's New York Pizza, Sardi's Authentic Italian food, Max's Hot Dogs, the Clammery that sold ice cold clams on a half shell, Fanny Farmer's candy store, salt water taffy, one or two sit down restaurants, and a dozen or so games of chance, ranging from the dart throwers to the wheels. Nobody ever won at anything. The wheels were rigged, and even if you won, the prize was worth less than you bet. One game I recall was ski ball. You rolled a ball up an alley and the ball sloped up a ramp and into a series of circles, each with a certain value. At the end of the game, the machine spewed out ticket points depending on score. The tickets could be redeemed for all kinds of prizes. And the prizes shown were bicycles, blenders, a .22 lever action rifle, dinner ware, sets of glasses, everything sparkly and nice and requiring high numbers of points, more than one could earn in the summer. The tickets were good from year to year. Sure they were. Because next year the point value of everything had increased. It was a sucker's game so nobody ever won. Another game set seven balls rolling down a ramp, each ball numbered. To win, you had to score more than fifty points. The croupier did the addition, of course, and no one ever hit fifty. At least if they did, they never knew it. The addition was rattled off so quickly no one could dispute the final count. It was a real art form to hear the vendor rattling off numbers that did not really add up correctly.

The wheels didn't have to be rigged. The odds did it all. Sometimes, the wheel didn't have numbers. It had suits of cards, hearts, spades, diamonds, clubs. To win, the gambler had to pick the right suit and card. Of course, the promised pay off was the big bear or rabbit or some flashy piece of jewelry, but it didn't matter what the prize was because nobody ever won. Not unless he was a shill.

Just for the record, a shill worked for the house. He wandered up to the gaming table, made a bet and walked away with the big prize. If you returned to the game a few days later, the winning prize would be right back up there on a shelf, and the shill wandered back and won it all over again. So profits piled up, collected by Pete's sons, Chenzo and Pasquale.

Pete was always in his restaurant, attending to business and making certain that food was prepared to the liking of his customers. Never did one of his friends pay for a meal there. Traipsing into his establishment on any given day were mayors, commissioners, judges, senators and nameless dignitaries who dined on his fare. I often saw Municipal judges from Newark sitting quietly at a secluded table. One of them was reputed to have a serious stomach ulcer so I often wondered how he could eat spicy Italian food and not suffer for it. I think the envelope he always received there probably had a lot to do with his health. Pete loved to cook but he did not get his name by cooking.

Rumor alone has it that Pete was very handy with a .38 and unafraid to use it. In fact, his nickname was based on his habit of carrying three or even four snub-nosed revolvers on him and when the need for shooting occurred, Pete blazed away with a gun in each hand . . . and hit what he aimed at. He was not a robber. He was not a thief in the conventional sense. But Pete knew how to use the persuasion of a firearm to battle his way to the head of the power chain. I never glimpsed so much as a bulge in his pockets when I visited with him, and he was always intriguing me with stories of Newark's history and how the Italians battled their way into the power chain. I never doubted his skill either with a gun or his hands. I never doubted the authenticity of his stories, either.

Still, those of us who knew him, the kids, the youngsters, irrespective of race, only knew the good side of him. Who can speak ill of those who do us good? Pete had a summer place in Long Branch. A small, unassuming home that could have belonged to anyone. It was a place of respite from the pollution and summer heat of Newark. There was never a time I walked by on Sunday that they were not having a large barbecue in his rear yard. There was never a time he did not rush down the long sidewalk leading to the yard and hustle me in for some food and drink. I recall once I was passing by with my friend, Herbie. Herbie was black and we palled together at time when blacks and whites just did not associate with one another.

Pete came down the long walk on seeing me and yelled I was not to pass by without stopping in. I put my head down and muttered:

"Can't, Pete. Where my friend goes I go and vice versa, you know."

Pete looked at me and smiled at Herbie.

"Listen to this kid," he said turning to Herbie. "Listen to him. Loyalty, huh. That's good." Then, to me, "Hey, Russie. Your friend is welcome. And don't you ever leave him out. Got it?"

With that he snugged an arm around Herbie and hustled him into the back yard.

"Listen here!" He commanded.

"This is Russie. Gonna be a lawyer, huh? And this is his friend, Herbie. They are my guests so make them welcome."

And that was that. Herb and I ate and drank the afternoon away, and I never saw a single glance or look from anybody. It was as though we were privileged people, guests of royalty, and in a rough sense, Pete was royalty. All his guests were royalty. So they dined on steaks, chops, short ribs, lobster, crab legs, shrimp. Beer, wine and whiskey flowed along with soft drinks. Yet I never saw anyone so careless as to be inebriated, nor did I ever hear anyone vulgar or rowdy.

If there was anything that characterized the mobsters I personally came in contact with, it was their low-key image, their quiet respect for women and their stony silence. They all had a way of saying a lot of words without really saying a meaningful thing. The bosses were affable, even jovial. Yet, if you gazed deep into their eyes, there was some terrifying evil that said these men were capable of anything. Pete had it. Joe P had it. Even my grandfather had it. It was a seamless web of men forged from need and from personal sense of power. They had a generous side and a dark side and how long you lived really depended on which side they saw you from.

I knew Pete because of my grandfather and he seemed a quiet, untroubling man. Always, he mentioned my grandfather and what a great man he had been. Always, he told me that respect was the most important commodity one can gain in life. I did not understand the need for respect but I know it now. For the respect of which he spoke was loyalty. Those who are loyal do not plot against you nor challenge your authority but serve well.

Throughout my life our paths would cross, through high school, college, law school, even at my job at the A & P Bakery. For it was there that I saw the other side of Pete, the dark side. It was a fitting place for such discovery. I was twenty then, in college and struggling to pay tuition. So I labored in an old, turn-of-the-century, red brick building, black with soot and chimney smoke, nestled on a back street near the railroad yard. Trains shunted their box cars off, leaving them to be filled or emptied and then removed again. But the trains could not be seen from within for the windows were clouded and dull and seldom opened. And it was as if a hive of ants cuddled within its structure, coming at the various hours and leaving at others, each ant with its own life, its own story, its own destitute morality. One of the ants was called Big John, a slovenly man of forty-five, sagging jowls, belly hung over a rope belt and the faded white baker's clothing that heralded his occupation. He stuffed an evil smelling, black wrinkled stogie in his mouth (a stogie is black tobacco raised in Italy and hand rolled into a crooked affair that resembled a broken stick rather than a cigar), and his dark, stained teeth yawned at you when he smoked. He smelled of smoke and sweat and had the disgusting habit of picking out bits of tobacco from between his teeth and flicking them off to the side. Worse, he always seemed to be sweating, and the sweat dripped from forehead into a channel that rutted right down to the tip of his nose.

John was a baker, manning the complex ovens that spewed out hundreds of bread loaves per hour and pounded and thudded the red hot pans along the broad canal until they emerged, brown and tasty from the far end. There is nothing so delightful to the palate as fresh baked bread. It has a warm and secure aroma, tears easily in your hands and wafts up into your nostrils. If he had stayed with baking, John would have fared much better, for it is better to work in a hell hole than be buried in the cool shade.

He was good at his job but his spare time and all his waking hours, including those which should have been devoted to his family, were spent handicapping horses. This was not a pastime. This was a disease. Big John was hooked. He poured over tally and performance charts like one designs a rocket engine. And every day brought a new tale, of some horse that lost by a nose, or some combination that would have paid two thousand dollars if only the five horse had come in. He snorted his tales of woe and borrowed when he could. More than once, I took bets down to Pete for him. More than once, I sympathized that this illness might lead him to trouble. And being the inveterate preacher I am, more than once, I tried talking reason to him. After all, I loved horse racing too. But it was not an illness I could not control. John was simply out of control and dealing with dangerous people. And he borrowed from the wrong people. Small potatoes at first, then larger, more dangerous fish.

"Russ, can you lend me three dollars? Got a hot combination that cannot lose and got some debts to pay," he oozed with as much charm as possible for a fat man.

"I'm light, John. Had to pay tuition. Anybody else you can tap?"

"The Mick," he answered, "but you know what he charges."

"Sweeney? He's scum. I borrowed five bucks from him. I was just trying to be one of the boys. The louse charged me seven for the five. And I paid him back in two days."

"I got to have money. Got to hit this horse or I'm in trouble."

The desperation in his face was intense. In the end, I loaned him the money rather than see him borrow from a loan shark. Gamblers are what they are because they dream of success. It's not riches or money that compels them. Gambling is the desire to be "right" and the extent one goes to be "right" is often disastrous.

So Big John had to be "right." Each day, he took the last of his money and wagered it on one horse or another, on one combination or another. Each day brought some success or some failure. Mostly failure.

Every time I saw him he was pleading for money. Asking a loan. Asking me to place a bet for him and waiting until he made a minor hit to repay me. He was on a collision course with fate and seemed undeterred by the risk he was running. Even that day when he came to ask me to place a bet for him, it was apparent the collision was not long in coming.

"I'm into Pete pretty heavy," he snorted, wiping the sweat off his nose with a sudden swipe. I was shocked by what I saw. Both eyes were puffed and blackened. His nose was flattened and red. And a huge crater ran down the course of his lip, blotted with dried blood.

"Gees John, what the hell happened to you?"

"I fell off a ladder. Painting the house. Just missed my footing and fell."

"Bullshit."

"I was just working up there and forgot what I was doing. Went down real hard. I headed for the hospital as soon as I got up. Russ, I need a few bucks. Need to make a bet. I been watchin' these two horses for a month now. They're both ready. I play the daily double and hit it big, and I'm out of dutch." He held out the tally sheet to show me his selections.

"John, you're nuts. You are playing with the wrong guys. Let me talk to Pete, get you out of this mess. But you got to stay off the gambling. John, it's a sickness. You need help. I'm telling you."

He grunted, then turned his huge head, swiping the sweat like a bothersome fly. "I just need one hit. Just one. Got the combination. The six and the four at Monmouth. Com'on, Russ. Ten bucks will do it."

The large brown eyes were deep and sad and in them I saw the history of destruction, a man bent on destroying himself. I knew nothing about John except that he worked in the A & P Bakery and that he had a sickness. I wondered about his family. Did he have children? A wife? Was the gambling his escape? Or just an attempt to make ends meet? I gave him the ten dollars knowing it was not only a waste of money, but feeding an illness that knew no bounds, no satisfaction.

Giving him the money was like buying the old story that a derelict wanted a quarter to get a meal. The derelict only wanted that next drink. One quarter would buy him a shot. Four, a bottle of cheap hooch. There was no meal to be eaten because I'd seen a hundred bums along Mulberry Street all crying for the same meal. It was a meal that came out of a bottle. In the end, the cops found them curled and stiff in every corner alley along Mulberry Street. And gambling was no better a disease.

So John placed his bet and fared no better than the derelicts on the dirty streets of Newark. Nor did he win more than a few dollars, until desperate and out of answers, he had asked for help from everyone in the shop.

"I'll do this for you, John. I'll talk to Pete, work out a way to pay off your marker but only if you get some kind of help." I saw the light in his face emerge. He agreed. I wonder how I could have been so trusting to believe him. Afterwards, I felt like the trusting wife, beaten, marked with bruises, who forgives and forgets because she fears being alone, so she suffers all the indignities of a drunken husband.

Pete seemed to know what I wanted as I ambled through the front door. He was sitting at a lunch table, snacking on lobster he imported from Maine. Pete made a salad of it with vinaigrette dressing and dipped generous amounts of Italian bread into the dish. He called it *scungele*. Once or twice a month, he sent his underlings up to Maine to ferry lobster down to his Jersey bar. It astounded me that anyone had the authority to command such obedience.

"Have some, Russie," he mewed, so softly I felt he was reading my thoughts and not really focused on me at all.

I scooped some into a plate and then we sat and ate. He whipped up a bottle of red wine and poured some in each glass.

"Russie, one thing I learned early in life. I learned people come from different backgrounds. They don't think the same, look the same, act the same. Some got honor, some don't. Take your friend, John. He's got no honor, no loyalty. He can't see further than the next bet. Russie, he's a loser. I know you got to practice being a mouthpiece so you come to talk for your friend. That's loyalty. I respect that. But money is business. We don't mess with money. Your grandfather would be the first to tell you that if he were alive."

"You're right, Pete. But I feel for the guy. Let him off the hook. C'mon, just this once."

"Sure. You're a good kid. A nice kid. But he's a loser. We wipe out this bill, and he goes right back. In the end, he finds himself a hole in the Bay or a slot in the swamp and that's where he winds up because he's a loser. You can't change destiny, kid. You can delay it but you can't change it."

"Yeah, Pete, but what kind of a lawyer will I be if I can't persuade a friend to let another friend off the hook?"

"Kid, you got me all wrong. I just want to collect my bread. Nothing's going to happen to your friend. Scout's honor."

It was not easy but I worked things out with Pete. Got him to do the unthinkable, wipe out the marker. Pete cut him off at the bookies so he couldn't bet. I saw relief on John's face, heard the promises, the hundred promises. He was like a great big lap dog slurping thanks all over my face. And then, he avoided me. I saw him and he'd look the other way, pretending not to see me. The reason was not difficult to discern. He was gambling with another bookie. He had used me. But like all roads lead to Rome, all bookies led to Pete. It was his turf and his turf alone.

When I saw John, he was deeply troubled but continued avoiding me. A faint hello was the most I got. Then he was busy and moving quickly away and so the contact lessened. It was just as well. My college work took much out of me, and I cut back my hours. Instead of working the four 'til midnight shift, I worked weekends and sometimes did double shifts to make up some of the lost time. I never saw John again. But I read his epilogue.

MAN DROWNS IN BAY AREA

> The body of John De Mario, of 122 Walnut Street, Newark, N.J., was found floating in Newark Bay. Officials said he had been dead for several days. The deceased is survived by his wife, Theresa, and two children whose names were withheld for privacy consideration. Mr. De Mario was employed as a Master Baker at the Newark Division of Atlantic and Pacific Bakeries. Police are investigating the possibility of a homicide.

I never questioned Pete about the death. It was common knowledge throughout the bakery as to what occurred. John was leaving work after the night shift ended at midnight. Two men met him in the parking lot, and the three of them left in a dark colored sedan. Witnesses had nothing further to say and refused identification. Some habits die hard.

Somehow I never quite looked at Pete the same way again. It was difficult to believe this generous man who fed me, furnished rewarding tips on sure horses, or granted me an accommodation of letting John off the hook, could also issue the command to end John's life. Knowing Pete furnished me a sense of power. I knew why he forgave the debt, and I knew that in the end it would do John no good. The power to accomplish things. It was a power that frightened me because I searched his eyes for signs of remorse, and there were none. What I saw in those eyes frightened me. Something cold, dark and ruthless. Something I had never seen before. Death. It was as if I were gazing into the eyes of a windowless soul. I would see that look many, many times and always, it was when death was nearby.

But Pete was not the only ruthless man in the business, and John was not the only man on the run. When nineteen, I was smitten with the urge to buy a car. A bright, new shiny, black 1951 six cylinder, overhead valve Chrysler that on its best day could not get out of the way of a three legged turtle. My father insisted that I work to make the payments, and, in keeping with his philosophy on child rearing, he placed me in the most abominable hell hole imaginable. That was when I went to work for the A & P Bakery and people like John came into my life. I called it the Black Hole of Calcutta, but it was on Queen Street just off the major highway and consisted of one three-story building in which bread and cake and doughnuts were punched out of steaming ovens, and men, overcome with heat and exhaustion, keeled over dead. My point is not my early work history but that I worked in such a place and frequented the only eating establishment within seven blocks, Willie's Diner. The incomparable Willie slashed out hash, hamburgers and other fine epicurean delights so long as one did not inspect the merchandise too closely or expect that it was completely stationary when being eaten.

It was a boxcar shaped diner, soot ridden from years of existence and pollution, with grease-smudged windows that never seemed untarnished even when cleaned. There was a single entrance with a sliding door unless one counted the rear entrance behind the kitchen. A row of cushioned seats lined the counter, and fronting on Queen Street, more seats and a narrow counter space. If one went at the heavy lunch or dinner hours, he was likely to wait so long that he carried his food back to work, punched in his time card and ate on the run. But off hours, Willie's establishment was a focal point of conversation and debate. And part of that debate became the mystery of George. He had no last name because he never offered one. And no one knew where he had come from or why he took residence in a shabby shack behind the railroad tracks.

In its hey day the railroad brought loads of goods to the bakery, supplies with which to make the vermin-infested food packaged in clear plastics and distributed to the public. Hence the shack and hence the diner which had been erected in the early 1900s. And to that place, George had come. He simply appeared one day, buying a small meal and offering to earn his keep washing dishes or running errands so long as he did not have to leave the confines of Queen Street. The shack in which he took residence was more than weathered. It was hardly standing. It ascended from the grimy earth that trudged along the railroad tracks, forged of splintered boards and corrugated metal sheets bound together with rusty nails. Some hobo fashioned a window and framed it with glass and thus it became the residence of every itinerant bum who rode the rails and found his way to the shack. And each man added something to his comfort, one fashioned a wooden door with bent squealing hinges while another improved the structure, and yet another smoothed the earthen floor. At some point in its lifetime the building tilted from the bay wind that curled down around the railroad yard and from wearied boards that groaned with age, but still other visitors poured enough labor into it so that it stood from generation to generation and from bum to bum. Stood like a bastion to the homeless, the wretched and the destitute. Stood with its flat metal roof like an incongruous jewel in a sea of swamp and sludge.

They did not stay long, the bums. Railroad detectives beat them about the head and face with flinty truncheons, leaving them to crawl off railroad property. Behind them another wave of hopeless men, hoping only for a night's rest, a meal, perhaps a slug of whiskey. Men broken by the fortunes of the Depression. Yet others by the Wars. Still others because they were born to have no hope. Yet each of them contributed something to the shack, and thus it stood, old and gray, surrounded by high swamp grass, some times sopping with rain water soaked in oil.

To the building, George added himself. And settled into housekeeping because the bums and the refugees were long gone. He must have been a carpenter or builder at some point in his life because he straightened the building so it stood proud and tall. Then added a floor of scrap wood and metal. Somewhere in the vast meadow that surrounded the yard, he found a bed frame and fashioned himself a bed, lined with newspaper and old cloth. From a large drum he sculpted a wood stove vented through the ceiling and this provided him with heat and a surface on which to cook.

What I recall most about George was wavy, steel-gray hair and greenish-blue eyes. His was not a face to be forgotten, thick features, a long line creasing the side of his nose, sloping down into a stern chin. He was broad-shouldered and barrel-chested with his torso tapering to a slender, almost feminine waist. But George was no female. He had strength, and yet he slunk around the diner and glanced furtively at each new opening of the sliding diner door so that one noted he was a man afraid, a man on the run. And he was educated, for one day, when I was quoting poetry, he finished the line, a stanza from "Dover Beach" by Matthew Arnold. He would never say where he gained education or where he came from. He had no accent to speak of, and, when he did speak, it was in whispered tones so that no one overheard.

He enjoyed the races, but he never left Queen Street. His favorite place was a dark corner of the diner where he could view the narrow alley and handicap the races for the forthcoming day. He owned only a single pair of charcoal gray pants, rumpled and dowdy appearing, though the two shirts he owned were always starched and neatly pressed. Often I made the bets for him, keeping his secret and tendering his winnings when the diner was devoid of curious patrons, and no matter how small the winnings, he always offered me something for bringing him luck. Occasionally, I took a small recompense but not often. I liked the mystery of George, and I enjoyed his conversations. He must have been very frightened of something because he once hit a parlay on the horses that won him fifty-five hundred dollars (a fortune in the 50s) and he would not collect it when the bookie said he wanted to see him personally. It wasn't often someone hit a three horse parlay, that's betting on one horse, putting the winnings on the second choice and the winnings from that on the third.

George risked the entire amount but he adamantly refused to leave Queen Street and I finally prevailed on Pistol Pete to release the funds. He vouched for me with some trepidation, wondering why any man would refuse to collect six Gs in person.

Most days, George worked at the diner. Washing dishes, making repairs for Willie, but keeping out of sight at every opportunity. He was a chain smoker, lighting one cigarette after another. Drifting smoke curled up his nostril which he inhaled, then, blew some of it in circles from his mouth. He never flipped the ashes either, allowing them to creep toward his upper lip until they plummeted from their own weight. When short of funds, he'd quit the habit and did not smoke for months.

Studying George did little good at all. He defied explanation. He was perhaps in his 50s, muscular, and somewhat flat features. The quizzical eyes that fixed you revealed little except when strange men came around, and then, they revealed a vast and unfathomable fear. George literally shook when two detectives came around investigating drug use in the bakery itself. He was not seen for days, holed up in his makeshift cabin. When he reappeared, he excused himself by pretending illness, and, in truth, he did not appear well. After that he visited the diner sporadically, working at odd hours and seldom appearing two days in a row. In time, he settled and appeared more frequently. And then he became a fixture as with the stools and stainless steel that decorated the place. He sometimes appeared unshaven. His hair extended in length and required trimming. When in better spirits, he trimmed his own hair, staring into a hand-held mirror, snipping the long, gray waves with long, rusted scissors. He always did this behind the diner, though, so he was not observed. When finished, he slunk into the eatery, perched in his solemn corner and breakfasted on coffee and toast. He seldom ate lunch, and it was rumored, he took the leavings from the plates of others that Willie stored for him in the kitchen. But that was only rumor, and I never learned the truth of it.

If George knew anything and he seemed to have a ubiquitous knowledge, he knew literature and he knew sports. He wagered on boxing matches with uncanny accuracy, following a fighter's career and carefully selecting the fights on which he wagered. On one occasion, he let slip a comment: "They won't let him win tonight. Odds too narrow." And then he immediately froze, aware of the slip and muttered unintelligible mitigation intended to retrieve his indiscretion.

"George, you were a boxer or a trainer or something, right?"

"Un huh."

"You know a lot about fights."

"Some. Yeah. I follow them like the horses."

"Always been a gambler, huh?"

"Not always. I did other things." His eyes narrowed into ribbons. "Why?"

"Nothing. You're just a mystery. You know literature and poetry. You know fights and horses. Wide range, that's all. Provokes curiosity."

"No mystery. I'm just a loner. I found this shack. I live there. Nobody bothers me. No hassle. No rent. No mortgages."

"What happens if the railroad tosses you out?"

"I go somewhere else. I don't need much. I can live anywhere."

And there the conversations ended because George wished it to go no further.

George did not always slink around the diner. There were times he surged along the linear confines of the elongated dining hall as if he were a business executive hurrying to a meeting. In those times, he seemed fluid and confident. His stride matched his confidence. The frowning lines that flowed along his face on most days receded into a relaxed countenance. The elongated creases that cut deep into his cheeks seemed to cut less deeply. Even the furrowed frown around his eyes surrendered to the brightness there. And then, the diner door slid open, George froze, staring at the entrance, and the harshness returned.

What I learned from George were all the things my mother did not wish me to learn. What eight-to-five odds meant. Why not to bet a favorite at the race track. When the odds determined whether or not to bet. To watch the odds board just before the race went off to note whether or not some betting action was developing on a particular horse. That the last race of the day was always a 'boat' race because the mob knew people would plunge on the safe bet trying to make back their losses. And it was the race, I learned, that paid the best if you knew which horse the fix was in for.

And on the fight game, he taught me to ignore the press.

"The sports writers are in on the fix. So they crank up the other boxer, make him look good, focus the public eye on him. Yeah, when you get a fight and the press is pushing one guy, pay attention to what the other guy is doing. Is he out boozing it up or is he home nights? Is one fighter being seen around town? That's a sure excuse for losing a fight. And you watch the betting. The mob doesn't lay money. It rakes it in off the losers. So they pump up the odds on one fighter because gamblers are greedy. People like that three-to-one bet and they get suckered. The mob doesn't put out a quarter, and they rake in thousands. Next time around, the public loses faith in the loser and he rebounds and beats the favorite."

"You know a lot of stuff, George."

"Well. You watch this Tory-Polaris fight. Who's getting all the play in the papers?"

"Tory."

"Five-to-one favorite. The odds will narrow. They don't want too wide a gap. It will come down say to five-to-two or even three-to-one odds. Then watch the action. They bet Tory and you lose. Just watch? The betters won't bet an underdog on those kind of short odds. So they bet Tory because they think they're getting sure money. And they never figure it out. Not ever."

The above conversation took place in the English language. Translation into Newark brogue would be: *They fix the fights. Some of the media buy into it because they know what's going on. They hype the public up. The suckers latch on to the odds and the sports page. Next thing they know the favorite takes a dive and the mob is in big bucks. You don't fight without the mob telling a pug how the fight comes out in advance.*

And he was right. I bet a few dollars on Polaris and won. Tory went down in the eighth round and never looked up. And I won again on the rematch when Tory became an underdog, and he floored Polaris with a single punch in the third round. And the odds were two-to-one for Polaris. The same system worked at the race tracks in the big stakes races. The newspapers played up the favorite and splashed him all over the front of the sports page. But he never won. I never lost picking the second favorite in a horse race. It was like gold. And George gave me the key to the chest.

At each new fight, though, it seemed George slid a little further into wretchedness. He aged more than his years. His stare seemed more distant. In mid-sentence, he would suddenly halt, forget his thought and become morose. We were in the midst of conversation about the numbers racket when a car backfired outside. Slowly, quietly, George slid off the diner stool until he lay prone on the floor. He was near comatose with fear, his heart literally pounding out of his chest, his face a ghoulish gray color. Willie produced a flask, and we revived George with some spirits. I had a time clock to punch but when my shift was over, I returned to find him seated in his usual place but still very pallid. Willie and I assisted him home, through the long, trampled grass that led to his shack, through the brisk night air that swept in from the sea. We lit the kerosene lamp that was his only light and laid him on the cot where he slept. Rats scurried into the shadows, their feet scratching the earthen floor.

He did not return for several days. When he did, he was not the same George. He said little, drinking his coffee with a quivering, trembling hand, slopping a little over into the saucer, then replacing it until he steadied himself and began again. He lived a threadbare existence, in a dilapidated old railroad shack, a bed, table, a wood box for a chair, makeshift shelves that held a few canned goods. I wondered how he got them since he never left the street but there they were. A bottle of rye whiskey, half full. Dinty Moore's stew, some soups, beans, canned corn, a tin of coffee and tea, two metal cups, worn and dented. On the stove, two frying pans, a tea pot salvaged from the junk piles in the swamp. One can find riches in the refuse that floats down from the great city. So we carried him back to his dwelling, and laid him down amidst his treasure trove and left. And like Lazarus, he came back from the dead, and we were friends again but he was failing.

I did not always see George. My school schedule conflicted with work, and I became nimble at altering my schedule in order to do both. Sometimes it was weeks before I saw George again. And yet, each time I saw him, he seemed less and less like George. The shirts were no longer starched and crisp but wrinkled and stained. His pants smelled of mold. His skin seemed darker and more coarse. There were times when he was near normal and other times when the strain of just being George carried him down into the depths of despair. And then, as suddenly as he appeared, George was gone. At first, his absence was nothing unusual. But it spanned a week, then two, then three. I shifted work hours, and Willie's was closed when I had lunch. When I returned to daytime schedule, George had still not returned. I spoke to Willie who visited him before and after work hours. "George had a stroke," he said. "Paralyzed him on the left side. He refused to go to the hospital."

He would not even let Willie call a doctor. For days, he languished in his little shack, able to take no nourishment, able to only occasionally swipe from the bottle of rye.

"I went in yesterday," Willie said, "George was just lying on his cot. He didn't move. The soup I brought him the day before was still untouched. I shook him awake. He was lethargic, his eyes real glassy. Incoherent but he was trying to tell me something. I couldn't tell what the hell he was saying. I had some fresh soup for him. Pea soup. He always liked my pea soup, but he wouldn't eat. " Willie was lean, a narrow-faced man with jutting chin and quick, brown eyes, one of those staunchly independent men whose determination was second only to his sanguinity. He was not easily rattled, but George's condition obviously perplexed him.

"He was near gone. I sat with him for an hour and he didn't move. Not at all. And then he just slumped down and stopped breathing. I figured he was dead so I called the ambulance. The City didn't want to bury him because he had no identification on him so I took up a collection to bury him. They didn't say when they'd do it. Rotten government officials. Never get a straight answer from any of them. Think they'd give a damn, wouldn't you?"

"I'll put in, too," I said, shaking my head. All I could think was that George lived as a mystery and died as a mystery. I couldn't live with that. I had to nose around for the truth.

Where had he come from, this mysterious man? And why had he burrowed into a wretched little shack in the soggy meadows? What frightened him so that he would never leave Queen Street? Who or what was he afraid of? Some answers come easy. Some come in time. Still others never come at all. Eventually I entered law school and abandoned my work at the bakery. Yet I never forgot George or the mystery that surrounded him. He wrapped the cloak of life around him and simply disappeared from its folds and yet the mystery of the man peaks the interest like a persistent thorn working its way out of the skin. Although dead, George remained alive . . . in my investigative mind.

Men like George are not unique. Many are on the run. Some escape. Others do not. When I spoke to some of the tough guys from the mob, they conjectured that George had been a boxer that double-crossed the mob. He was supposed to throw a fight, but he got smart and bet on himself. The mob didn't like that. They assigned a hit man to find George and make an example of him. From that fight on, George vanished. He was so frightened it's unlikely he would have talked to the police. I often wondered what his days immediately after that fight were like for George. He had to know the mob was after him. Did he sleep in the streets? Travel from town to town? Find work wherever they asked no questions? Or did he slink into the marshes or the bayous? Or ride the rails? If they had found him, would George simply have ended up floating in Newark Bay?

I saw men such as George and Pete as part of an underworld current. The one man rules it. The other is dominated by it. For Pete, it was the power of money, the power to control. For George, it was simply survival. And to survive, he lived like a rat in a cave.

As for Pete, he lived well into his 80s and died from natural causes. He thus escaped the investigations by Rudolph Giuliani which sent shock waves into the Mafia but did not demolish it. Several of my clients were harvested as a result of technological advances in tapping telephones, even pay phones, and are still guests of the federal government. Because they are Italian, they will die in prison.

Chapter Three

◆

Sicilian Roots

It was a four hundred fifty acre wetland farm that lay just off Lord Stirling Road, Stirling, New Jersey, long before the urbanization that settled over the State. There was nothing distinguishable about it. Just a dingy, red-brick, two story house, with dark lifeless windows and aging vines spreading over the front. Across the second floor, a balcony cordoned by black wrought iron coursed the length of it and at the pinnacle carved in white stone were the initials RV, Rosolino Vassallo, and the date, 1934—the year of my birth. I remember in dead winter pushing open the French doors, stepping out onto the balcony and studying the animal tracks that lay in the snow beneath. Raccoon, deer, fox and rabbit that had visited during the night and evaporated with dawn.

It was a farm house with twisting corridors and small rooms tucked away in odd corners, a large, warm kitchen and a cramped living room with sliding doors. Suspended on one wall were rifles and shotguns of various makes from all

FARMHOUSE – The farmhouse itself appeared small but was very large inside, with rooms along the corridors and separate bedrooms upstairs.

over the world. Outside, and a distance from the house itself, lay twenty-seven dog houses, housing beagles, retrievers, hounds, pointers and setters. They were never silent. When some were silent, the others were barking, and it took very little to set them chorusing. My grandfather loved to hunt and, therefore, raised and stocked pheasant, quail and doves. It was not unusual to see him releasing them before a hunt. Indeed, during the hunting season, men came there as guests and shot game. So it was not unusual to see men toting pheasants, quail or partridge which had been carefully raised and then released a day or two before the event. As a wetland, it housed ducks as well as other marsh birds. Rabbits abounded as did deer, raccoon and squirrels. When there was nothing in season my grandfather sharpened his eye shooting small sparrows and cowbirds.

Although there were twenty-seven dogs, only two were allowed to roam loose: Rusty, an Irish setter, and Queenie, a German Pointer. They were both affable dogs except when eating. One Sunday, I left the table to feed Queenie some table scraps. I made the mistake of approaching from the rear. Thinking I was taking her food away, Queenie spun and bit me behind the left ear. It wasn't a bad bite but it did shock me. Not as much of a shock as the sight of my grandfather's anger at the dog. And no amount of pleading could prevent him from shooting her. Disloyalty carries a high price. In the end, he raised the gun, and I hugged the dog by the neck. By then, Queenie knew she was in trouble, but she had no concept that her life was in danger. If ever a dog does something right, she did the right thing that day. She licked my face.

"She's sorry, Grandpa. See. She's sorry." The tears I shed must have touched him. He slowly lowered the gun and nodded. Then he patted me on the head and hugged me and the dog.

"I think you be a good lawyer." He turned to the rest of the men and announced. "This is my grandson. See how he protects his friends." And he squeezed me until I thought the breath would leak out of me.

I thought my mom would banish me to the cellar beneath the main house but she settled for the water closet. The cellar itself was more frightening. It held the Italian products so prized by the Sicilian palate. Parmesan, provolone and mozzarella cheese. Italian hams, salami, mortadel and other imported processed meats. Canned plum tomatoes, puree, fava beans and other goods of Italian vintage. Wild game hung to age. Oddly enough, my grandfather was not much of a wine drinker. He preferred straight rye followed by seltzer water. So there was no wine in the cellar. It was a dark, damp place, frightening with all its unlighted corners. I always thought of it as musty and lifeless, and I avoided it because it frightened me. At times, it was unlocked. Other times it was locked. The significance had to do with men hiding from the law. But my mother did not dare incarcerate me in the dark cellar with my grandfather there. Despite the shrew that she could be, she would not defy my grandfather's love for me. I still remember bits and pieces of my grandfather's farm. I think mostly it was a place of freedom for me. It was a place where my cousin, Peggy, and I had many fun-filled times. For years she was my only friend.

There was a single oak on the front lawn. Its massive branches seemed to cover the entire yard. I recall it because they hung large jugs that captured thousands of Japanese beetles during summer, beetles that clutched my soft skin and pinched until it hurt. Along side the house lay a five hundred foot well with a hand pump that never ran dry and produced gallons and gallons of frigid, delicious water. Sixty years later, the well is still there, though the State of New Jersey has locked it away from the public. Just before the gravel drive stood a circular, screened pavilion, a place where my cousin and I spent hours playing. Especially on rainy days when the farm was submerged in mist and steady rain, the pavilion was a place of comfort and enchantment. It was abandoned by day and so became our refuge. My cousin and I made many a fantasy come to life in that round dormitory with its wicker furniture and Persian carpets. In it, we could chase the barn cats, bounce on the sofa, race around the perimeter or play hide and seek. So by day we children held possession because the adults wanted to be rid of us, and by night the adults rested to gain the evening breeze. Many nights, their punctuated voices lulled us to sleep in our rooms above. There, my cousin and I found sanctuary in the pavilion where we were safe from the watchful eyes of the adults. We were free.

FARM BUILDINGS – The farm in Basking Ridge had a number of buildings on it as well as twenty-seven dog houses. Even the caretaker had his own home.

Though it was distant and remote from Newark, the farm was part of the streets as well. This was a working farm. A farm that produced. Beyond the main house were the cow barn, the milking barn, the pony shed, the pasteurization room, the caretaker's cottage and a corn crib. Each building had its purpose. Chrome, electric milking machines squeezed milk from over-laden cows. Captured in metal urns, the milk was poured into a hopper and then raced along long, steel pipes which formed a grid. At each pipe the temperature of the milk cooled until it slid frosty and ice cold into the bottling machine. There is no taste as that of clean, frothy ice cold milk with all its fat content. And thus, my cousin and I often visited there.

The farm had several fields, one to the left of the farm house where goats and ponies dozed in the noon sun. To the far right, cattle grazed in most of the field. A solitary bull resided in another. My cousin and I often raced that bull across the paddock. He could easily have caught us but he never did. I suspect he enjoyed playing with us. A solitary bull must suffer boredom when he is not in his season. But while he liked us, he held no love for the Polish caretaker. Neither did Peggy and I. On one occasion, during mating season, the caretaker went to lead the bull into the mating pens. It must have hurt being yanked by a ring in the nose but perhaps the bull's hormones were up so he was oblivious to the pain. The bull pulled free and charged the caretaker sending him scurrying through an open gate. He managed to stay ahead but barely by whiskers. Convinced the bull might soon run him down, he scurried up the flimsiest clothes pole on the farm. It bent with each breeze, let alone a massive bull butting it. The caretaker saw us watching and implored us to fetch help. But in every child there is the potential for evil, and my cousin and I were soul mates in crime. We agreed to summon help and casually sauntered away, leaving him to sway with every head butt the bull delivered. Help, eventually, did arrive but the caretaker was slow to forgive the tardy pony express that so long delayed his rescue.

Behind the farmhouse lay a single road to the rear pastures. Here the cattle wintered, safe from the winds that sheered across the front fields. Along that road, I rode my circus pony, Lucky, which my grandfather purchased for me. I'm told it was a gift for surviving a near-death operation on my mastoids. All I know is that I raged with fever and had to be brought to St. Michael's Hospital in Newark for care. My dad told me that my grandfather spoke to the doctor just before the operation and suggested that if his grandson died, the doctor would accompany me to heaven. Obviously, I survived. So did the doctor.

GRAPE ARBOR – The arbor at the Basking Ridge Farm. Under this arbor all family functions occurred. Sunday meetings of the Family also occurred under its shade.

That is the grandfather I knew. A man deeply loving of his family and with the soul of mischief that belied his mob affiliations. He employed a local woman as a cook at the farm, and he teased her without mercy. They obviously enjoyed a close relationship as he was always teasing her about the quality of her cooking. On one occasion, he and I were near the grain silo, and he discovered a catch of baby mice. He suggested I deliver them to the cook and place them in her hands. But when I went there, the cook was not in the kitchen, and the only activity was a pot boiling on the stove. I removed the cover, popped in the mice, replaced the lid and left. When the cook pulled the lid off the pot, tiny mice were popping out like popcorn. The horrendous screaming echoing through the windows signaled to my grandfather that he and I had better make hasty our retreat. It was two weeks before he persuaded the cook to return and a month before we rounded up the singed and scalded mice that had scattered throughout the house.

If it can be said that a farm has a heart, the heart of this farm was the lengthy row of picnic tables sheltered by a long arbor. In the summer, the arbor harbored grapes, the leaves of which shielded the picnic tables beneath. This was the farm of Rosolino Vassallo, my grandfather, born in Alia, Sicily, once a cobbler and later a man of honor in what is now dreaded as the murderous Mafia.

There is not much to Alia. It's a small hill town of rocky terrain and steep hills. Like so many remote villages in Sicily, it has its ruins; its rocky landscape; its archaic, under-populated town. There are caves that could tell a hundred stories of murder and mystery. Caves where people dwell. The roads are narrow and the land mostly barren. Still, the people eke out a living from the earth. It was not always so. Once, Sicily was luxuriant with green grass and stalwart trees. But the hoards who invaded and conquered the land pilfered its resources until there was no timber. With no timber and the constant winds, including the sirocco, the earth dried and crumbled into dust. Today, Alia is pock-marked with caves and dry land, but it thrives still because the spirit of the people who live there refuse to let it die. It is still a friendly land. Its people still hold to their old traditions.

Earning a living there is difficult, yet the people cling to the village tenaciously because it harbors the tradition of a thousand years of farming. Like many such towns, every one knows everyone and, like every town, the inhabitants protected what was theirs from those who were dishonest. In my grandfather's childhood, his family took the farm mule into the house at night to sleep with them, lest robbers steal

ROSOLINO VASSALLO – My grand-father, Rosolino Vassallo. Stern looking, kind heart.

it and leave them with no animal. In time, they had several mules and enlarged the house to accommodate them. That he came from such humble origins and still managed to etch out wealth and authority in the United States is to his credit. Unlike many other immigrants, he did not come to the United States merely to milk it of its opportunity. He learned the language and the customs. He became a citizen. He suffered the prejudice and taunts of immigrants who had come before. He worked for substandard wages, established a shoemaker's shop, expanded it and moved on when the occasion arose. He was not a dread man to me. He was a vested man, one who came from Alia with his parents who were unable to read or write, unable to earn a living in Sicily.

Land was his dream as it is the dream of every noble Sicilian and life held no illusions for him. For many peasants, the dream of land was an impossible one. Sicily, inhabited by the Greeks, Romans, Carthaginians, Moors, Normans, French, and even the Germans for a short time, learned to distrust conquerors because they took more than they returned. Peasants who rented the land paid as much as two-thirds of their crops to the wealthy conquerors who lived off them, stripped the land, and denigrated the soil. So when my grandfather's family settled in New Orleans, he quickly affiliated with the toughest Sicilian youths in town and commenced using the hormone capability that later in life sired seventeen children—five of whom survived to adulthood. That his miscreant behavior was a discomfort to his mother was never in doubt. Nunzia Manno Vassallo was a woman who could neither read nor write but clutched a massive determination that her children would be honorable citizens free of crime. When Rosolino became entrenched with local toughs and brought the police home more than once, Nunzia had a relative write to Alia asking if one Concetta (Esposito) Cortese was yet unmarried. And while this young tough was able to push his way to the top of itinerant gangs and intimidate others into rendering him fealty and financial support, his mother brooked no rebellion and packed him off to Sicily where he married Concetta.

Marriage must have settled him. The diminutive woman he wedded bore him seventeen children as I have previously written and idolized him into sainthood. Years later, he traveled to New Jersey and settled there, continuing his learned occupation of cobbler and opening a store on the main thoroughfare of Newark's busy metropolis. This continued only for a short time. Money was difficult to come by, and Rosolino had a family to support. The Depression did not end until well after 1934. Some still say that Franklin Roosevelt forced us into war to bring about an economic recovery. Sicilians who came to this country were regarded as little more than blacks—even by the Italians. They banded together out of necessity, for survival. And they brought with them the customs of the old country, even those that trafficked in illegality. Since the lottery was legal in Italy but illegal in the United States, Sicilians banded together to bring the Italian lottery to their adopted country. To them, this was no more immoral or illegal that lifting a whiskey glass during Prohibition. This land, America, was not like their native soil. It was unaccepting of newcomers and a difficult place to find work. People scorned the manner of their speech and ridiculed their staunch Catholic faith. Where did they come from? Where did the Vassallos come from?

My father always told me that we descended from the French and that our name was D'Arsal. Though I cannot prove his recitation of the family origins, my father's credibility gains respect with each passing investigation into family history. A genealogist in Malta has traced some of the Vassallo name and confirms that there were Vassallos in France. I once asked my father about a crest on wrought iron, interior family gates, and he told me we had originally descended from a French family of nobility. In one of the various French revolutions, the family sided with the wrong nobles and escaped France barely ahead of the sword. They settled somewhere in Sicily (no doubt hiding in the remote village of Alia) and never returned to France. He suggested the name was changed to Vassallo because it defined a feudal lord of lower stature, sort of an underboss. The name

Vassallo derives from the Latin word vassal or a servant, feudal subject or retainer, but it could have applied to any position within the feudal system. From the email of Count Charles de Branchforte Said, this quote:

> The Vassallo family are of direct Royal descent from the Ancient Lombardian Royal Family. One branch went to the Byzantine Empire and were created Counts. Another branch went to Sicily. It is known that they were exiled from Lombardy and some ended in France where they became Counts of Orleans for a century or so and then were invited back to Milan. One branch was invited to Sicily, another to Greece and others remained in Milan. Later, the faction that settled in Greece later traveled to Sicily.

There is no hard evidence to confirm my father's version as true; there no hard evidence to suggest it is not true. On the other hand there is just too much coincidence involved. It's likely that my dad's version was correct. We are descended from royalty.

There is in fact a lineage of that name still living in France, but it is near impossible to connect it to the Vassallo family in Sicily. What happened to the D'Arsal family as they settled in Sicily is unknown and probably never will be discovered. I do know that my grandfather was seventeen when he arrived in New Orleans, that he returned to Sicily to marry and remained there for two years. He returned to New Orleans and opened a shoemaking business which is not so strange since there were other leather workers in our lineage.

My aunt's recollection is that two of the Vassallo children, both named Nancy had perished in New Orleans. One in a fire and the other Nancy when a hooligan threw a rock and struck her in the head. My grandmother, Concetta Vassallo, felt the place was jinxed, and she wanted to be away from the painful memories associated with New Orleans. More than likely my grandfather connected with Concetta's brother, Sal Cortese, and moved into Newark because he was assured a better way of life. Sal was living in Newark then and eventually purchased a farm in Florham Park. He was perfectly placed to help my grandparents establish themselves in Newark.

Census and birth records for Virginia Vassallo, the youngest child, revealed that Rosolino migrated to Newark in 1911. Information related by my father, Tony, also indicates that by 1930 the Vassallo family was living in Newark, New Jersey. My father, then age twenty-eight, was listed as owning a shoemaker shop while my grandfather, Rosolino, was listed as a realtor. There is no way my grandfather was in the real estate business. He might have made personal investments in real estate or given mortgage money—which I am sure he did—but the likelihood is that he was already in the Mafia.

Why do I conclude this? He came to New Jersey in 1911. He opened a shoemaker's shop on Hill Street, and my father worked for him. My dad always said he worked until he was twenty-nine and handed his entire paycheck over to my grandfather. That wasn't so much because Rosolino needed the money but to maintain control of his sons. The shoemaker shop was legitimate enough, but it was also a front for betting operations. People who wanted to place bets on the horses, or sports, or even the Italian lottery dropped in from time to time. In 1918, an ultra-conservative United States Congress passed the Prohibition Act outlawing liquor. It was a golden opportunity for Italian immigrants to raise their status in the financial structure, and, since a large contingent of Italians had immigrated to Canada, it was natural for relatives to link up and establish a conduit for passing illegal alcohol across the border. Many of them made the liquor in their homes or on their farms, all without intervention from the Canadian government. The liquor was then bottled and sold through outlets in the United States. Sometimes it was sold in clear bottles while other times, one could find such hooch in legitimate bottles such as Canadian Club. The notion of recycling is not a new one. The frugal Italians pilfered as many empty bottles as they could find and sealed their own liquor in such containers. That my father still had such contacts in Canada was the reason he traveled there with me when I was five and six years old. Prohibition had long ended, but the same Canadian/Italians who had supported rum running also supported the gambling industry. And they also wagered.

With the advent of better international communications, lottery information could be passed over the wire as could horse racing results and sports results. Liquor, untaxed cigarettes, prostitution and, to a small degree, illegal drugs funneled huge amounts of income into the mob coffers. But not all of these operations were of the vintage seen in *The Godfather*. Many of these small operations existed long before the mob organized and consolidated their holdings. Rather than disturb a way of life that was dying with the older generation, the mob bosses chose to let these businesses die of attrition, filling in their own people as the senior members died off. Of course, sometimes they did

CHESTNUT STREET HOUSES – The Chestnut Street houses were wooden frame, some with slate tiles covering the front. All had brick stoops and looked very much alike.

stand in the way, drunk with their own power. When they did, old age and a natural death were not usually the end result.

In this setting, my grandfather rose in power, establishing a "policy" or "numbers" racket in New Jersey and organizing a tight, efficient band of loyal Sicilian friends and relations to police it. There were bookies, collectors, runners, accountants, wire operators, stoolies, politicians and, yes, enforcers. Within a short time of entering the rackets, he purchased land and constructed three tenement style homes, joined to one another but with separate entrances. I lived in the third unit of these dwellings until my marriage.

One thing, certainly, is true. My grandfather welded the might of power that spanned the generations. I did not always know the reasons why nor do I really know them now. I only know that normal men turned white at the mention of his name. I only know that men are dead because they disrespected him. Many years later, too many, my present wife, Virginia, and I were dining in a local Italian trattoria in Montclair. We were usually seated in the front of the restaurant, but on this occasion, we were taken to a smaller back room with about ten tables. Two musicians, a violinist and a clarinetist, were playing old Italian tunes. Both were in their seventies, white haired, affable, with the earmarks of men who had played for so many years, they no longer needed sheet music for they had blended into their instruments as though they were one. As the smaller of the two men moved to our table and began playing, I studied his face intently. When he finished, I nodded and clapped. He bent near to ask for any requests.

"I know you," I said. He shrugged disinterestedly as if to say, "many people think they know me." But I persisted.

"You needed a favor, and you came to my grandfather's house. He met you in the living room, upstairs, and the two of you spoke in Italian. You seemed troubled, and he put his hand on your shoulder and patted you. After that, you calmed down and shook his hand and kissed his ring."

He stared at me with an incredulous look on his face. I read it well. *Who is this usurper that he speaks to me like this? He could only have been a boy. How could he know such a thing and who is he?*

"What was your grandfather's name?" He smiled benignly.

"Vassallo. Rosolino Vassallo. Chestnut Street, Newark."

His face blanched white. A pure white. A bloodless white. The pallid color of age that had been there moments before now drained into mask of fear. His right eye began to twitch. But he said nothing. He only glanced at his partner and moved to another table. They played a tune, and Virginia gawked at me with shock written in her eyes. Moments later, the duo was gone and, though it was early evening, they did not appear again. I often wonder what he knew about my grandfather that I did not. Why does a man turn white so many years after another man is dead?

That man's reaction imbued me with a sense of the power my grandfather must have held. After so many years, because I could have been no more than five or six at the time, that man was terrorized at the mention of a man long dead. And that was but a single example of my grandfather's reputation.

Another case in point occurred with two Irish toughs who learned Rosolino wore a five carat diamond ring on his finger. The Irish had little respect for Italian immigrants. The police were hard on them. The Irish gangsters were just as tough. These two punks approached my grandfather and stuck a gun in his stomach. The other grabbed his hand and tried pulling the ring off.

I was there that day, a child of seven. What impressed me most was Grandpa's calm demeanor throughout the entire robbery. When they snarled at him and heaped disrespect on his attempts to reason with them, he showed no temper at all, only a sullen glint in his eyes. But these were contemptuous men. They did not merely want to steal. They wanted to degrade him, humiliate him, shame him in front of his grandson. I admit I was disappointed when my grandfather took no action. On the contrary, he seemed most cooperative, and I distained his fawning subservience.

"*Paisans*, are you sure you want to do this?" he cooed.

"Listen to the dago," one said to his partner. "Shut your wop mouth. Don't give me that *pisano* crap or I'll bull ya with this gun." The shorter man had an Irish face, youngish with blue/grey eyes, red hair flopping up over the top of his forehead. The other was built like a boxer, brown hair and eyes, a short scar on his chin, a bulge in his nose where it had been broken in a fight. He menaced my grandfather with his gun, but my grandfather showed no fear.

"Give me the damn ring," the taller one said, yanking it off his finger. My grandfather grimaced a little, then regained his composure.

"Wait," my grandfather said calmly, "you shouldn't rush something like this. Do you want people to think you are amateurs?" A strange twist grew on his lips, a stern yet humorous twist. "My wallet is full, too. Here. Take." He held out the wallet to them. The short one yanked it from his hand and dug out the money. My grandfather watched quietly. He held an air of self-confidence that was strange given the circumstances. Then, he dug into his left pocket. "And more. More money. See what you miss by rushing?" He handed them a large roll of bills which the short one snatched, his own confidence somewhat shaken. In all that time, the two Micks stood quietly, wondering how this man held at gun point had suddenly assumed control of their robbery. But he had. He had wrested control, was giving them more than they demanded. I was astonished. I knew he never carried a gun. I did not know if he needed one, but it seemed maddening to have him giving away his wealth with such serenity.

As they turned to leave, he spoke to them again: "Hey, Irish. I give you a chance to give it back. You are *sfacciato*,

DIAMOND RING – The present size of the Rosolino's diamond ring is 3.04 carats. Originally, this ring was five carats. In a fit of temper my grandfather pounded the table and struck the ring on the edge, cracking off a piece. The ring had to be re-cut to a smaller size.

you know, bold, eh? So I give you a chance to return everything, and we forget the whole thing."

There was a little smile on his face, almost imperceptible. His eyes did not retain the same smile. They were lifeless, spiritless. I did not understand why . . . then. For a moment, I thought the taller Mick would strike him. He raised his arm to cuff him with the back of his hand. But something warned him and he desisted. They left, shaking their heads in disbelief. Within several days though, I noticed my grandfather had his ring on again, and he again carried a large roll of bills in his pocket. My father told me the Irish boys repented their error and decided to leave New Jersey. The newspapers said they had gone swimming in Newark Bay and accidentally drowned. That they were wearing street clothes and dress shoes as they swam seemed to strike no one as odd except me.

I often wondered whether those robbers connected the dots when they decided to swim with lead weights around their feet. Did they recall my grandfather's sardonic smile? Did they understand he had led them into a fatal trap and swiftly slammed the door behind them? Did they wish for a second chance to return the goods and apologize? Did they even get to spend some of the money for a goodbye spree?

1939 CAR – This 1939 roadster shows the degree of luxury and wealth enjoyed by the Vassallo family in pre-war times.

My father would say little of the affair. Only that the men thought better of their actions and returned the ring and the money. Today, the ring is in my possession to be passed on to whomever I decide shall merit it. It is more valuable in terms of memories than dollars. And when I see it, I often wish I could have witnessed the demise of the unfortunate hoods.

To me, my grandfather was kind and patient. When my cousin and I burned out the car battery playing elevator with his electric windows, he exhibited a mirth unparalleled. And we so loved him and his mischief that, in gratitude, we painted the convertible top of his new roadster a bright red to match the color of the Chestnut Street home. For this, he swatted my Uncle John because he left an open can of paint and brushes nearby. But to us, he smiled a pained, understanding smile and soon became his tractable self. He loved us, and he loved his farm, the land being a symbol of status far beyond the wealth he accumulated, and his grandson representing the continuation of his dynasty.

The farm was freedom to children. Free of adults, we could roam the farmlands as we saw fit. Sundays were even more special because on those days we would pile into the pony cart and trot the long distance into Morristown. There we attended movies, ate ice cream and walked the length of each and every unoccupied park bench. On other Sundays, the stolid quiet of farm life was suddenly interrupted. One moment, the dirt road leading by our farm was quiet and still, and, in another instant, it brimmed with a long cavalcade of black, ominous roadsters, slowly rolling down the long, straight road. Not even the dust was much disturbed as they motored on. My cousin and I saw other cars enter and leave the farm on other days, but we never saw such a proliferation except on Sundays. To us, it would mean merriment and noise and boccia games where we could steal the money off the boccia ball and scurry away with our profit. The change was placed on top of the target ball to signal any touching by another ball, the object being to get close but not to move or touch the stationery ball. My grandfather made good the losses and never asked for the money, though, I suspect it found its way back after nightfall when we were asleep. At least, it was never in my pocket when morning came.

Farm life was quiet, often boring unless you were a child with a pony to ride, and goats to be bucked off, and barn cats to chase, and bulls to tease. For those not inclined to that sport, it could be very boring. So the sight of so many cars motoring up the dead still road brought excitement to the once quiet farm. My grandmother and the women shifted into high gear. My grandfather took his place near the well where they would park, and my cousin and I stood on top of the picnic tables so we could watch from our favorite vantage point.

PARKING AREA ON FARM – On certain Sundays this parking area would be filled with sinister black limousines.

The cars, it seemed, were hardly moving at all, moving as if they did not even wish to disturb the road. We waited. Impatient and anxious to see who it was, we waited. So Peg and I watched in excited revelry to see who they were.

Then, the cars arrived, long black limousines, moving slowly into the parking area on the farm and stopping near the well where my grandfather stood. He was near six feet, slightly overweight with deep creases in his sagging cheeks but that day, he seemed so much taller, so much prouder, that I hardly knew he was that big. Men alighted from the black monsters, and other men took their places by the cars, swarthy, muscled, sinister men, men without feeling or humor in their eyes. Even when they tried to be polite, there was something foreboding in their demeanor, as if they were automatons that operated by pushing a button. If ordered, I felt they would kill me as easily as squashing a gnat. And so as all evil is fascinating, we watched them with apt attention, entranced by the happenings.

We espied these men, all with bulges in their jackets, as they stood by the vehicles, searching the roads as though others were soon to be coming. But none did. The men who alighted from the cars were sportily dressed in very expensive suits. All had elaborate watches and still others had very bright diamonds poking out from behind their vests. They, too, had bulges, under their shoulder or in their pants pockets. And all seemed kindly and courteously disposing. There was nothing conspicuous about them, just something that told you there was something different about them.

As they approached my grandfather, they did a strange thing, shaking hands and kissing the ring on his finger. My cousin and I wondered how it felt to kiss a warm ring so we stood in line, and, when it came our turn, we bent and kissed the diamond ring on his hand. He laughed and said something Italian to the other men, and, for the first time, they laughed too. Then, he patted me on the head and hugged me. I did not understand what he said in Italian. Mom and Dad could never agree on how to say something so I never learned. But I understood that whatever he said was a lesson to the other men because they all nodded.

They filed under the arbor in perfect order, the well-dressed men sitting nearest my grandfather, the muscular soldiers still posted by the cars. All of them were Sicilians, some with thick, brushy mustaches, others clean shaven and all with a limp smile and dark, frightening eyes. They banded together in the new country as they had in Sicily. Distrustful of strangers by heritage for all who conquered Sicily took from the peasants, thus they learned to trust no one but their own and, perhaps, to trust family before friends. Outsiders were not welcomed. Respect and loyalty were valued highly and silence even more highly. So these men came to the table of my grandfather and spoke their native language. The family stood at the base of the tables far from my grandfather. And the conversation droned on, each man speaking in turn, some softly, others vociferously. They banded together because they were men of honor.

But there was one man who wasn't there. We didn't know who he was but my cousin and I saw him in the early morning hours, walking along the pathways leading to the paddocks, never on the road. He seemed nervous and watchful, peering over his shoulder every now and then, stopping a little, never quite at ease. He seemed mole-like with deep beads for eyes, an elongated nose and sloping cheeks that disappeared into a sharp chin. Sometimes we thought we heard a strange voice after we were in bed but we never saw anyone. He was just always a dark figure walking in the shadows around the farm. And he was not there, not at dinner, not at our regular meals, not during daylight hours, but he was there. He didn't stay very long, but he was there.

The table conversation went on for hours, droning into the early evening hours. For children, dinner was endless. We could not leave the table until given permission to do so, and my grandfather seemed too preoccupied to give such permission. The antipasto came first, each person passing the plate and taking his fill. Then a second course, insalata they called it, consisting of lettuce, chicory, water cress, sometimes dandelion, tomatoes, green peppers and basil. After that was served some form of pasta, rigatoni, or fettuccine, linguine or fussili with the rich, thick tomato sauce and covered with romano or parmesan cheese. Then the sauce meats, meatballs, flank steak, Italian sausage, floating in bolognese sauce. All served with Sicilian round

ROSOLINO VASSALLO AND MEN – My grandfather with a number of his friends and business associates.   He was, indeed, an imposing figure.

loaves of crusty, brown bread and followed by fruit, nuts, pastries and rich, black demitasse served with Anisette or Sambuca liquors.

The men by the cars did not all sit to eat. The women brought plates, two at a time, while the others fidgeted to alertness as if they expected something to happen while they alone were on guard. Some stood watching the woods, the houses, the roads... even sometimes, the sky. Others studied barns and the road from the back fields. I wondered who they were, but even as a child, I knew one did not ask them questions. They were not friendly men.

Children were served last unless my grandmother was serving. She had my aunts make plates for my cousin and me and set us at a separate section of the table. Now here was this diminutive little woman, no more that four foot, ten inches tall, and probably not more than one hundred and thirty pounds and she had born seventeen children and could cook for upward of thirty people on a Sunday afternoon. She operated four open barbecue pits, basting and roasting chickens while running back and forth to the house to supervise her helpers on the remainder of dinner. So these men ate until the sun went down, from antipasto to soup, then a helping of something in-between, then the main course, and coffee, desserts and pastries, and finally a large bowl of fruit and nuts passed down and around the long tables. The men ate and drank, all the while continuing their discussions.

This dialogue was not social talk. It was animated and argumentative. There was much motioning of hands, grimacing, some outright pounding on the table. It seemed that the winning of such points was not won by logic but by the sheer force of personality. My grandfather often resorted to smashing the table with his fist to make a point and when he did so, the others seemed to cower. Then, the conversation waned soft . . . pianissimo, very soft, and reason returned to the table. When day was done, the men shook hands. The men who had stood by the cars all through the day and early evening, looking none the less for wear, not even sweating from the long hours of a hot day, stirred to action like marbles rolling across the floor, opening car doors, scanning the road, the woods and the farm again. The suited men smiled, shook hands again, and hurriedly disappeared into idling cars. Then, the cavalcade wheeled slowly out of the driveway, disturbing no more dust than when they had arrived, and motored away into the evening dusk. All the conversation then was hushed, and children were hurried to bed. Since my cousin and I were the only children, we often felt targeted.

I did not know for many years who those men were or how they came to be there or what affiliation Grandpa Vassallo had with them but it was obvious they were important to him. Bits at a time the lessons are learned, not all the lessons, for much is lost because no history is preserved and thus, I write this now so that my children will know.

I have provoked curiosity about the strange man on the farm. And perhaps now, even he will be unknown to you. He was one of the originators of an organization called Murder Incorporated. Lepke, along with Abe Reles, enticed the mob into hiring their contract staff of hit men. Hundreds of hits occurred under their auspices, and they were not above contracting with private persons who were trustworthy enough to engage their services. I understand Lepke (Little Louis in Yiddish) was a very cold-blooded man who did some of the murders himself and contracted as a hit man to the various mobs. Yet, he was also a devoted family man, and, needless to say, his family never knew his occupation.

Lepke was on the run. Both the local police and the F.B.I. were chasing him because of his crimes. I don't know what the connection was between him and my grandfather but somehow he had gotten to the farm to hide out. This was the strange man we had seen from time to time. He avoided everyone, took his meals in one of the rooms which was always locked, and seldom ventured out. We just knew he was there.

We were still visiting the farm when another group of vehicles pulled up. These men were less discreet. They rushed the farm from both sides of the road, plummeting out of the doors like gushing water and spilling all over the farm. What was conspicuous about them were their machine guns.

They all had them except the one, heavyset man with wrinkled jowls and a rather large nose. He seemed to be the leader of these men and directed them on where to search. They had no regard for property or privacy and stormed into the house, kicking in doors and occupying the downstairs rooms like invading forces. They shoved my grandfather and my father into parlor chairs and motioned with their guns for everyone to sit. The women were huddled into a corner of the same room but were permitted to sit where they wished. The impression I formed was not that these men were so brave, but that they were really frightened of whoever or whatever it was they were looking for. As a child of five I had little idea what was going on. So I sat on the floor besides my grandfather's chair and watched.

The man in charge was questioning my grandfather. He was nodding to each question, saying very little. Although he always spoke with a slight accent, my grandfather was an American citizen. Two of the men came in from searching the outside farm area and called:

"Mr. Hoover . . ."

Then, he walked over to them, and they whispered and gestured. Hoover returned to questioning my grandfather, telling him they knew that Lepke was there and wanted to know where. My grandfather denied knowing anyone of that name. It seemed as though hours went by. The men refused to go. They continued searching, even through the extensive woods surrounding the farm itself. No one was found. I often wondered where the man had gone or when he left, but I was never to find that out.

One of the men bent down to question me. I looked at him when he asked me if there were any strange men around the farm lately?

I nodded yes.

"Where is he, sonny?" he crooned, his eyes constricting.

"Right next to me," I answered, looking at him.

He didn't think it was funny. He straightened up and repositioned his gun. My grandfather held a stiff smile on his face but his eyes were admiringly bright. He was then perhaps sixty and had suffered a slight stroke not long before. It was difficult for him to hold his water, and he needed a bathroom. As he started out of the chair, the F.B.I. agent who had questioned me shoved the machine gun into his stomach and pushed him down again. "Sit down there!"

How dare he! I thought. How dare this man come onto my grandfather's farm and shove my grandfather around.

I inched my hand under the chair where my grandfather was sitting. I was groping for something. The agent looked in my direction. I stopped. He looked away. My hand inched again. This time it touched a cold feel of steel. The metal felt cold and reassuring. My tiny hand closed around the butt. Slowly, sliding it out, I stopped when the gun reached the edge. The agent looked again. I put on my most innocent look. Stopped. He looked away. I slid the gun out and squirted. Dead aim. In the face. Water pistols in those days delivered a lot of water and a hard stream. He sputtered, fumed. He turned the machine gun on me and for a moment . . . just a moment . . . I thought I was dead. But I had avenged my grandfather, the indignity.

The man in charge laughed. He thought it was funny. The agent did not. Hoover sent him outside for a smoke and put another agent in his place. Hoover patted me on the head and said something about bravery. I always felt a lot of pride about that but, many years later, I heard he was a homosexual and wondered if it were such a compliment at all.

Lepke was not the only criminal at the farm. There was also public enemy number one ... me. At least from the number of times I was incarcerated, one would think I was enemy number one. Off the small kitchen was a water closet, probably three feet by three feet. They later converted it into a small toilet, and, if I had to pee, I had to hold my elbows down or bump them into the walls on either side. Whatever my crime, I was summarily sentenced to the water closet, there to remain until someone was able to entreat my mother to spring me. Of all the times I can recall, only once did I deserve solitary confinement. Watching the three stooges gave me the ploy of pulling a chair out from under someone just as they were sitting. Mom seemed a likely candidate so just as she was sitting at the dinner table, I pulled the chair out from under her. I really do not know what possessed me to do this but she hit the floor like a load of sand. I can still hear the gawumppp as she landed.

I can tell you that as soon as she regained her decorum— for she was an aristocratic woman with a penchant for social stature, she came up swinging, cuffing my ears on both sides. Sentenced immediately to solitary confinement. And from the confines I heard my Aunt Virginia and my Aunt Josie, both of whom knew full well what I had done and suppressed smirks extremely well I am told, argue that I was trying to be a gentlemen and push the chair under her. That she bought some of the argument and escaped more embarrassment by not pushing the issue is evidenced by the fact that I was not more severely punished. Of course, I lied convincingly that I was merely trying to push the chair under her when I lost my balance and tipped the chair backwards. It was the last time I enacted anything I saw in the movies, especially on my mother. As she was not in a position to refute this, I suffered only nominal punishment, unlike Lepke who was to suffer a more terrible fate.

Lepke eventually surrendered on lesser charges but the government, being what it is, double-crossed him and tried him for murder. He was convicted, refused to recant or give information on any of his associates and was executed. In fact, he was the only mob affiliate ever to be executed. That he was sheltered on my grandfather's farm was always a source of pride to me. After all, he was a celebrity. Too, my altercation with the F.B.I. man left my pride undamaged as well. In my grandfather's eyes, I was a *pezzanovante*, a pistola at age five.

All this occurred on my grandfather's land ... a land we called the farm. The men gathered on Sundays to discuss business, and there was merriment and argument. The women scurried around to serve the food and then retired to the main house where they ate their own meals. But the men remained.

Of the men who came to my grandfather's table, I knew two of them better than most. One of them, Dominick D'Elia, lived around the corner from me and had married the sister of Don Salvatore Messina. Dominick was part of a legitimate contingent of mobsters who had fanned out into respectable businesses. When he married Messina's sister, he was brought under the Messina Family. It was easy to spot Dominick. He was pudgy, so much so that he waddled down the street. And he wore a starched white shirt which was buttoned to the top, a black tie that was usually crooked and half opened, and a wide black belt. Of all the men who came to the farm, he was the most affable, thick cheeks, clean shaven, smiling eyes and a soft, kind voice.

Every day, Dominick walked the eight blocks to the Down Neck paper mill. Every day, he'd stop to say something to me. During the summer, he'd sweat a lot and seemed uncomfortable. I often offered him a ride once I started driving as he seemed to be part of the neighborhood forever. He always declined. I think he enjoyed strolling along the streets, watching the various changes in the neighborhood. If we were out there playing boxball or street tennis, he'd stop and watch, comment when he saw something that impressed him. In the days when my grandfather was alive but disabled, Dominick frequently stopped to visit with him. I think he enjoyed talking about the old days. I know my grandfather enjoyed the visits. The man who was once so proud and powerful had been brought down by a third and more damaging stroke, and, although he was not bedridden, he did not often leave the house.

The paper mills were nothing more than hollow buildings filled with bales and bales of crushed and packaged paper and cardboard. The trucks pulled into a garage that was open at both ends and onto a scale. The paper or cardboard was then dumped into a large pit. And the truck weighed empty. The difference was the amount of load that it carried. When the truck pulled forward, a huge machine pounded the paper into a solid mass, and another machine wound it tightly with metal bands. All in all the bulk was eight feet high and five feet wide and probably weighed a thousand pounds. Most of the guys who worked there often referred to the bales as dirty or clean. I always thought it meant the condition of the paper. Later, I learned that a dirty bale contained the body of a mob victim. If it was clean, it was just regular paper.

I was fifteen and it was 1949. I remember Irish Joe, thin, blond, blue-eyed, because he offered me a job riding with him and gathering newsprint and cardboard. I didn't need the money but riding in a truck, at fifteen, with a grown-up guy was high living for me. Joe didn't work every day during the summer because he had another job. He trucked small items from the docks to warehouses within the city. Usually we worked Thursday through Saturday.

Joe needed a permit to pick up paper products. The license was expensive, costing one hundred dollars and only granting the right to obtain paper within a single city. If one wanted to gather paper in a neighboring city, he had to get another license. So Joe had to spirit along the city lines, grab the booty quickly, and get out before the cops saw him working that area. That was where I came in.

We'd circle the block, looking for cop cars or some beat cop walking the streets. If the coast were clear, we'd sneak back. I'd hop off the rear of the truck, toss the paper and cardboard into the truck body and run back to sit in the cab. Joe and I always had a good laugh, and it made me feel great to know we had beaten the system. I guess it's a little like drinking under age. The minute one turned of legal age, alcohol just didn't have the same appeal. And I enjoyed gathering paper with Joe, but the real excitement was when we crossed the city lines.

There is another reason I remember Joe. He had a son called Daniel, but for some reason, Joe called him Megadootz. Now this was a five year old kid who had a vocabulary worse than any sailor or longshoremen I had ever met. The string of four-lettered words that this five year old could spew out would shame the toughest of the tough. Joe seemed to get a kick out of it too. I know we disagreed on that because I felt he should be reprimanding the kid, but it was not really my place to say anything because it wasn't my kid. The child could be reasonable enough if you didn't tease him about something. He was a bit stumpy for his age, very short hair, and ears that pushed into the side of his head and made it difficult to see them at all. He'd sit between Joe and me, and, every once in a while, his father would tease him and out would come a string of nasty words, none of which are contained in the Bible.

I often wondered what happened to the kid. Joe was Catholic so they probably sent him to a parochial school and I can just imagine the first time the nuns crossed him, and Megadootz had something to say. Back in those days, they were still allowed to punish a child physically if he got out of hand. The nuns in my school were not shy with the bar soap. Not that I ever had trouble with profanity. I only used it when I reverted to my Down Neck voice. Even the kids in my school weren't apt to use profanity. We were a pretty tame bunch back in those days.

I don't recall how long I worked with Joe, but working with him I was able to trace a lot of changes within the paper industry and within the mob.

I mentioned that there were two men I recalled who came to my grandfather's table. The second man, Don Messina, was totally unlike his brother-in-law, Dominick. The Don hailed from Roseland where he had a thirty room mansion set deep in the woods and surrounded by high brick fencing. The entrance ran through a quarter mile of pines on a winding driveway that led to the circular drive in front of his home. Unlike most homes, it was built of grey blocks and resembled a French or German church with its two stories and high spires. The windows were Victorian, the kind they put into Tudor homes, dark mahogany. Everything about the place spelled money, class, aristocracy. My grandfather brought me there as a child. I was astonished by the long, walnut handrail spiraling to the top of marble stairs and the vastness of the foyer. There must have been ten separate doorways leading out of that foyer. One of them led to the kitchen, and that is where the children were brought and fed. Afterwards, I was allowed to play in the rear garden which was large enough to house a fenced-in swimming pool, a garden maze, picnic tables, an outdoor bar and patio, and a fish pond. The area was fenced in by a high brick fence, so no one could sneak up and fire a shot.

Don Messina was not an affable man. His eyes were serious and business-like; his hair, wavy and closely curled. He was darker than most of the others, and he often ate sparsely and refused alcoholic beverage. Neither did he smoke. His body guard did not remain by the car, but stood very near him facing away so that the Don's back was vigilantly guarded. Incidentally, I should comment that the term Don did not always mean the head of a family. It was a term of respect also used for someone high up in the organization. Just as some people refer to a close friend as "uncle" or "aunt", the term Don meant 'sir', someone in authority and entitled to respect.

In later years, his youngest daughter, Rose Marie, often visited Dominick when the Don was inclined to slum in lower Newark. Unlike her father, she was friendly and docile. Rose Marie attended the best of private schools. I never knew what I fell in love with, her looks or her education. She had both, for Rose Marie was slender, almost willow-like, slightly taller than me, light brown hair, soft, beckoning eyes and a sultry voice. I didn't see her often but we saw each other often enough to spend hours talking while her family was upstairs visiting.

Sometimes the Don had to come looking for her, and, when he did, his looks at me were not inviting. I had the distinct impression that the Don had marital plans for his daughter, and they included no one from the lower end of Newark. I am not being boastful if I speculate that Rose Marie had an interest in me as well. I think she did. But our worlds were just too far apart.

I recall asking her to attend a school dance with me when I started driving. She wanted to go, but she knew her father would never consent. I think he may have said something to her about our relationship because our little talks seemed to end right about that time. I'd see her; her face would brighten, and she would hurry by to visit with her aunt and Dominick. She seldom came out, and, when she did, it was usually to get something from her father's car and, then, disappear into the dark hallway that led to Dominick's home.

I am sure that when Rose Marie was given permission to marry, her wedding and reception resembled the scene in *The Godfather*. I had not seen her for years. When I did, she had a small child she was holding by the hand. Our eyes met. She cast hers downwards and hurried by. I said hello to her. She turned and stared at me, and it was then I could see she was crying. It choked me up, but I had nothing to say. What could I say? Her father ordained her future, perhaps even selected the man she was to marry and messing in that kind of situation, and with that kind of man, would only bring me some concrete shoes.

Rose Marie was docile and loving, the kind of woman who accepts adversity and moves on. When I consider the shattered existence women have brought into my own life, I often wonder if things would have been different with Rose

Marie. Then, again, I recall that her father was a Don, and life might not have been so pleasant under his watchful eye.

Don Messina did not come from Alia, but he was Sicilian, and I am sure that whomever he selected for Rose Marie had his complete approval. It's not that he did not approve of me. In fact, I did not exist to him at all. He was not one of my grandfather's underlings, and he did not cow-tow to anyone. He was, as they say, the man.

And he was a man of unique financial abilities, a foresight that was almost legendary. Six months before Prohibition ended, he was already moving in political circles to engage in other enterprises. Like all the others, he made huge sums of money during Prohibition. And he knew how to invest it. He was not one of those who got caught short during the Depression. Even then, as a young man, he had wisdom and an uncanny knack of predicting the future. While many of his compatriots were investing in the stock market, Don Messina was investing in foreign companies, mostly those handling fuel and energy. When people were defaulting on their mortgage loans, Don Messina was purchasing properties from bankrupt banks and renting them out at low rentals. When the market was at its high, Don Messina was selling stock short and buying it back at lower prices. I never knew if he was just very intelligent or whether he knew how to fix things. He just had the Midas touch.

It was said that he was like some massive spider, spinning a web of influence and investments that reaped more and more money. Prior to the First World War, he began acquiring small paper mills and obtaining government contracts for paper supplies. The need expanded during the war itself. He was a strong supporter of Franklin Roosevelt and contributed catastrophic sums to his campaign. Again, the rumor had it that it was Don Messina's organization that arranged the assassination of Huey Long, the infamous Senator from Louisiana, and that it came about because Long was expanding his sphere of influence into other states and might actually challenge Roosevelt for the presidency. Whether or not there is truth to that rumor will never be resolved, but it would not have been beyond the pale of the Don.

Joe told me that during the World War II itself the price of paper reached one dollar and ten cents per hundred. He also told me that he would frequently unload his truck, douse the cardboard with a hose to wet it down, then stack the dry paper on top of it so the buyer wouldn't notice. He frequently increased his profit by cheating a little. That he could have ended up buried in his own wet coffin probably never occurred to him.

The government was the biggest customer of finished paper products for many years. They were not only the Don's largest customer, they were Joe's. That was when Joe saw an opportunity to work the system in his favor. He bought a second-hand, two-ton truck, purchased a license and began gathering paper. It was a difficult move for him to make. He had just moved to a more expensive apartment and had a wife and small child, but Joe was happy-go-lucky and willing to take the chance. People kept telling him that with the war over, the price of paper would drop. On the contrary, the price remained stable.

As Joe was building a small fortune, Don Messina embarked on an even more aggressive program. He began buying the smaller paper mills throughout the country. By the time he finished, there were few left large enough to compete with him for government contracts. In fact, few were left to compete in the general market. Raw paper was melted down into pulp and used to recycle the materials into new paper and cardboard. Although the timber companies were unrestricted in their cutting operations, recycling made sense from a financial point of view because the finished products could be sold for lower prices. Despite this fact, there were not many centers capable of turning the raw material into a finished product. There were not even many outlets where such raw material could be brought and packaged. There was little enough competition.

But the Don wanted no competition at all for what he had in mind. He artificially raised the price of paper. It wasn't based on the law of supply and demand. The price was based on attracting all the truckers into bringing their products to Messina's outlets and no where else. When I met Joe, mixed paper was selling for one dollar eighty per hundred and cardboard for two dollars and ten cents per hundred. Rather than dropping the price, Don Messina started cornering the paper market in 1939. He continued through World War II. By the time Joe and I were collecting paper, Don Messina had driven the price through the proverbial ceiling.

To Joe and me, these prices were a bonanza. If Joe made good money, he could afford to pay me a better wage, and, though I really had a separate income in the firecracker trade, the extra money did help. With his plethora of mills, Don Messina was in a position to take as much paper as the market could supply.

The prices continued to increase. His competitors could not match the prices he was paying because their purchases were based on the law of supply and demand. Messina had created a false demand, and he was drying up the paper supply. Thousands upon thousands of pounds of raw material accumulated in his warehouses and storage facilities. His supply of money seemed endless.

Those adversaries that attempted purchasing paper at his prices were soon bankrupt. They either closed or they sold out to the Don's offers of purchase. Those that refused to sell went into foreclosure, and the Don was able to purchase their facilities at foreclosure sales.

Once he had eliminated the competition, Don Messina simply pulled the plug and flooded the market with paper, killing off the last of his competition. The price of paper dropped overnight. One day we drove a load in and received two dollars and fifty cents per hundred for cardboard. The next day we brought in another load and were docketed at thirty-five cents per hundred. The day after, the Don's mill would not even take our load. All the other mills were in such poor financial condition that they couldn't buy the raw material even at the reduced price.

During World War II, the price of recycled paper rose dramatically. Timber and wood were needed for other purposes and pulp was in sparse supply. The Don lapped up the government contracts and supplied goods at extremely high prices. As the war wound to an end with the bombing of Hiroshima and Nagasaki, prices stabilized and fell. Don Messina, however, continued operating his paper mills, along with his other enterprises. So, as Don Messina rose in power and importance, jolly old Dominick rose in prestige along with him.

Every morning, I saw Dominick turn the corner and walk toward me. His wife had made him wear a white shirt and a black tie which she pulled up tight around his thick neck. He didn't mind the tie because black was a mourning symbol for his dead mother. But he did mind having it crushed up to his neck along with a tightly buttoned shirt. By the time he reached the corner of Pacific and Chestnut Streets, he had unloosened the top button and pulled the tie away from his neck. He made a comical picture with that slanted tie and open collar. I often thought that his wife pictured him some kind of executive heading to his office. In fact, Dominick only had a cubby hole where he had a small desk and chair. More often than not, he sat on a bale watching the trucks pull in and out. When business went slack, as it usually did between eleven a.m. and one p.m., he sauntered down to the corner luncheonette where he imbibed at least two submarine sandwiches, three or four bottles of soda and a quart of French vanilla ice cream.

It was Dominick's job to make certain that the weights were right and that truckers were treated fairly. It was not unknown for some of the Don's workers to shave the weight of materials being delivered, stack them up under an assumed company name and make payment to themselves as if they were the heads of those companies. Dominick could not afford to have people complaining to the higher-ups. If he caught a worker short changing a trucker, he fired him on the spot. No trial. No explanations. Just out.

The gist of the matter was that unhappy truckers would spread the word to other truckers. Feeling cheated, they might bring their loads to other mills. Although most of the mills were done for, there were new ones springing up. They were not troubling enough to cause the Don to drive them out of business, but he didn't want disgruntlement among his suppliers. Often, Dominick would take a trucker down to the luncheonette for lunch. It was his function to test the waters and make sure that the suppliers were satisfied with their treatment.

It was also Dominick's job to make sure the scales were tested and accurate. In the beginning days there were no state agencies to test the scales. That was a later invention of government as they found the need to make jobs for political workers. That he found a lot of favor with the drivers is without doubt. Every one liked Dominick. He had a nice way about him and probably the most endearing factor about him was that he lived to die a natural death, untouched by any of his mob activities. Of course, the Don could have intimidated the truckers to deal with his shops. Exploding trucks and cars was not a novelty back then but an implement of fear. Those who conducted the protection rackets knew well how to use the weapons of intimidation. But the Don insisted that the working man be treated well, especially if he were Italian.

Dominick was enterprising enough to start his own booking operation at the outlet on Chestnut Street. His brother-in-law knew of this, of course, but since it didn't affect his operations, he permitted Dominick to run his little business unimpeded. For Dominick, it was extra income. For the Don, it kept Dominick happy and self-sufficient.

What the Don apparently saw, that others did not, was the turmoil transcending the Far East, namely China, Korea, and Russia. Apparently the Communist nations wanted a unified Korea under the auspices of their Korean sympathizers. North Korea was, in fact, a rural and agrarian culture while South Korea was more industrial. I am not a historian so I do not understand all the intricacies of the political situation, but it surely would have been a feather in the communist cap if an agrarian culture could incorporate an industrial area into its sphere of influence. That the

Korean conflict was inspired by the Chinese and Russians is without doubt. I think that is why Truman fired Mac Arthur rather than let him fight past the thirty-eighth parallel, though I still believe the General was right to finish off the enemy while we were able.

The Korean conflict created a new demand for paper products and thus, the Don's insightful wisdom again prevailed as the war progressed. The price of paper again rose. Joe and I were there to reap the benefits. Lord knows what the government was paying for finished products, but one has to marvel at the business acumen of Don Messina. He was just uncanny in predicting market demands and needs.

For me, the Korean conflict had a different significance. I graduated St. James Grammar School in 1948 at the age of fourteen. One of my friends there, Lefty Brohen, a tough Irish kid of muscular vintage, joined the service probably within three years of our graduation. Lefty had pale blue eyes and dirty blond hair that hung over his forehead. I can still see him blowing out the left side of his mouth, trying to get the hair up off his face.

Lefty was a pretty good ball player. And he had a flair for boxing and the military. When he could, he always wore khaki jeans, though we were rarely allowed to dress in anything but what the nuns dictated. Lefty lived at home with his mom. I don't know what happened to his father. Someone said his parents were separated, but Lefty said his father was dead, killed in the war. I never knew much about them. I never saw where they lived. I do know that Lefty's mother didn't have a lot of money because his clothing had to last him the whole school year so he couldn't play a lot of games with us.

264 Russell A. Vassallo

Not long ago, as I was writing this, I realized that within five years of our graduation from St. James, Lefty had joined the service and had been killed in Korea. He was his mother's only child. The impact of this thought brought me to the realization that at age fourteen, one of us was only steps away from death. I mean, one minute we were kids just learning that the girls we had attended school with for eight years had grown into little women and had breasts and curves in the right place, and, before we had a chance to live, one of us was dead. Lefty had been a true patriot. He wasn't drafted; he joined. Lefty was one of those guys with a lot of patriotism. He loved his country, enough to die for it. I guess a lot of guys who ran to Canada wouldn't understand that kind of patriotism. We just had it then. Something about the waving flag set off a spark of emotion in us, like it did in Lefty, and we wanted to die for our country. My Uncle Sam, who was in the Second World War, told me General Patton once told the troops that nobody ever won a war dying for his country. Wars are won by making the other guy die for his country.

I had that kind of patriotism too. I guess it's just inherent in some people. Back then, in the 40s, we loved our country and were proud of her. When the Japs bombed Pearl Harbor, I was seven. I remember Roosevelt's speech. I remember wanting to join to fight for our country. The thought of a sneak attack on unsuspecting people angered every single American in the country. Kids like me scoured the neighborhood for scrap metal that could be used to make guns and planes and ships. We listened to news of the war on the radio, and we watched the newsreels in the movie houses. All the time the battles were going on, we were patiently waiting to turn seventeen so we could fight for our country. Even the games we played were patriotic. It wasn't cowboys and Indians anymore. We were fighting Nazis and Japs, blowing up ammo dumps and watching Duke Wayne and Randolph Scott lead men into battle.

I do not think we will ever see such patriotism again. I do not think we will win any more wars. We have grown weak and been divided by the left-over communists of the 50s, and they are still as determined to destroy us as they were back then. Today, of course, we call them Liberals, Left-Wingers, left of center. I have other names for them, the least of which are cowards, back-stabbers and anarchists. Those are the tamest of my names for them. They defile God, the flag, our sense of patriotism, our sense of morality and our beliefs in freedom. Even men like the Don were patriotic. He donated to War Bonds, bought a substantial number of them. He insisted that his men support the war effort by conserving gas and donating care packages to the war effort. If he saw a soldier, sailor or marine on the streets, that man got a first-class meal and a hand full of money to spend in town. If they wanted a woman, she was furnished. If the soldier and his girl needed a night out, the Don had a room for them.

The Don, of course, had other enterprises which sprang from the World War II. All materials were being diverted to the war effort. England was being bombed. They needed war materials as well as food and supplies. Even in America, it was difficult to get meat, butter, eggs, milk, tires, gasoline. We had ration stamps for the amount of our weekly gas supply. It was near impossible to get tires, and one either had them retreaded or recapped or purchased them from the black market. Tires on the black market were new tires. But some scammers cleaned the tires and sprayed them black, then re-cut the treads to make them look new. Needless to say, it didn't take long for the tires to blow out or wear down.

1932 VASSALLO FAMILY – 1932 Vassallo Family photograph. Although the Great Depression started in 1929, this photograph shows the degree of wealth of my grandfather's family circa 1932.

It was tougher to get black market gasoline. One had to have real connections within the mob. Since my grandfather was still alive, we seemed to be able to obtain more gasoline than our ration stamp allowed. I know my parents had a secret cache where they kept contraband foods that could not be purchased in the markets. Where they got the canned goods from is a matter of speculation. But I do not doubt that the Don had something to do with supply and demand.

Many of the Don's people engaged in private enterprise. Merchandise pilfered from factories making government goods often found their way into the market place. My aunt worked in a factory that made shaving and paint brushes for the armed services, and she often came home with extra items. If she could do that working for the Rubberset Company, others could do it at their factories.

So while the Don was closing down mills and controlling the price of paper products, he had also spread his tentacles into rationed items. There were rumors of huge warehouses full of tires, gasoline cans, oil, grease, eggs, ham, meat, dairy products, canned goods and the like. Even rubber heels could be obtained for a price. And the black market was not confined to the mob. My uncle served under General Patton as one of his medics, and he would frequently obtain goods from various sources and sell them to the French or the Dutch for escalated prices. In fact, he put himself through school with the funds he earned in the Army.

So while America was fighting a war on two fronts, the mobsters I knew were supplying goods to the public. I don't know if my grandfather was part of this operation, but we never seemed to want for anything. While others could not obtain meats and diary products, we had them. Nothing in our lives seemed to change. We still visited the farm. We still had large dinners for my grandfather's associates. Dominick still attended the meetings as well as Don Messina.

When I first saw Don Messina, he seemed inordinately young to hold such power, but I think his power sprang not so much from his army as from his wealth and intelligence. He was excellent at infiltrating the political landscape and sewing up all the connections. So when the public demanded crackdowns on certain areas of crime, his operations were discreetly untouched. And he was adroit at spotting financial trends and knew how to manipulate them to his own purpose. While banks were failing during the Depression, he was lobbying for the Federal program to prevent future failures. When passage of such a bill occurred, he began buying the buildings and equipment of the failed banks and starting them up again. Although there was nothing illegal in this kind of investment, the funds that supported these enterprises came from illegal betting operations, stolen booty, hijackings, fixed horse races, prostitution rings, and fraudulent documents for illegal immigrants.

From the latter, he drew dozens of loyal workers, dedicated to Don Messina because he had smuggled them into a country they could not enter without his aid. No matter what illegal business Don Messina established, his contingent of immigrants was there, not only to work for him, but to protect his interests. He commanded respect as well as loyalty. But if one of his soldiers faced a prison sentence, the soldier's family had nothing to fear. All their living expenses were paid by the Don. He educated their children because he recognized the need for professionals. Thus, while he was founding one business after another, he was also laying the groundwork for Italians to become lawyers, doctors, architects and others. Those who could not cotton to formal education were sent to vocational schools where they learned some skill. His mechanics sprang from the ranks of the children he had educated. His accountants found themselves with permanent work after their graduation from school and owing their degrees to his funding. Nor did he hesitate to encourage his people to trickle into the ranks of law enforcement. The Don did not leave a single stone unturned and yet, when he visited my grandfather's farm, he did not sit at the head of the table. On the contrary, he sat next to my grandfather as a sign of respect to the owner of the land. Only on neutral territory did he sit at the head of the table.

When my grandfather suffered his first stroke and his active life in the mob was finished, they sometimes used him as a mediator between warring families to resolve differences amicably. Because he was known as an honorable man, both trustworthy and dedicated to the family, even the most ambitious Mafioso were inclined to heed his advice. I recall once they met while I was visiting my grandfather. Four men sat at the living room table, somber, lightless men with anger and ambition written on their faces. As they talked, my grandfather listened. The dispute, it seemed, stemmed from a territorial claim over boundary lines, one man claiming he was entitled to it by right and the other claiming it by right of succession. Rosolino was able to recount the entire mob history of that particular area. He discussed the origin of the boundary lines and the men who agreed to them. He traced the lineage of each family and how they came to be involved in the rackets. He also traced the original ownership of that territory and how various negotiating sessions ended in confusion as to the proper ownership. When he had done, he asked for a map of the entire territory and proceeded, with a near-useless hand, to mark in the lines of ownership from the inception of the agreement to the present day. When he finished, each family agreed to revised lines, and the dispute was ended with no one gaining or losing financially.

It always seemed Don Messina entered our lives again after such a negotiating session. I suspect he merely came to thank my grandfather, perhaps even to reward him financially. Although my grandfather was disabled, he apparently still had some connection to the racketeering that went on. There is no way he could have supported his family without some kind of income, though he had amassed a good deal of money. Inflation must have made a dent in his fortunes. He still owned the farm which produced milk, but our family's financial destiny was to change dramatically after his death.

The farm he owned was in excess of four hundred acres. At the time of his first stroke, he owned more than one hundred and twenty-five cows, all good milk producing cattle. He produced milk for the Guernsey Company. I remember the huge metal cans in which the milk was stored. By four a.m. they were filled and set along the road for the milk company to collect. Smaller quantities were bottled and stored in cases which were also placed along the roadway in front of the farm.

When my grandfather died, my father was no longer able to assist at the farm, and my uncle had his own business. The farm was leased to a scummy local farmer who proceeded to milk more than the cows. He would take a good producing cow and exchange it for one of his own that was near slaughter. He pilfered some of the guns my grandfather had collected over the years. The goats disappeared. My pony was sold off. Most of the farm equipment seemed to degenerate faster than the laws of nature allow. It took some years before my uncle discerned why the farm income was decreasing with every passing year, but when he did, our position within the mob no longer existed. My uncle had never really been involved, and my father had given up his connection with the rackets to please an irritant wife.

In the end, my grandmother sold off parts of the farm when she needed money on which to live. I think she sold the last of it just before her death. Since she outlasted my grandfather by some twenty-five years, she must have been a frugal woman indeed. A law suit against the mendacious farmer failed for lack of evidence. It was fortunate for him that all this occurred after my grandfather's death. I do not think the matter would have been settled in a court of law had he been alive.

The only thing that saved my grandmother was the rising land values in the Basking Ridge area which became a very exclusive suburb of Morristown. After my grandmother's death, the State of New Jersey declared the farm a wetland and purchased it under the Green Acres Act. It now serves as a wildlife refuge for marsh birds. The well is still there, but it is locked to prevent people from drinking from it. The buildings are all gone. The screened pavilion that once furnished so many happy hours for my cousin and me was removed. There is no more roadway to the back paddock. The caretaker's house was torn down. All the bird pens are gone. The main dwelling with its red brick exterior and wrought iron porches was demolished.

I could only go there once to see what had become of it. All I recognized was the pump. It stuck up from the ground as if shorn of all its clothing. The brick basin built up around it, the one with the double sink where one could plug the hole between the sinks and watch the water rise, was also dismantled. The arbor where we saw so many important people and spent so many hours feasting and talking had rotted and disintegrated. If there was anything left at all, it was the stately oak that stood in the front yard. It looked sad and abandoned as if all the life had been drained from it. As I looked around at what once had been, I saw the devastation of uncaring men, and I lamented because a part of me was gone, too. It seemed sacrilegious to me that my grandfather's dream should be shorn of its meaning and left to wither.

Still, as I stood by where the arbor used to be, now overgrown with briars and weeds, I could not help but drift back to those idyllic Sunday afternoons. The men were always a great fascination to me. Watching my grandmother command her little band of helpers, seeing the endless supply of food lifted onto the table, listening to the animated voices of the men as they discussed business, all filled my cousin and me with a sense of importance, that something vital was occurring, almost history being made. We didn't then understand what it was, but we came to understand, down the road, when all of it was gone. To us, the farm was freedom and play. It was goats to ride and a pony and cart. It was ice cream visits in Morristown and lazing around the farm. It was rainy days in the pavilion. It was escaping the massive bull in the small paddock. It was stuffing a wooden peg into the hole between the sinks on the outside pump, filling one side with water and sailing little boats. It was standing on the bridge looking down at the dark water, wondering how deep it really was. It was watching fresh milk come down the pasteurizing pipes, catching it in a tin cup and enjoying the frothy, ice cold flavor of milk and fat. It was walking along the edge of the pump until I slipped and fell, incurring the scar on my chin that I still carry today. It was meeting the new visitors who always seemed to be coming. It was sitting under the shade of the arbor and, sometimes, plucking off some of the dark purple grapes that grew there.

We little understood who the men were or why they came there, anymore than we understood anything about the mysterious figure that walked the farm by night but was never seen during the day. We did understand that these men were there for more reasons than socializing. We did understand that the men stationed around the limousines were there to watch and to protect. It would be years before we understood that they assembled to discuss business and, sometimes, to discuss power. And more years before we understood the real nature of my grandfather's involvement. When we did learn, it was not a source of shame but one of pride. I was proud of my grandfather for surviving in a harsh land with all its prejudices and discriminations. It was hard understanding why Catholics were reviled, or Italians discriminated against. It was completely understandable why men such as my grandfather and Don Messina banded together to succeed in this new country.

When the Second World War broke out, the Mafia had its business interest, but it also played a major role in organizing resistance within Sicily. Without that cooperation thousands more American troops might have died taking the tiny stronghold off the coast of Italy. How did the American government treat us when the war was over? Just about as well as it treated the American Indians or the Branch Davidians at Waco, Texas. It broke its promises and double-crossed the men who had been instrumental in assisting them. Is it any wonder that the Sicilian has a deep distrust for government? Is it any wonder that they joined together to enact and enforce their own form of justice? Just as in the hills of Sicily where there was no law, they had to protect their own, and there is no honor as valued as the loyalty of a Sicilian. He will lay down his life to protect a friend.

All the voices are still now. All the men are dead. No longer does Lord Stirling Road carry the sleek, black limousines down to my grandfather's farm. No longer do they move in unison into the parking lots and onto the patches of grass firm enough to hold them. No longer do they sit, gesturing and arguing as the day wears on. They are now only distant and fading memories in the mind of a child . . . a child who is vastly proud of his family heritage and who is now grown to manhood. Only the memories remain. Only the hint of power remains. In the annals of time, we age and we become less than we ever were. We age. We grow old. Memories become jumbled. We become afraid. And it is then that we have just the memory of those fading times to stir us back to life.

∽ ∽ ∽ ∽ ∽

What did I know of the family "business"?

I know they engaged mostly in the numbers racket. The Feds called it the policy racket.

That my grandfather, my father and my Uncle John were involved in this is without question. They were among the originators in northern New Jersey, and I imagine it was prompted by the fact that Italians either reverted to their own money making ideas or they starved. Back then, most Italians were Catholics, and the large Protestant companies like Coke just did not hire Catholics. Either the Italians made bathtub gin or, when Prohibition ended, they fended for themselves in some other way.

Anyway, these were the rackets. No drugs. No murders. Well, maybe a business murder here and there. Just gambling without taxation. Then it was illegal because no taxes were paid. Today, the state has its hand in the till and everything is legal. It is strange how morality seems to change with new revenue. That the Mafia afforded work to ignorant and hungry people never seemed to influence the Government, but that was the kind of racket Grandpa Vassallo was in. He kept his sons working. And he helped a hell of a lot of people.

My dad seemed to have stayed in the rackets longer than Uncle John. With my grandfather dead in 1943, only my father kept contact with the powers that be. I know this because, on at least one occasion, he took me to the home of a very wealthy man, Don Santo. We had dinner with him one Sunday afternoon. My father was disappointed because I could not greet the man in Italian, and he expected me to learn the line in one day when he and my mother could not agree on how to speak the language. I don't know if mom was with us. I can't imagine her not going, and yet I do not remember her being there.

Whatever took place at the meeting I will never know. I only know it was very similar to the meetings my grandfather had on his farm. I also know that when the big boys like Luciano and Capone started moving into the rackets, the small rackets started getting very hazardous. Some of them wanted to contract out for murder, and others were already dabbling in drugs and prostitution. Grandpa Vassallo wanted none of this, and he was respected well enough to be permitted to retire with dignity and his small operation in Newark was left untouched. When he suffered his third stroke, he retired from the entire operation. My dad continued working for those who took over.

I remember every Sunday afternoon we would take a ride out to Elizabeth, N.J. My father would go into a small, drab-looking house, stay a while and come out. He went in with a bag and came out with a leather pouch. He never spoke in front of the children so we never knew what was in the bag—not until later. In those days children really were seen and not heard so you did not question your parents the way children do today.

On one Sunday, we were making our usual run when my father noticed a black, two-door sedan tailing him. There were two men sitting in it, and the sedan pulled in front of

TONY AND PHILOMENA

**My father and mother,
Anthony and Philomena Vassallo,
in one of their happier times.**

us, neatly forcing us over to the curb. One of the men started getting out of the car.

My father shoved the bag into my mother's shaking hands and asked her to conceal it. She was so scared she stuffed it down along her seat where it would fall out if they opened her door. I grabbed it and jammed it down into my pants right under my testicles. The police made us follow them to their precinct where they searched my mother and father. There was a detective with me. He seemed friendly enough. I asked him if he wanted me to empty my pockets and he laughed, "Did I want to?"

So I emptied my pockets. "Could I go and pee?" He pointed the way. Sometimes I get the feeling they were just looking for a pay-off because the cops really were not very thorough. The bathroom had all the décor of a prison cell, concrete floors and cinderblock walls, windows with metal frames, scarred and faded tile over the sinks. Like most bathrooms, it stank of Lysol and urine. The stall doors were damaged so the locks could not be secured, and I spent half the time relieving myself and the other half, keeping the door from hitting me in the rear. As I gazed down into the toilet water, it occurred to me that some very famous posteriors had probably sat on the very seat before me. I conjured the names of John Dillinger, Baby Face Nelson, Machine Gun Kelly, Clyde and Bonnie Barrow, even though none of them had ever been anywhere near Newark, N. J. I wondered how any of them would look sitting on a toilet, but since I had never seen pictures of any of them (other than movie actors), it was difficult to envision. Now, years later, I realize that I was a unique person to have drummed up such a thought. Years later when I tried cases, I asked a theatrical actor how he dealt with opening night. He told me to imagine the audience sitting on a toilet seat with a bucket over their heads. I had to keep from laughing the first time I tried a case, but I have to admit it worked. I saw the jury sitting on a toilet, pants down around their knees, and buckets over their heads. I found myself staring into their eyes, pleading with them, romancing them with my soul, tearing up just at the right moment. Perhaps it's why I won ninety-two per cent of my trials and lost very few appeals. All from an inane suggestion that aided me in overcoming my fears of facing people. But that was years later, beyond the purview of an ten year old boy, beyond the comprehensions of a man to predict his destiny.

When I finished urinating, I peered out into the deserted bathroom, then tore the betting slips into small pieces and flushed them down the toilet. Some of them clung to the sides of the toilet and I flushed again. To make it sound as if there were more than one person in the toilet, I changed stalls and flushed more down the bowl. I still had the bag to contend with, and that was much too large to flush away. I tossed the bag out an open window.

I really felt quite proud of myself, but it was hard concealing my emotions when the detective looked at me. I gave the most innocent, child-like smile I could and sat across from him again. He was completing a form of some kind and occasionally looked at me as if grinning secretly because he knew something I didn't. I squirmed. He grinned. Suddenly, I felt like confessing everything, even the dirtiest thoughts I ever had.

I asked if they had a water fountain, and he pointed to a corner of the squad room. It severed the tension. The squad room itself was laid out with metal desks, linoleum floors and oaken chairs that wheeled squeekingly away when pushed. Each desk had a telephone and a typewriter, a dingy lamp, scads of loose papers spread out like stepping stones, ashtrays smothered with stale cigarettes to compliment the dull grey finish that had once been shiny and new. Most of the desks were either dented or scratched and resembled something you would see in a second hand shop—a very second hand shop. I wondered how anyone could work in such an environment. The swinging overhead lamps were hardly bright enough to see when night enveloped the outside. It could easily have been a crypt where the corpses of living men were buried in an occupation that sealed them into an interminable fate.

I stood on my toes, trying to reach the fountain. Being short was no prize, and I swore as the water drizzled down my chin or spurted up my nose. I didn't really want the water anyway. It was just a diversion.

When I got back, my mother was standing there waiting for me, her face sallow and drawn. All they did was ask her a few questions, and she looked like death warmed over. Eventually, they let us go. My father asked my mother what she did with the slips. She told him she slipped them under the seat. I volunteered that I took them from under the seat. The cops had searched the car while we were there. When I told my father what I had done, he seemed very proud of me... mother, of course, thought I was becoming a hooligan, and the numbers racket was a bad influence on me. At ten, the Sicilian law of helping one another and protecting the family was already ingrained in me, so much so, that I destroyed evidence and protected my father. My mother had been shaking and pale during the entire episode. She chastised my father for praising me, said I would amount to nothing but a crook and slapped me for my good deed. In point of truth, I learned a lot from my small connection with the numbers racket. Mom didn't have the stomach for it but it was the only thing Dad ever succeeded at. Without that, he was destined to be broke and struggling the rest of his life. When we were alone and he could speak without my mother hounding him down, he patted me on the back for my fast thinking and told me I probably had saved him from going to jail. It became one of those solemn secrets Dad and I always kept, like sneaking into the cheap movie houses to watch cowboy movies and the time I caught him bringing flowers to a woman in St. Michael's Hospital. He seemed surprised to see me there and stammered that he was visiting a sick friend. I nodded and gave him a knowing smile, but I didn't have to tell him that my lips were sealed because he already knew that. We were partners. If he cheated on my mother, it was all right with me because I understood. Besides, there was the code of *Omerta*, the code of silence. It was ... and is ... as sacred to me now as it was then.

Years later, I was the last family member to see Dad alive. If mom felt anything, she really never showed it. Nor did she adhere to his wishes, which were to be buried in a pine box and laid in the ground. She didn't buy a pine box, and she laid him to rest in a stone vault high above the ground. I guess even in death he wasn't entitled to his last wishes. But in his hey day, when he was working the numbers and a member of the mob, Dad was quite the impressive man, so I wonder how mom wore him down until he was the weakened simp that he became. My aunt told me that once, when a certain young man was paying too much attention to her, my father went over to the boy, stuck his hand in his pocket and poked a finger against the material. "Stay away from my sister or you know what you get." It was funny because I know my dad never carried a gun. It just wasn't something he would do. But, seeing him in his pin-striped suit, with a finger poking out of the pocket like a gun, told me something about the man. Mobster or not, he was protecting his sister from the street scum. It worked. The guy never passed at my aunt again.

I don't think he was very high in the mob, more like a tag-a-long for my grandfather because he had been with him in his shoe business. Dad always told me that until he was twenty-nine, he handed his pay check over to my grandfather. I don't know if that was true or not. He seemed well-healed when mom married him. And he was always part of any meetings the gang had.

I will never know the extent of my grandfather's involvement with the mob. Two things have always troubled me with the family explanation that he was only a small time member of a local organization. For one thing, why would a local member of a very small organization be entrusted with the responsibility of hiding a notorious criminal such as Louis Lepke? Hell, the F.B.I. was looking for Lepke all over the country, and there he was, hiding on my grandfather's farm. Secondly, when my grandfather died, they did not lay him out in a funeral home. His casket was set up in the living room of his home, and people filed in to see him. In fact, they filed in for so long and in such numbers, that they had to hold him there for an extra two days. The only reason for such a private ceremony was because they didn't have the capacity to host all the people who would come to pay their last respects.

I remember the funeral well. Before they closed the casket, my father bent over the corpse and kissed him. Then, Dad lifted me up and held me so I, too, could kiss Grandpa. But he was not the same warm, loving man I had known during my lifetime. He was cold and lifeless, and yet, even in death, there was an imposing aura about him. My grandmother was beside herself. In those days, when your spouse died, you died with him. Today, a spouse is buried and, in most instances, the widow is off with her boyfriend or her kids. They can't bury the guy fast enough before they "move on." Romance and loyalty are just dead; they are embalmed and buried. Nothing is remembered because today's younger generation has been fed a diet of looking out for number one. But there are still women with old-fashioned ideas. They don't dress in black, but they never marry again and, in their hearts, the only picture is of one man and one man only. I am not being sarcastic, nor am I maligning women. I think of women as the vessels of life and humanity and I respect them deeply. I speak of a new generation. It used to be that children fought to have the parents move in with them. Today, they quarrel over the cheapest retirement home to shove the old bag in and the last thing they'd want to do is to give them a home. Italian annals are replete with stories of parents who signed over the homes to their children and were thrown out on the streets so I kid you not when I say there is a new kind of respect in the world.

Not long ago, one of my wife's relatives was already planning what retirement home my wife should go into. I'm not even in my grave and the family is thinking that far ahead. Just warms my toes to know I'm in the way. Shouldn't I have the privilege of living out my life without someone selecting a retirement home for my widow? Well, perhaps I've lived too long. That's one problem most of my dead friends did not have. They didn't get so old that their family argued over where to bury them. The Family buried them in definite locations.

My grandfather died with nobility and purpose. Not gunned down or executed by the Mob. A gas leak developed in the kitchen stove, and my grandmother was overcome by the fumes. At that time grandpa was recovering from a stroke and suffering with severe diabetes. When he saw her faint, he lifted a heavy oaken chair and heaved it through the window. The window shattered admitting air into the room, and he dragged my grandmother outside. But the excitement overcame him, and he suffered a massive coronary. I saw him lying on the sidewalk, my father standing next to him. I never saw him alive again. At that time he motioned the diamond ring to my father. He could not speak. He was paralyzed. My dad gave the ring to me, telling me grandpa intended it for me. I still have it. There are other versions of his death in the family, but those versions come from people who were not actually present when he died. I peeked out the living room window and saw him lying on the ground. There was no reason for him to be outside because he had been disabled by his strokes. It was not likely he would be dying on a concrete sidewalk unless he had to be moved out of the house.

That my grandmother loved him is without parallel. She mourned his death until the day of her own death. It was seldom she wore anything but black. When she spoke of him, it was as though he were still alive. She instilled a sense of pride in me, pride that he was my grandfather, pride that I had to make something of myself, to make him proud, to carry his name well. And when the guys were going off on a caper to steal copper, I not only had the mobsters making sure I stayed straight, I had my grandmother as well.

I recall that once, after her death, a woman was walking down the street. As she passed, she stared at me, studying me as if I were under a microscope. She was tall and stately, perhaps in her forties, dirty blond hair and cream complexion. She never hesitated a single step, but stepped toward me as she passed:

"You have a grey-haired protector," she said. I nodded. "Yes, it's my grandmother. She watches over me," I said and pointed my head skyward. As the years have gone by, I admit Grandma has had a full time job. Auto accidents, near-drowning, bridges collapsing under my tractor, thrown twice by horses, once with busted hip and ribs and the second time with those injuries plus a punctured lung.

The internal details of my father's involvement in the mob were not something my mother cared to discuss. Her dreams of high society shattered by the illusion of reality, she had no recourse but to pretend something that did not exist. She spent her entire life, seeking to climb socially, only to wind up in misery and as a very common woman. Years earlier, I asked her for more details about the family business. Reluctantly, my mom finally offered some information on the Mob activities. Her version is that during the economic depression, the City of Newark was beginning to fail and a mayor called Bill Moran wanted to save the city from failing. It's hard for me to believe any politician doing anything for the city without something to gain. Anyway, Moran supposedly contacted the Italian government and asked if they would send the weekly lottery numbers to Newark. He calculated that if people could play the lottery and win money, they would be able to afford taxes and to spend it in the Newark businesses. There may be some truth in this since the police seldom bothered the local racketeers, and most raids occurred only after Moran lost his position as mayor. But I rather think the connection had nothing to do with Mayor Moran. He might well have been on the pad with the associates who established the rackets, but I do not think he originated it. It is more likely that my grandfather was not doing well financially in New Orleans and moved to Newark to take advantage of his Mafia connections.

Paisani (compatriots) who had also come from Alia or other parts of Sicily saw an opportunity in the North that was not present in Louisiana at that time. They migrated to New Jersey and persuaded my grandfather to come with them. I am sure that Sal Cortese, his brother-in-law, had a hand in persuading him or he would never have made such a move. But coming there when he did, he would have been on the ground floor of the numbers racket as well as some bootlegging.

By the time Prohibition was in effect he would have already been established in New Jersey and purchased property on Chestnut Street. True, he operated a small shoemaker shop on Hill Street and then purchased a larger one on Broad Street and made shoes for a number of famous people. My father was in his 20s at that point and worked in the shop. When my grandfather sold the shop and moved entirely into the rackets, he took his two sons, Tony and Johnny, with him and gave them jobs. That my father was never able to succeed at anything after that indicates that my grandfather well knew his son's limitations and was providing for him. Johnny was able to establish his own legitimate business selling appliances. But my dad first tried a partnership in a leather factory that contracted with the Navy to produce goods. When the Second World War ended, he tried purchasing a confectionery store and lost his entire investment. He then tried another location and failed at that as well. With the last of his money, he invested in a carpeting business with a Jewish partner. When the business failed because of changing economics in Newark, the last of his fortune was gone. He studied radiology and worked the remainder of his life at the Newark City Dispensary taking x-rays, but he was never able to accumulate the fortune he once held.

That fortune kept my mother in diamonds and furs for many years, but Dad's repeated failures eventually brought her down to the status of a peasant. Only while my grandfather lived did the Vassallo family enjoy wealth and status.

I do know that my grandfather, as well as my father, held very strict rules of accountability. Loyalty was foremost. A man who was loyal would not betray you and gun you down. So fealty was as imposing as it was in feudal days when lords commanded the loyalty of their subjects. The concept might even have descended from feudal times. And the law of *omerta*, which is now so violated by the more modern Mob affiliates, was strictly adhered to. Today, it is given homage only in the gangs that are sweeping our nation as a result of illegal immigration. There was a time when the wives of such

SHOEMAKER SHOP – **The Shoemaker shop first opened by my grandfather. My father stands in the forefront as he had learned the trade from my grandfather.**

men risked jail rather than disclose any facts and, sadly, I would not risk my life or my freedom on the loyalty of any person presently in my life. Loyalty and respect are just not part of today's world, and I often long for the days when that code was a vibrant part of my life. Even now, when I think of it, I could have had a man's life simply for the asking. These days, I'm lucky if I can win an argument with my grandchildren.

I have seen this rule carried to ludicrous extremes in a drug case involving New York/New Jersey mobsters. A certain don could easily have saved himself and his associates from charges of drug dealing simply by testifying and clearing his name. He had more than enough proof and was so benignly charming and persuasive, he could easily have swayed a jury. Yet, he refused to testify, refused to defend himself or to permit any of his family to testify.

Conviction was easy in light of this ridiculous application of the code of silence. But it was his code. He died in prison. His power might have been on the wane, but he was a man of honor to the end.

This was a man who ordered the deaths of those who opposed him or sought to topple his reign. Still, the power of the mob is awesome. They control every facet of their business. It is difficult to understand just how powerful my grandfather was. I saw many people come to him for aid and, though they spoke in Italian, it was obvious they were asking favors. Strange men often came to the house on Chestnut Street and spent long hours speaking with him. I was present during some of these discussions that made it clear my grandfather was in charge. I don't know that he ever refused anyone. He was a man with a special quality. He stood out in a crowd. He never lost his individuality. It was obvious he was a man who controlled his own destiny.

Yet, he was patriotic and supportive of America. He learned to read and write in English, became an American citizen, insisted that my grandmother also obtain citizenship. He voted. He funded community projects. He donated to worthy causes. He doled out money for the less fortunate. Because of my grandfather, I had access to men I never would have known. The power of life and death is an awesome one, especially in the hands of ruthless men. And yet, they seemed so innocuous, so tame. Sometimes it seemed my grandfather's power reached from beyond the grave.

I am sure the history will be hidden. My children and grandchildren will never know what really went on. Like myself, they can only scrape together bits and pieces. No one will ever know the truth. Some of this I witnessed. Some, my father filled in. The bits and pieces fade with age. Some things do not fade.

In my teens I drove to St. Joseph's Church which was inhabited by the Franciscan monks. Often I saw this young girl staring at me. She was not especially attractive so I paid little attention to her. Later when she had become a famous singing star, she denied her birth origin of Newark and claimed to be from some neighboring suburb but she was from Newark. My sister knew her and told me she had a crush on me. I had no interest in her so I just never pursued her. At the time she seemed somewhat stunted with course features and far too many cosmetics. Yet, she became a fairly prominent singer and movie star. I might have ended in Hollywood if I had. Who knows?

It is not public knowledge that a young attorney with a very famous singer in the family was shot and killed because the mob believed he was giving information to the Prosecutor. Their scam was a simple one, involving a banker, bank lawyer, title agent, contractor and a dummy purchaser. The object was to obtain a mortgage far in excess of the value of a particular property. Once the money was obtained, the purchaser went into default. The bank foreclosed and found the buyer to have disappeared, and none of the assets he alleged on his original mortgage application. The property would be sold at foreclosure and a racketeer would purchase it for cash at a much reduced price. The property was then sold at a handsome profit in addition to the original mortgage money the bank advanced. It was not uncommon to reap a profit of half million dollars on the deal, and everyone cut a piece of the pie.

One may ask why the auditors did not pick up such a large amount almost immediately, but the fact is that banks have large and numerous transactions, and, while the auditor may know two or three million is missing, it's another thing to find out where. I am sure that today the banks have streamlined their auditing techniques with the use of computers, but I recall that once a six thousand dollar credit showed up in my attorney trust account, and I could find no record of any such deposit. It took me months to give the money back to the bank because they didn't know where it came from in the first place. Because it was my attorney trust account, I had to strictly tally and explain every dime that was in that account. In the event of an audit by the bar association, I would have had to explain where that money came from and what client it belonged to. After months, the bank accepted the return of the six thousand dollars. I am not sure even now that they actually credited it to the proper account.

The mortgage scheme worked for years, a pyramid-type fraud which had several deals working at any given time. In other words, more than one property was involved but the cast of characters never changed. No mortgage payments were ever made.

Eventually the crooked bank attorney had to foreclose on the mortgages which he did individually so as not to arouse suspicion. The property would be sold at a Sheriff's sale. Members of the mob appeared at the sale, buttonholing prospective bidders and suggesting that they refrain from bidding or suffer the consequences. A mob plant would then purchase the home for far less than its value, and a new pyramid would commence with different players. They did this to bring the first series of transactions to an end. But it didn't end the scheme.

Unfortunately, things began to unravel when bank auditors finally sifted through thousands of financial transactions and traced the discrepancies to the purchase and sale of one particular house. This was joined with an investigation conducted by the Sheriff's office which noticed the same properties constantly being foreclosed. Eventually the law closed in on the most prominent players, but, since the money could not be traced to the mob, only the players who were visible actually suffered.

The bank itself was innocent as well since only the bank lawyer had any knowledge of the fraud. In truth, the County Prosecutor's office—which single-handedly accounted for more mob executions than the Valentine's Day Massacre—was not even after the lawyer—who faced disbarment at the very least and, perhaps, ten years in the hoosegow. No, they were after bigger fish because they suspected that the mob had an interest in the transaction. They were after some of the very men who, as body guards and young apprentices, had met at my grandfather's farm and eventually risen through the ranks.

So they arranged clandestine meetings with Joey Falcone either to gain information or intimidate him into revealing information. The intimidation stemmed from Joey's knowledge of mob policy, that anyone who appeared too cozy with the gendarme was a risk they could not afford. As a lawyer, Joey knew the code of ethics for the Bar Association, a lawyer must avoid even the appearance of impropriety. The code of the mob was even more restrictive than that. If they even sniffed the prospect of a stoolie, no matter how groundless the suspicion, someone suffered. So the County prosecutors knew exactly what kind of pressure they were bringing to bear when they detained such men for hours at a time. Often, the sessions would go into the morning hours. They meant it to give every indication to the mob that the victim was squealing his lungs out.

Joey may have been a lawyer, but he was also a member of an elite group of people, and he well knew the appearances that were being painted. On one hand, if he kept silent, no one would really know he was loyal. On the other hand, if he stooled, they would certainly know it was him. Still, the law of *omerta* took precedence and he remained loyal. As dutifully as possible, Joey met with the powers that be, explained his silence, argued and cajoled the bosses that he spoke no evil, that the prosecutor was setting him up. The scenario probably went something like this:

Joey: "We need to call a meeting. I need advice. They're making me look bad."

Voice: "Things are hot right now. Difficult to do. The product is not selling, and the merchants are afraid of a recession."

Joey: "I'm loyal to the cooperative. Haven't I always sold the product well? Given good advice? Let's think about the balance sheets here. How much did the company earn on my ideas? Millions? If you put bread into someone's mouth, don't they at least owe you a hearing before they fire you?"

Joey well knew that without conversation he had no chance at all to survive so he had to persuade them to at least meet with him.

Voice: "How does the company know this is not a set up? C'mon, Joey. It's a risk. If the competition has you wired or something, we would give up trade secrets, big trouble." The voice was like cold gravel. And Joey must have been sweating by then.

Joey: "So frisk me! If they find a wire, then fire me. If not, at least hear what I have to say. I'm telling you they're setting me up."

Voice : "Good point. I can't say yes or no. I'll meet with the Board of Directors and present your proposition. Play it level until you hear from me. And keep your mouth shut about our product."

Joey: "*Gratia. Bona Sera.*"

Voice: "*Chao.*"

Joey was boxed in. If he cooperated with the police, the mob would find him and execute him. Even the witness protection program was not infallible. The mob once planted one of their operatives in the F.B.I. center where she had access to the names and locations of all federal witnesses under their protection. Needless to say, this was discovered when witnesses started disappearing. No, Joey's only chance was to reason directly, persuade the Don he was loyal, perhaps even enlist his aid to abscond and later rejoin his family outside the country. And such conversations were routine, never directly alluding to the actual subject matter, but always speaking in the language of the underworld.

The Board of Directors had no need to meet. They only had need to persuade Joey he had a chance of convincing them. To send a hit man might really alert him that his life was in danger. If the hit failed, Joey was sure to ask for the witness protection program and start singing. To tell him to meet somewhere would equally alert him to danger. So several telephone conversations occurred in which Joey was permitted to "persuade" the company that a meeting would be fruitful, and, in each conversation, doubts were expressed that the company might be taking an unnecessary risk. In the end, Joey persuaded them he was trustworthy, and thus, thinking he was relatively safe, a late-night meeting was arranged which would occur in front of Joey's home with the Board convening in their limousine and Joey standing in the street next to the vehicle. Getting in was just not something he would have done at that point. He offered to submit to a search. They were condescending. No need for that among friends. He probably smelled a rat, but his only hope was to convince the mob he wasn't spilling to the cops. So he talked. He talked about the deals they had mustered. He talked about what the prosecutors were asking him to do. He submitted that his wife could verify the late telephone calls summoning him to their offices, the cops visiting the house and picking him up, the impromptu notes left in his mail box. He talked because his life was at stake, and he wouldn't even know if he succeeded—even if he walked away alive.

He must have seen a familiar face, one that caused him some relief because he trusted the face. They would not have sent a stranger or someone prone to rash action. On the contrary, they would send a negotiator, someone willing to listen, someone with whom Joey could reason. It had to be someone Joey knew was high enough in the organization to give him a pass. Such men always carried a gun, and they always had a body guard so the presence of another man might not necessarily have alarmed Joey. The conversation would drone on and on, ceasing only when the lights of a late night vehicle interrupted the flow of discussion. At first, the quiet arguments bantered back and forth, the visitor winning some points, Joey winning others. As each point accumulated in his favor, Joey indeed must have felt very smug. After all he was bargaining for his life, and he was winning.

Finally the conversation droned to an end.

Voice: "*Paisan*, how much time do you need to get out of the country?"

Joey: "I can be out of here by noon tomorrow. A few things I need to do. Draw some cash . . ."

Voice: "No, too risky. The Company will pay your expenses. Some place warm and sunny. Keep your mouth shut with your family. You can't let on the Company is sending you somewhere. I'll meet with you again tomorrow night, say nine p.m. right here. We'll make the arrangements. That's the safe way. The Board wants to use your ideas again. Likes the way you deal. Maybe things cool down, six months, a year; we get your family out and find you a new location. Got me? But hey, Joey, not a word to anybody. Understand."

Joey finally emitted the breath that had welled up inside him. But did he believe? Or did he believe because there was nothing else left to believe? As a lawyer, did he conceive that a risk undone is no risk at all, but a risk remaining is always a potential hazard? Those thoughts die with a man. They died with Joey. The car inched forward ever so slowly. Joey turned his back to the face he trusted. The sharp whump, whump, whump hammered the back of his head like a rivet, nudging him forward ever so slightly. The shock of it caused him to sag and slump, inch by inch, to his knees, then feeling the blood spurting from his head wounds, his eyes rolled back into his head, and he uttered a surprised cry. He swayed while on his knees, refusing to go down completely. To go down completely was to die. Then, whump, whump, whump, like soggy firecrackers igniting the night, and all the determination went out of Joey because then he knew the truth. The tiny bullets fragmented around in his brain, tearing vital capillaries and grey matter to shreds. The bullets would not even exit his head.

He leaned his shoulder into the ground, met the earth and then lay still. He lay still even as the headlines broadcasted that the brother of this famous movie star had been executed by the mob. And Joey was a risk undone. The little play acting was totally unnecessary, but a vital part of the hit. The mob needed an unsuspecting victim. Joey was standing next to the car, but in the street. To alert him to a problem might cause him to bolt and begin drawing attention to the people in the car. No, they wanted a victim both relaxed and unsuspecting. They wanted someone near enough to be hit without a commotion. No alarmed screams. No outcry identifying them. With Joey silenced, there was no one to give evidence because a similar meeting had been established with the title agent at or near the very same time. But they didn't find him in the streets. He simply disappeared. Some say he is buried in cement in a construction project. Others say he was laid to rest in quicksand in the New Jersey Meadows, though this was usually reserved for the honored dead. Still others say he became a floater in the Newark Bay and never surfaced. The title agent was, in fact, revealing information to the prosecutor and agreed to cop a plea in return for the information. Thus it was that he, too, became a risk undone. The mob has its own witness protection program. But the witnesses seldom survive.

The purchaser was an integral part of the mob and a vital connection to drugs being brought from Sicily to America. His role was more than just buying a house. Because he was an innocent dupe, he could be useful in other areas. He was spirited away to the land of sun and warmth where he remained for a time, returning long enough to the U.S. to be arrested in a sting called the Pizza Connection. He is still presently serving time for his indiscretion, though the territory opened by this gap in the Italian Mafia opened the floodgates to ruthless killers from the Haitian, Jamaican, Chinese and Russian mobs. They are infinitely more dangerous because they do not hesitate to kill politicians, police or rival competitors. Car trunks are stuffed full of their victims. Thus any hope of eliminating the drug trade by disenfranchising the Mafia has opened a wound of infinity. More brutal men with no code of honor, no rule against killing police or politicians or even family members of competition, now abound. For that, we can thank those men with the courage to eliminate the mob, but not the courage to face more dangerous foes of our national health and freedom.

The banker knew very little of the people involved. He suffered a short prison term. But he walked away with his life. The last I heard is that he was released early for good behavior and was selling used cars.

The farm from which these men sprang, the farm from which these men drew their roots was not so much a physical place as with my grandfather but a tradition rooted in the very history of Sicily itself. In the history of Sicily there were many conquering nations, the Phoenicians, the Romans, the Moors, the French, the Greeks, the Carthaginians and so on. Each invader, each conqueror took more and more of the land and worked the people to their detriment. As Sicilians evolved as a people, they learned that no matter who controlled the land, their plight was never a good one. Thus they learned to resolve their own differences without the intervention of government or the political controlling entity. And they learned the value of *omerta*, the law of silence, because speaking the truth could only gain them punishment or death. Just as nations conquered Sicily so, too, did the Mafia conquer Sicily by infiltrating every aspect of the economy and politics. Ruthless in its quest to achieve power, the Mafia executes those who stand in its way. A dead competitor is no competitor at all.

But if this was part of mob history, it was no part of my grandfather's small operation. He confined his activity to bootleg liquor and the numbers racket. His sense of honor and morality would not permit him to delve into prostitution, drugs or murder. I say this knowing that the men who heisted his diamond ring were the worse for wear but, if my father is to be believed, my grandfather only asked for an accommodation from some longshoremen who knew the culprits and nothing more. That they met their demise could not entirely be laid at the door step of my grandfather. In a sense, they tried and convicted themselves and earned their executions. On the other hand, he may have been involved in much more than the family ever revealed. It would be difficult for me to accept the fact that my family murdered people for financial gain. Still, brutal men did associate with my grandfather. I cannot deny that. And there was that musician who turned pale at the mere mention of my grandfather's name.

How did I view it? How do I view it today? I was always immensely proud that justice was served. The Irish were crooks. They stole. If they came to a bad end for stealing, it was a fate deserved. If my grandfather participated in that fate, I am not adverse to his role. With mob affiliations comes a power. Sometimes, it is the power of life and death.

Was this the grandfather that I knew? Mine was a grandfather who owned a large farm. He purchased a circus pony called Lucky for his two grandchildren. There were ten or even fifteen small goats that we often tried to ride. He was the grandfather who stood and watched the billy goat butt us in the behind when we bent down and that bucked us off when we tried riding him. He took us with him when he sharpened his eye by shooting crows and sparrows. We

ROSOLINO AND CONCETTA

Rosolino and Concetta Vassallo, my grandparents were widely known. My grandfather ran one end of the business, and my grandmother made up for it with her deep religious faith. Concetta never got used to the fact that she could move when her picture was being taken. She would stand absolutely rigid until the photo was taken, a throw-back to the days of old cameras where the slightest movement would blur the picture.

watched him when he fed his prized pheasants to be released during hunting season. He built us the screen pavilion in which we played and especially enjoyed during rainy days because it was ours, and we were free of adults there. He drove us into Morristown in a pony cart to see movies and enjoy ice cream. He filled the room with laughter at our antics. When my cousin and I painted the roof of his brand new convertible, he did not punish us but the uncle who left the paint unsealed.

He was as mischievous as a child and a titan in business. And never did he raise his voice or a hand to either me or my cousin. But he had no problem slamming his fist down on the oaken table to enforce his rule of law. He once slammed the table so hard he chipped off a piece of his five carat diamond ring. It had to be recut and is now 3.04 carats.

My grandmother Vassallo was as religious as my grandfather was irreligious. She had a small room in which she maintained an alter with a crucifix and statue of the Blessed Virgin Mary. Two candles adorned the dresser, one on each side. She'd light these when she prayed. Her faith was great. Each morning, she arose at five a.m. and walked eight blocks to Mass at Saint James Roman Catholic Church. She did this well into her eighties even though it was not an easy walk. This four-foot-eleven woman had an interesting history in her own right. Her father, Giovanni Cortese, and mother, Guiseppa Scalfani, had at least eight children. Concetta was the youngest. When Concetta was approximately eleven years old, Giovanni went to the court in Termini Immerse, Sicily, and filed papers asking to have his name changed from Cortese to Esposito.

When the children ventured into the United States, they assumed the name Cortese. But when Rosolino Vassallo married Concetta in Alia, he had to marry her as an Esposito as that was officially her name. The name Esposito means "exposure" which can roughly be translated into "orphan." Every year, the small villages would gather all the children who had been orphaned or who were illegitimate. They were parceled out to families that would then care for them.

I am not sure exactly what occurred, but at some point in time, Giovanni petitioned the court to have the name change. He took the name Esposito and abandoned the name Cortese, though all records in the United States pertaining to my grandmother show she always used the latter name as did her brother, Sal Cortese. My assumption is that to be an "Esposito" was a source of shame. It literally meant you were a street child. Such name changes were not unusual in Italy or Sicily, but why change from Cortese to the more common name, Esposito.

Concetta did not enter the clergy as did her brother and sister. One of them became a priest; the other, a nun. In fact, she had to use her maiden name when traveling because the Italian authorities required it. When she booked passage with my grandfather to come to America, she traveled under the name Esposito, her legal name.

When my wife researched the record and discovered the name change, she was at a loss to explain my great-grandfather's actions. Such an action at that time in history simply wasn't done, much less to take the name of a street waif or orphan. I conjecture that a rift developed within the Cortese family, and my great-grandfather broke with them. This is not unheard of in Sicilian lore so it's entirely possible that this is what occurred. In relinquishing the name Cortese and taking the name of Esposito, my great-grandfather intended an insult to the Cortese patriarch. He was simply thumbing his nose at the family who had raised him, but why, we will probably never know. Knowing the Sicilian mind as I do, there can be no other explanation. Sicilians are very proud of their heritage and their names. They do not abandon either lightly.

I have to assume that my grandmother remained friendly with the Cortese family even after her father broke off relations. I say this because she simply got along with everyone. She wasn't just religious in faith. She practiced her religion with enormous patience and love.

In later years, I stopped by to confide in my grandmother that I was divorcing my wife, Angela. She hugged me for having been admitted to the New Jersey Bar and told me she was proud of me, even though I had been away from the law for ten years, and I passed the examination on the first try. She wanted to congratulate me on being admitted to the NJ Bar Association as it was my grandfather's dream—and hers—that the grandchildren amount to something. This was especially true of the grandsons as the girls were simply expected to marry and have children. I recall that she took time from her Italian soap operas and *Il Progresso*, her Italian newspaper, and gave me a vigorous hug, much more robust than one would expect from such a tiny woman. She then dug in her small purse and unfolded two one dollar bills, handed them to me, and said: "Who pays me respect, gets. Who no pay me respect, no get." It was her way.

We sat together for a long time, discussing the reasons for my divorce. I thought, being the strict Catholic she was, that I was in for a drubbing. Instead, she held my hand and told me she would pray for me. And then, she confided in me that she had never thought Angela was the right woman for me. It shocked me. I felt so close to her then I wanted to ask more about the family business. I knew so little.

"Grandma," I asked, "how did you feel about grandpa's business?"

"He worka hard, you grandfather." She pitched this in that soprano tone that was always hers. "It's no easy maka shoes and boots, but he do. We have seventeen children, but only Tony, Josie, Johnny and Virginia survive." She turned and faced a young girl's picture on the wall. "You Aunt Francis. . . . This one," pointing to the picture, "she die in a fire." Then looking out the window, she said: "Nancy, she's a little girl. She ride on the vegetable wagon and da Irish kid, he throw a stone and hit her head. She suffer for three days. Then, she die. God rest her soul. I pray for her every day."

"I don't mean the shoe business. I mean, you know, his other business."

She shrugged. "He do what he have to do to feed his family. Da children they have to eat. He maka money and he feed us. He was a good husband."

"I know," I said, touching the picture on the wall and tracing the gold-toned frame around it. Francis wasn't especially good looking, but I have never forgotten her face. "But I mean the family business."

"The family was his a business."

"But you know, he had to . . . ah . . . hurt people, sometime."

"He no hurt a nobody," she shot defensively. "When we come a here to dis a country, no work, no job. He maka shoes, but the Irish cops, they wanna da pay or dey break windows. Pretty soon, you grandfather get disgust. He calla my brother, Sal, in Newark. He tell you grandfather to come. He find work. So we move. I don't know what he do. He no hurt nobody."

No matter how I plied her, she would never say more.

The public hears of mob executions and regards them with shock and fear, but when we heard of mob executions, we understood there were reasons that made the killing necessary. If you were Italian and someone disappeared or was executed, you were a mobster. If someone shot himself and then walked to the park to lie down and die, you were President and not a mobster, though I venture that the same forces which perform the executions, also elect presidents. I do not condone the Mafia or justify their actions. I merely understand these actions and see them as the Liberals see everything else, with shades of gray. If there is no longer any morality in marriage or in the priesthood or religion, what is worse: a killer who kills to protect his business interests or a zealot who rails against the morality we have known since time immemorial? The Mafia corrupts power and bends it to its own will. They are no different than any other men in power. If one is inclined to condemn them for mob executions, one should also consider such things as the Waco massacre by government officials or Ruby Ridge where a cold-blooded federal agent shot and killed a woman holding an infant child ... and was later awarded a medal. No less than the United States Attorney General ordered the mass execution of Branch Davidians. How can anyone say that one murder is better or worse than any other? Murder is murder, whether it's for business or for politics. But if I had my personal choice, I'd say there are more Mafioso in Heaven than politicians.

But the immoral, they corrupt the soul, the very life blood of existence itself. And therefore who is the worst criminal, he who corrupts the mind and body or he who corrupts the soul? At least the Mafia is straightforward, and its aims are open and understandable. But those who corrupt a way of life, the morality of man, through their insidious wearing away of the stone, those who make a mockery of democracy, they have no souls and therefore no salvation. And those who choose to represent the people and do their own will are more despicable than the worst murderer.

Chapter Four

◆

The Demise of the King

The streets are hard, the streets are cold
Endless conflict, bitter and bold;
Seek out a friend
Seek him, be kind
But never, ever leave an
Enemy behind.

Trixie King could well have been described as Dapper Dan. He literally glittered as he walked. His dress was casual but elegant, sporting Havana, open-collared shirts, sterling white trousers and brown and white oxford shoes. Everything was neatly starched and crisply creased so he glittered when he paraded along the sidewalks. I never knew if he was called King because that was his name or because it was the manner in which he surveyed his domain. He wore more diamonds than his wife, exhibiting a three-and-one-half-carat diamond ring on his left pinkie, a diamond studded wrist watch, a gold bracelet around his right wrist dotted with diamond chips and with T. K. engraved on the back plate. He left no doubt as to who he was, nor did he leave any doubt as to what he was. If anyone were ignorant of that fact, they had but to look at his array of automobiles which included a 1950 Cadillac, a 1949 Chrysler New Yorker and a Cadillac limousine. If anyone doubted his affiliation, they had only to consider that he never worked at a trade.

And yet, his dwelling was unimpressive, as he lived in a non-descript tenement-style house in lower Newark, with plain exterior and faded red brick steps. Most of the area, in fact, was mixed residential and light industrial, with homes stashed covertly between warehouses, converted livery stables, grocery stores and bakeries. The houses crammed together like frightened children huddling against the cold. Garages came at a premium when they could be found, and most vehicles enjoyed street parking, with some even territorially cordoning off their spaces with garbage cans and wooden horses. More than one range war began, not over the stealing of cattle, but the pilfering of a coveted parking space. The rule, however, did not apply to Trixie. His space was inviolate, and he carefully protected his space and his car as he did himself.

Nor was he any less impressive than his vehicles for Trixie was just short of 5'8", muscular and trim, square face with a rather prominent Roman nose. His eyes were so inset that it was difficult to see what color they were, but they were brown and somewhat somber. He possessed a manner of looking at someone with a smile on his face while his eyes were narrowing into the gloom of one who is plotting something evil and sinister.

Trixie carried himself like royalty. Not just with his mob friends or his underlings but with his family, Maria and two boys, both of whom walked in his shadow and one of whom aspired to be much like his father. The other, alas, was wimpy and a disgrace to Trixie. The older boy often demonstrated his disdain by slapping the younger boy soundly on the nape of his neck. Anthony had his father's Roman nose, but his mother's dark brown hair and rapier-like features. She was a beautiful woman, so lovely that even in a house dress, she outshone the other neighborhood women. She disassociated herself from them and carried herself with the same dignity and aristocracy that the King did. After all, she was married to royalty. Not that the King's sampling of his whorehouse wares did not spur deep and resentful arguments, but Maria was discreet enough not to discuss such events in front of others.

Anthony, or Tony, was not discreet at all. He openly bragged of his father's notoriety and boxing skills and occasionally got to drive his father's Cadillac. But, not often. Bobbie, on the other hand, was slight of build, narrow of face, with thin, dark brown hair and mournful eyes. He whispered rather than spoke, and one had the impression that something had gone far amiss in his hormone structure as he was more female than male. In later years, he became gay and left Newark for San Francisco. Unlike his seventeen year old brother, Bobbie's thirteen years had served to teach him nothing. His sole associate was a gargantuan young girl of twenty-one who toppled the scales at four hundred sixty pounds, wore pig tails and flashed seductive brown eyes at anyone who demonstrated the slightest interest in her at all. The story told of her is that her mother never sent her to the bakery on Sunday because Dollie would munch as she walked, and, by the time she made the slow and painful journey home, there was but a single jelly donut remaining. We could often hear her mother's shrill voice, shrieking out the window and shattering the Sunday silence: *Dolly, finuda jelly don!* (You finished the jelly donuts.) I spent more time dodging her advances than I did working or in school, for it was apparent she had a crush on me. I suspect it was my corpulent waist that attracted her, the implication being that a fat boy didn't have any better chance of finding a girl than Dollie had of finding a man.

What I recall most about her is that she dressed in button-down shirts and had coal black curls that hung down in ringlets around her ears. She made her attempts at being sultry by speaking in low, intimate tones, and she used those large, brown eyes to flirt the language of love like a snake enticing a bird from a tree. To me, she was not hypnotic, but frightening. The thought of loving such a woman scared me to death. I once made the mistake of taking her for a ride in my 1938 Chevrolet. That particular model had a trunk that could only be reached by lifting the inside rear seat, uncovering a space where the spare tire and equipment was kept. If the lower seat were not level, the trunk could not be opened.

Dolly's weight was so great that she caused the seat to rise, jamming the seat back so that it could not be pulled open. We had to politely request that she sit on the other side so the seat would return to its original position. One did not antagonize Dolly for she had a choke hold that brought stars to the eyes and blood rushing to one's head. That she was closely associated with the King family was well known, and Mrs. King applauded the fact that her younger son had a friend he could relate to. Later, there occurred things between them that Mrs. King did not applaud, but by then, the King was dead, and she had no control over either of her children.

No matter what the King's family situation, it was always known when Trixie was leaving his home because an entourage of wife and children paraded out with him, sauntered up to the Cadillac, seeking last minute favors, entreating him for money, and dutifully kissed him good-bye. That he shuttered when kissed by his sons was common knowledge, but they utilized his frequent absences to enjoy the freedom his absence gave them. His wife, in particular, viewed his absence for business purposes as an excuse to tap him for funds he would not normally give. And he had no qualms about refusing except not wanting to be embarrassed in public; he dipped into his pocket, produced a well-padded roll of bills and peeled several off. He made such a display of this event that everyone near enough could see he was ripping off hundred dollar bills. Then, he rolled the car slowly forward, peering right and left to observe who had been watching all this and drove off to attend a business that kept him well into the hours of the morning.

Where he went and what he did was not a matter of public record. Trixie was a mobster. That was common knowledge. His pugilistic face illustrated that he had more than once defended himself. There are some who say he had a criminal record of various sorts, but such records were never available for confirmation. His interest lay primarily in the numbers racket, gambling and brothels, but he also dabbled in contraband and stolen goods. His main enterprise was as a bookie and a gambler. He did well at both. He was not part of my grandfather's clan, and I am not totally sure of which mob he belonged to, but he never worked and, yet, earned a comfortable living.

Kids who admired him often saw him with other men such as the Pistol and, on occasion, he visited top Mafia men living in the respectable suburbs of New Jersey. He offered the mob protection from prosecution primarily because he had grown up with most of the local police, knew who to tap with money and gifts, and established a powerful network of influential friends that were of use to the underworld. In a strict sense, he was not really Mafia, but was affiliated with them because he inspired bureaucrats, police and even judges to make legal determinations much to his favor or the favor of his friends. He did not have to make his "bones". He was never inducted into the society. He swore no oath of allegiance or *Omerta*. He did not attend meetings or conferences unless the subject matter was within his terrain. Still, he was one of them.

Privately, he engaged in gambling and booking, more particularly with longshoremen and others who frequented the Four Corners Tavern. In fact, it was the tavern where he held court, each day awaiting the arrival of some debtor or potential client or dispensing one of his toughs to persuade a reluctant patron that money loaned was money to be repaid. Vigorish is the life blood of the loan shark. So, if a mob guy loaned a hundred dollars, the vigorish (interest) was ten per cent or ten dollars per week.

Loan sharking was very profitable. I know from personal experience. In later years, one of my clients came and asked me for a loan of five hundred dollars, not for himself, but for a friend. Each week he delivered the sum of seventy-five dollars. When he made the seventh payment, I was aware that the repayment totaled more than the loan, but I assumed that the additional money was interest of some kind. When he came the following week with an additional seventy-five, making the total repayment six hundred dollars, I discussed the matter with him and understood, for the first time, that his friend was merely paying the interest and still owed me the original five hundred. Moreover, he confided that the friend was a Newark detective. In essence, John had backed me into a loan sharking operation with a Newark detective. I could see the headline: *Local attorney arrested for loan sharking.*

It is noteworthy that Trixie actually started out in life as a longshoreman with a penchant for boxing. He frequently bet on himself and won. On one occasion it was suggested by the mob that he suffer a fall in the sixth round. He did not. Not because he held any loyalty to honesty, but simply because their offer was worth far less money to him than winning the fight. Had it been otherwise he would have gladly thrown the battle. Two bruisers were assigned to meet him near a dark street and teach him his erroneous ways. Though never confirmed, rumor had it that Trixie met the bruisers and opened up on both of them with such a voracious lashing that flailed the two of them into wilted hulks. He then went after the local mob boss himself, redeemed himself by smashing the boss's face, and promptly invited any others to join the fray.

When a loyal bodyguard accepted his offer, Trixie invited him outside for a private discussion. There was a single gun shot, heard by all within the nightclub. There was little doubt in anyone's mind that Trixie had been put to rest. But he had not been. Not to be outdone and not being a complete fool, he then sought an audience with the Don himself, presented his case as an aggrieved victim of Italian descent and suggested to the Don that he could be of greater service alive than dead. He was assigned to the local boss whose face he had indeed disfigured but instead of hard feelings, he earned such respect, even from the boss he had beaten, that he was enlisted as an aide, a runner and earned good wages. From that point, he ventured into one business after another. His stevedore friends pilfered goods right from the very ships they unloaded, with huge shipments accidentally dropping into the water. The currents, of course, were said to be so treacherous that none of the goods could be recovered, and thus the claims were submitted to the marine insurer whose only respite was to continually raise rates to compensate for the losses.

Remarkably, shortly after one of these catastrophic losses, merchandise began appearing in the parking lot of various shopping malls. Wrist watches, low cost jewelry, perfume and colognes, shaving lotions, bathing suits, suit and sport jackets, radios, television sets, stereos, imported cigars and wines, not to mention assorted guns and cases of ammunition. It was not infrequent that a small truck backed up to a location and sold hinds and quarters of fresh beef right off the rear of the truck. Nor was it unusual for a surreptitious vehicle to cruise the parking lot until a customer was found. The truck was opened. The prospective buyer selected from an assortment of revolvers, semi-autos, shortened shot guns and even an occasional machine gun. From each new enterprise, the Don reaped the benefit of high profits, and, while Trixie would never succeed to the throne, he was held in high esteem by ranking authority.

There is much speculation as to how an Italian came to be known as Trixie King. Many conjecture that he was so devious that he earned the name because of his chicanery. In truth, I don't know how he got the name Trixie or King. I know he was considered king of the gamblers. His luck was phenomenal. He had one of those lucky hands that could pull four aces with a single deuce sitting in his hand. He was a

FOUR CORNERS BAR – The Four Corner Tavern is now a restaurant but in 1953 it was a tavern with steps going up into the building.

moneymaker and the schemes he concocted produced income. Though not enlisted in the Mafia, he was their golden idol. And he was the idol of every kid who saw him.

It seemed Trixie was an inescapable part of the landscape, as if he had always been there, like God, and would never perish. Though in his 40s, he dominated his family and his domain and he still used his fists liberally. Usually he displayed his boxing prowess in the Four Corners, displacing unruly drunks with a punch or two. There was nothing especially dramatic about the club. From the blackened exterior one could hardly surmise it was a drinking establishment. The interior was straight forward and unembellished, with a dark, oaken bar stretching the width of the rear. Near the left side, the bar curved into an opening where the bartender entered and exited with drinks destined for the tables that littered the interior. A few bar stools near the right side of the bar, not enough to prevent men from standing there for drinks. From the entranceway, one could view the bar, the tables and even the stools.

Nor was there anything especially appealing about the bar itself. It was neat and clean, counters behind it displayed both hard liquor and cordials and the usual taps for drawing beer from ice cold kegs. It was dim inside. A dimness that precludes light and mirth and merriment. It was a dimness that shadowed the business transactions of futile men etching profit and loss on each new scheme. And it was in the Four Corners where such business was done, by furtive, bold men who feared, not the lawful authority, but each other. To be a mark, to be taken by another in business was unpardonable. The lives and futures of people depended on what these men ruled. And like the old Roman Emperors they determined whether the gladiators lived or died. But they were not interested in politics. They were interested in profit. And when vacationing from the motives of profit, they enjoyed the helpless drunks that Trixie batted around the bar, solely for the enjoyment of his associates and to flatter his own ego. Boxing was a manly sport, and the mob guys enjoyed it.

On one such evening, he was shooting dice with several patrons, one of whom had a temper like an enraged water buffalo. Not only was the man drinking heavily, but he was obnoxious about losing heavily at the crap game. He openly accused the players of cheating him of his pay check. When things got out of hand, he accosted Trixie who promptly set him down with several shattering blows. The beaten man left in a rage, returned a short time later with a shotgun and proceeded to open fire on the remaining players. The King had left by that time, and the infuriated shooter stormed out into the streets looking for his enemy.

Like all such incidents, Trixie did not even file it away for future reference. He no more paid attention to the men he beat than he would to a penny on the ground. And when months elapsed with no retribution, the incident was far from his mind that Saturday when he joined several friends for drinks and cards at the Four Corners Tavern. Besides, Saturday was collection and payoff day. Losers had to pay for the bets Trixie booked during the week. Winners could collect their bets as soon after winning as they decided. Gamblers, being what they are, the winnings usually were parlayed, and the next week, they were the losers who had to pay.

Other bookies sometimes resorted to violent tactics to compel losers to pay their debts. This was not a problem Trixie had. He did not go after the gambler. Not as a rule. He went after some member of the family. A wife, a sister, a brother, sometimes even a adolescent child. Although the Don was not especially fond of Trixie tactics, he did respect his ability at collection. For that reason and for reasons of profit, Trixie was permitted to operate pretty much as he saw fit.

Zeke and I met at the Four Corners on weekends. It was our movie day when the pocket money I earned from selling firecrackers and the money he earned from shining shoes at the Club, which is what we called the Four Corners, coincided with double features at the Rialto Theater in lower Newark. Back then, thirty-five cents during the week and fifty cents on Sundays brought the News Reel, a cartoon or two, another chapter in the latest serial, and two full features. And, you could stay all day until the evening performances started.

So Zeke worked the Club because the men were flush from their weekly earnings and tipped well. The gambling winners were anxious to pass off their ill-gotten cash and lavished Zeke with bucks simply to impress the bookies who met there. Zeke usually did not need to work more than two hours and he had sufficient money to attend the movie and live for the oncoming week. But on that day, fate was to intervene and teach yet another lesson on how fragile, how very fragile, life really is.

As we entered the Club, Zeke with his shoeshine box in hand and me traipsing slowly behind him, Trixie stood at the bar. He motioned me to join him as he usually did when he saw me. He had known my grandfather, and he traded in my father's store. He had a fondness for me and enjoyed seeing me belly up to the bar for a birch beer. But his fondness was born of a respect that comes only with men who exhibit courage and I had done so by confronting his son, Anthony.

The incident involved a black Cocker Spaniel named Blackie whom I found wandering the streets of Down Neck Newark and promptly adopted. She was an affectionate dog, and, since childhood allergies had precluded me from owning animals, she was the first since the farm days. So I set her a place in the basement of my father's grocery store and made her as comfortable as possible. A few months later she rewarded me with ten puppies, but since that is not the point of this story, I will pass on. In any event, about two weeks after I adopted the dog, a friend advised me that Trixie's son, Tony, was making noises that I had stolen his dog. And it was further stated that he was "looking" for me, which meant there was to be a rumble between us.

Anthony was not especially brave, but he hung out with a dangerous crowd at a candy store called The Lair. This was not the name of the store. I think it was Chestnut Confectionery but it was called The Lair for obvious reasons. Tony's association there was not determined by his bravery but by his father's reputation. In other words, he was admitted because of his father's reputation and not for any accomplishments of his own.

Without a second thought, I drove to The Lair and barged into the womb of destruction. I called Tony outside and invited him to settle the issue of dog ownership right there and then. The dog had been running wild. No one claimed her. I did. Did he want to make something out of it? Some of his associates milled outside, watching the proceedings but, because Anthony was not really one of them, they chose to remain mute. So Tony cowered and declined ownership of the animal. I generously permitted him to retract his statements, and the issue died there. The dog stayed with me.

A week later, Trixie saw me coming out of my father's store and motioned me over with the command of authority that only such a one can have.

"You stole my kid's dog?" he queried, his eyes hard and unyielding.

"I found the dog running loose. It was on Malvern Street, sniffing for food. I asked around. Nobody claimed it. So I took it in. Anyway, Anthony and I talked about this, and we agreed I should take the dog."

"Bullshit," he barked. "It's my kid's dog. And you went to The Lair and called him out."

I hedged. "I went down to talk. He was calling me a thief. What would you do?"

"You called my kid out in front of a gang of his friends, right?"

"I guess that's right. I asked him if the dog was worth fighting over, and he said it wasn't. We shook hands and that was that."

Then, he broke into a grin and roughed my hair. "You got courage, kid. Any guy who calls another guy out on his home turf is tough. I respect that."

"Anthony just didn't think it was worth fighting over."

"You must be a foot shorter than Anthony, and he was afraid to take you on. Don't make excuses when you got guts, kid. Don't be sorry. That wimp Anthony of mine takes after his mother. No guts. He'll amount to nothin' I don't make him."

Then, his face relaxing, a slight smile creasing the corners of his mouth, he said: "You come see me anytime you need somethin'. Got me? Anytime."

I felt my heart beginning to beat again. Before that, I conjured up cement shoes, or quicksand pits at the Newark Bay or maybe a body full of machine gun bullets. My fear abated, and I knew I had the respect of an important man.

"I don't know. Maybe we could help each other," I said.

His faced furrowed but lightened into a smile. "What?"

"Well, I got this little business going. Fireworks. A friend has a contact at the port, but I have to rely on him to supply me. Sometimes he does. Sometimes he doesn't. I need a steady supply. I can sell all I can get from May through July, maybe even into August. We pay ten bucks a case for a thousand packs when I can get them. Maybe you could get me a steady contact."

He burst into laughter, solid laughter, not feigned. King didn't often laugh, at anything, but here was this twenty-year-old negotiating a deal with him for firecrackers.

"You're cutting out your partner. You little skunk, you got it all figured. You make a hundred per cent of the profit."

I blushed. The louse had me figured. I was cutting Del out of the picture and going on my own. Besides, Del had other interests. I could move his supply and still sell on my own without him knowing.

"Go down to Port Eleven and see Brownie. Tell him I sent you. Tell him if he does me this favor, he can forget the last marker."

He was as good as his word. He furnished me with a name and instructions to contact the man at a company depot on the docks. That man would supply me with whatever I wanted and whenever I wanted it, and I would pay him directly. Del was elated with my success, and it did raise my status with him since he understood then I had my own influential mob contacts. Del and I were not close friends. Not friends at all, in fact. He was my protection, and I was his supplier. We did business. It was to my advantage for him to know I had my own connections. It kept the wolf at bay. A business that was occasionally earning fifty to one hundred dollars per week expanded into earning three or even four hundred dollars per week. In time, I increased the price of firecrackers to as much as seventy-five cents per pack and raised our profit level even more. I can remember lending my father money when he was short. One of my aunts got married and couldn't pay for the bridal breakfast (they could not afford a reception). I dipped into my pocket and flashed the one hundred and thirty five dollars for the event. My father was stunned. My aunt was eternally grateful. So, there was power in having mob connections and in enjoying enterprise.

Thus, that Saturday, when I walked in, Trixie was standing with his back against the bar and his arms outstretched.

He leaned back over the bar. "Have a drink with me."

"Sure thing. But let me buy. I'm working"

He waved me off, then turned toward the door where a ruckus of some kind had developed. "No, kid. I'll pay the tab."

But the conversation did not continue for long. Not that day. In a mad burst, a tall, drunken, muscular man rushed into the bar, shotgun in hand, pointing it at Trixie. Since I was directly next to him, the scatter-gun would also take me as well as him. We were both stunned. I glanced at the stricken mobster expecting a miracle. His eyes were focusing on the double barrel shotgun, searching his recollection as to who would want him dead. To be sure, he had enemies but none within the mob. I waited for a miracle. There was none. Slowly, the man's features penetrated Trixie's mind. He recognized him. He was, in fact, the Pollock he punched down several times when the drunken man went on a rampage. And now, the Pollock was poking a double barrel shotgun, the most lethal of close range weapons, at Trixie's stomach. He was menacing Trixie, and there was nowhere for him to go.

It is said a man's life flashes before him at the moment of death. Mine didn't. I thought of my mother's words about hanging around social degenerates. I thought of how she would feel when they broke the news I had been gunned down as an innocent victim. I wondered how much pain a scatter-gun would cause on impact. I thought of all the rabbits, squirrels and pheasants I'd shot at my grandfather's farm. In a moment or two, I would know exactly how they felt when shot. I stared into the barrel of that shotgun, knowing that death could be a frozen moment away.

The Pole's eyes were cold, void. There was nothing but death in them. With the barrel of the shotgun, he motioned to me to move aside. When Trixie side-stepped with me, he held him with a movement of the gun. Trixie understood what he meant and froze. The Pollock motioned me further aside, never taking his eyes from the frightened man. And at that moment, I understood there were no brave men in the underworld. That they were as frightened of death as any other man. Trixie was sweating; his mouth was working as if he had palsy. His arms were still outstretched along the bar as if he were Jesus, impaled upon the cross.

"C'mon, have a drink," his voice hoarse with fear.

I wondered what he thought about in the interminable moment before death. Was the moment filled with regret of things left undone or left unsaid? Did he think he'd never feel the warmth of his wife snuggling next to him? Did he feel anger and frustration at being helpless? Was he repentant before God? Or was the pain and the certainty of death so great that he merely turned desperately internal, seeking escape rather than resignation? In the end, it didn't matter what he thought. He was frozen in time, and an angry man with emotionless eyes was glaring at him with determination and the will to kill.

I moved well aside. A second later, a cannonade of thunder erupted within the small enclosure. The thunder did not roll off the walls but rather resonated and saturated the entire room. The stinging, acrid odor of gun powder fumed like a volcanic eruption clouding visibility. Despite the fog, the form of a man being slashed in half by a gunshot was still discernible. The dark red blood that characterizes a gut shot was evident as it splashed its way through Trixie's body and to the mirror behind the bar. He did not slump to the ground, but rather bucked backwards, pinned to the bar. There was stunned silence. Gun shots were no strange phenomenon in lower Newark, but a Saturday night, shattered by the thunder of a shotgun and in the close quarters of a bar, astonished the wide-eyed patrons.

But only for a moment. In seconds, they recovered, ganged up on the Pollock and wrestled him to the floor. The shot gun was torn loose from his grasp and had there been more ammunition, they would have assassinated him on the spot. I beat it out the door. Anyone who is streetwise knows enough not to hang around for the cops. Besides, I was underage and in a tavern.

The police arrived, gathered information and arrested the killer. The ambulance came and, from it, spewed hastening, faceless people in white garb. Some of them came away blood stained when they touched the corpse. It amazed me that they had to pronounce him dead since anyone could see the man was cut in half. The man who had been Trixie King was reduced to a bloodied hulk, grotesquely displayed along the bar. They placed him in a black body bag and rolled him away. Zeke had passed out from fright when the gun went off. He had not recovered so the ambulance people attended him and drove him home. I wandered about the streets for hours, comprehending what had just occurred. I finally returned home. My father was there. He had not heard as yet. When I told him what I had seen, all he could say was: "When you want life most, you lose it. Trixie's day was today."

My mother had a lot more to say, all of it directed at me for being in the wrong place at the wrong time. Not a word of sympathy or understanding from her. I asked if we should do something to help the family. I was met with a stony silence that irritated me. I went to see the King family, but they refused to answer the door. Everything was dark and lifeless inside.

And I did not see them until the funeral, three days hence. When I saw them, they were not the people I had known and seen for years. The wife was lifeless and pale. The children moped as if retarded. People came and went from the funeral hall, offering condolences to the stunned family. The relatives who attended were few for Trixie was not endeared to them, but there were mobsters and bookies and even a few tearful prostitutes who attended. I paid my respects, remained the required amount of time for protocol and left. Somehow a part of my innocence had died right along with Trixie. Nor was it anything I could ever forget.

The months that passed convinced me that when the center of the universe is suddenly demolished, the moon, the stars, the sun, the clouds, all cease to exist. So it was with Trixie's family. His wife was seldom seen. The children did the shopping and the chores. No one visited. The murder trial came and went but none of them attended, for, in truth, there was nothing they could say. Their world had been shattered. No one could put Humpty Dumpty together again.

Anthony, of course, inherited the Cadillac, but, somehow, it did not seem nearly as grand or as luxurious as when T.K. drove it. Nor, did he seem as cocky or flagrant as he once had been, as if he bore the shame of his father's death and had been humbled. The younger son took up with a local lesbian and was often seen with his face made up with mascara and lipstick. It seemed to trouble his brother and his mother not at all. The Universe had been shot-gunned to death and everything ceased to exist. They did not even attend the execution of the killer. Life just faded away and them with it.

In time, my life directed me to other pursuits and the memory of the great King faded. There are times now when I question whether I conjured the entire affair from fantasy. Perhaps the mind can only assimilate so much, and then it rebels with forgetfulness and causes us to question whether life is real or fictional. I know the time and place where all this transpired. I just disbelieve that it was ever part of my life's experience. It was all dream-like until I read a book recounting the incident. And then, I knew it was not dream, but reality. I have faced the issue and put it aside. It happened. I cannot change that. Yet, there are nights when the roar of that weapon bellowing into the cloistered bar is very real. Only then, I have not been moved aside. I am the target. And the great King lives on, while I pass on into oblivion.

Tears and Tales

Stories of Animal and Human Rescue

By Russell A. Vassallo

"Best Book Award 2006"
Finalist
Fiction/Short Stories

"*Tears and Tales* offers up a remarkable story of life, love, beauty, independence, and glorious relationships favorably acknowledging basic truths which simply make life worth living. *Tears and Tales* is especially recommended reading, particularly to cancer patients and animal lovers." – Midwest Book Review, July 2006

"Through 11 heartwarming stories of animal companionship, *Tears and Tales* is based on Vassallo's personal memories of the animals that comforted him in good and bad times."
-Seton Hall University Magazine, *Pirates in Print*

"Russell Vassallo presents these real-life stories with an attitude of respect for all living things. These are unforgettable creatures and the author has created an unforgettable book."—Vernon Tucker, Farrier, Liberty, KY

ISBN: 978-0-9776739-0-2   176 pages   paperback $16.95

See order form at the back of this book or www.krazyduck.com

Unsung Patriot:

How The Stars and Stripes Began

By Virginia G. Vassallo

Guy T. Viskniskki was the founder and first editor-in-chief of *The Stars and Stripes*, the newspaper for the American Expeditionary Forces during World War I. Virginia G. Vassallo is his granddaughter and based much of her book upon his unpublished memoirs and family history. *Unsung Patriot* weaves the struggle to establish *The Stars and Stripes* with a portrait of the man who was dynamic enough to accomplish the task. Guy was a complex man and the author grew up with many competing images of him. In writing this book she feels that she found her grandfather – a man she never knew.

> **"Guy T. Viskniskki is remembered for his patriotism, integrity and perseverance. He was a man of character. . . . Virginia's esteem and high regard for the accomplishments of Guy T. Viskniskki come through brilliantly in this tribute. She created a masterpiece in this well-rounded accolade of a dynamic, yet complex, man whose legacy is "The Stars and Stripes." Virginia is incredibly articulate. Her words are well-chosen, her organization meticulous, and her presentation is compelling."**
>
> *Richard R. Blake, Korean War Veteran*

ISBN: 978-0-977639-2-6   225 pages   paperback $21.95
See order form at the back of this book or www.krazyduck.com

The Horse with the Golden Mane

Stories of Adventure Mystery, and Romance

By Russell A. Vassallo

"Eric" – Sol Goodkin was freed from a Nazi death camp and came to America to escape violence. Mysteriously a Doberman pinscher appears in his rear yard, hungry and blood-stained. Sol finds himself befriending the very breed of dog used by the Germans to hunt and attack Jewish prisoners. In an ending that will shock and startle the reader, the friendship and conflicts between man and dog achieve sensational heights and race to a smash conclusion.

"Taj" – The bond between man and animal comes to full fruition when Grant Larsen pursues his horse, Taj, to prevent him from being destroyed. In the process he learns about the mystery of a crippled child and mends a broken relationship with his daughter. The story of whether or not Grant finds his horse will keep readers on the edge of their seats.

"The Horse with the Golden Mane" – A man's desperate love for his wife leads him into a strange bond with an unruly and abused horse. In rescuing the animal, he is also rescuing himself, but a strange twist in the plot, and the man's uncanny relationship with the horse, parallel a search for his wife that will baffle and astonish the reader.

ISBN: 978-0-9776739-1-9   240 pages   paperback $18.00
See order form at the back of this book or www.krazyduck.com

ORDER FORM

To receive additional copies of any of the Krazy Duck
Productions books, please enter the quantity and total on the
appropriate lines and mail this form to
Krazy Duck Productions.

Quantity	Title	Price	Total
_____	**Tears and Tales**	$16.95	_____
_____	**The Horse with the Golden Mane**	$18.00	_____
_____	**Unsung Patriot**	$21.95	_____
_____	**Streetwise**	$22.95	_____

Shipping ($2.00 per book)   _____

Total (enclose check or money order)   _____

Name: _____

Street Address: _____

City: _____ State: _____ ZIP: _____

Mail check or money order to:

Krazy Duck Productions

P.O. Box 105

Danville, KY 40423